About Island Press

Since 1984, the nonprofit organization Island Press has been stimulating, shaping, and communicating ideas that are essential for solving environmental problems worldwide. With more than 1,000 titles in print and some 30 new releases each year, we are the nation's leading publisher on environmental issues. We identify innovative thinkers and emerging trends in the environmental field. We work with world-renowned experts and authors to develop cross-disciplinary solutions to environmental challenges.

Island Press designs and executes educational campaigns, in conjunction with our authors, to communicate their critical messages in print, in person, and online using the latest technologies, innovative programs, and the media. Our goal is to reach targeted audiences—scientists, policy makers, environmental advocates, urban planners, the media, and concerned citizens—with information that can be used to create the framework for long-term ecological health and human well-being.

Island Press gratefully acknowledges major support from The Bobolink Foundation, Caldera Foundation, The Curtis and Edith Munson Foundation, The Forrest C. and Frances H. Lattner Foundation, The JPB Foundation, The Kresge Foundation, The Summit Charitable Foundation, Inc., and many other generous organizations and individuals.

The opinions expressed in this book are those of the author(s) and do not necessarily reflect the views of our supporters.

THE AFFORDABLE CITY

THE AFFORDABLE CITY

*Strategies for Putting
Housing within Reach
(and Keeping It There)*

SHANE PHILLIPS

ISLANDPRESS | Washington | Covelo

Library of Congress Control Number: 2020931763

All Island Press books are printed on environmentally responsible
materials.

Manufactured in the United States of America
10 9 8 7 6 5 4

Keywords: affordable city, affordable housing, homelessness, housing
affordability, housing finance, housing policy, housing stability, housing
subsidy, housing supply, "not in my backyard" (NIMBY), real estate
development, rent control, tenant protections, "yes in my backyard"
(YIMBY)

Contents

—

Preface

—

Quite a few friends (and my editor) have asked me, "Who did you write this book for?" My first intuition has been to reply that it's for anyone who cares about housing affordability, which conveniently describes the majority of coastal US residents and quite a few in the Mountain West, South, and Midwest as well. I look forward to the book sales bonanza.

But, truthfully, that's not right. This book is really for people who prioritize affordability and community over their own agenda, ideological purity, or personal ownership of victories and losses. It's for people who don't want only to identify problems and bad actors but who are also set on enacting solutions, even when those solutions may be incomplete or incremental or may require compromise. Admittedly, and unfortunately, that's a somewhat smaller readership.

And yet, I think, it's bigger than most people realize.

Most of us suffering from the high cost of housing don't care about factions, ideologies, or whose side "wins" the political fight of the day; we care about results. We want very simple things: homes that don't break the bank; the ability to live, stay, and thrive in the communities of our choosing; and strong, enforceable protections from abuse and exploitation.

To date, the housing policy debate in high- and rising-cost cities has been defined by its poles: if you support the development of more homes, then you mustn't care about tenants; if you care about tenants, then you mustn't support new development. But these are false choices. Cities grow; thus they need more homes. Communities change faster than some people can manage; thus they need protection.

The central argument of this book, supported by dozens of specific policies to help make it an actionable resource, is that more homes and stronger tenant protections are both indispensable. Furthermore, both of these efforts—with public funding to augment them—are mutually reinforcing. Each is more effective with the other. Supply, Stability, and Subsidy—the themes of this book—are all integral to realizing the promise of affordable and accessible cities.

The diversity of ideas in this book reflects my own scattershot background. I never finished high school, but I was the first person in my extended family to go to college, first at the University of Washington, where I majored in biochemistry, and later at the University of Southern California (USC), for master's degrees in urban planning and public administration. Before getting my bachelor's degree I worked at a grocery store, several restaurants, a city public works department, UPS, and Comcast, as a cable technician. (Please, no *Cable Guy* jokes.) During college I worked in a chemistry lab and a genetics lab, and after college I did tuberculosis research. I grew up in the suburbs but was then living in Seattle, and it was around this time that I began to develop an interest in cities and write about them in my blog, *Better Institutions* (http://www.better-institutions.com).

I moved from Seattle to Los Angeles to enroll in graduate school, and while there I worked in a city council office and later as a consultant on transportation, development, and sustainability projects. After graduating I worked on a Downtown Los Angeles transportation project, continuing to write and to grow increasingly interested in housing. As slow as progress could be, it seemed that LA and other cities were moving in the right direction on transportation. When it came to housing, it seemed to me that things were only getting worse, and I was motivated to focus my efforts there. I took a job as director of public policy for a Downtown LA advocacy organization, and there I had the opportunity to work on housing policy in what was arguably the only pro-housing neighborhood in a city of five hundred square miles.

Today I work on housing full time and then some, serving as the housing initiative project manager for the Lewis Center for Regional Policy Studies at the University of California, Los Angeles (whew), writing about how to strengthen rent control one week and how to build more market-rate homes the next. After seven years in LA, I believe I've made every housing advocate angry at me at least once.

I've taught public policy at USC, I advocate with organizations such as Abundant Housing LA and Streets For All, and I assist with local efforts including LA's citywide housing element task force. The work genuinely never gets old.

My views on housing policy weren't always so all-inclusive, and maybe that's true of you as well. In my case, I came to housing advocacy with a focus on supply, armed with endless statistics about the decades of underbuilding that plagued US cities and its consequences for scarcity, vacancies, and rents and home prices. I didn't believe that housing production could solve our affordability and homelessness crises by itself, but I didn't have much to offer beyond it. I bought into the argument that rent control was anathema to housing supply, and I had little to say about public funding and other government-led interventions.

My views began to shift as I saw, time and again, the consequences of redevelopment that didn't account for the needs of existing tenants. While not true of most development in my adopted city of Los Angeles, too many projects displaced renters with virtually no compensation and no promise of return to their former address. A new building would go up, replacing moderately affordable rent-stabilized homes with a mix of market-rate and truly affordable units, which was a genuine improvement, but the tenants displaced from the demolished buildings weren't the ones to benefit. Something was very wrong with the system we'd designed.

I also saw that housing supply, as essential as it was, couldn't match the pace of change in individual communities. A $5 billion stadium was proposed in Inglewood and rents and home values skyrocketed nearly overnight; even if the city had allowed for infinite development to meet the growing demand, thousands of households would be displaced before relief ever arrived. These changes were entirely outside the control of local residents, and yet they were the ones to suffer the consequences.

Around this time I was fortunate enough to buy my first home, a duplex. The building was rent stabilized, with a below-market tenant household in one unit and the former owners in the other. I moved into the owners' unit and made it my home. I also became a landlord, and I grew to loathe the entire industry. Every incentive was oriented toward profit maximization at the expense of tenants, with huge rewards for those willing to bend the rules or breach the limits of human decency. Again, this came down to policy choices that prioritized the wealth of landlords over the needs of tenants. For the record, my neighbor, my tenant, has stayed in his home at a stable rent, but protections dependent upon the goodwill of individuals are no real protections at all. If there's one section of this book where my passion veers into indignant rage, it's my discussion of polices that favor the interests of landlords over tenants.

After years of working in public policy, learning from market-rate and nonprofit developers, tenant and pro-housing advocates, academics, city staff and public officials, and many others, I began to grow frustrated. I saw the early signs of inclusive advocacy in cities such as Oakland, California; Minneapolis, Minnesota; and Portland, Oregon—places where advocates had come together to prioritize the needs of existing *and* future residents—but these examples were few and far between. Such partnerships were almost nonexistent in LA, though they're finally taking root here, too. There were precious few full-throated defenses of a comprehensive, all-of-the-above, practical approach to housing affordability, and there were virtually no policy blueprints for advocates and public officials who needed support. Heaps of credit are due to Data for Progress and its excellent report "Homes for All" for breaking early ground in this respect.

So I started writing.

My goal was to create a resource that can be easily referenced by readers, with detail on most of the specific policies you're likely to come across and big-picture explanations of the value of Supply, Stability, and Subsidy and how they can—and must—work together. We need everyone in this fight and every tool in the belt. It's a fight for problem solvers and coalition builders, and I hope this book will be of service to you who fit the bill.

Acknowledgments

—

This book is the result of countless hours of conversation and debate with friends, loved ones, colleagues, and acquaintances. And frenemies. I wrote the first draft in a matter of months (while otherwise unemployed, admittedly), but the concepts and policies at its heart were many years in the making. Thank you to those who have supported my ideas—the wacky as well as the mundane—and to those who have challenged me along the way. Every author says their book wouldn't have been possible without the help of some person or another, and I believe that's especially true for me. My understanding of the technical, financial, moral, and simply *human* aspects of housing policy has been shaped by those around me; my perspective would be impoverished and embarrassingly incomplete without their feedback. I'd like to offer a special thanks to Mark Vallianatos and Luke Klipp for their specific comments on my manuscript and a more general, but no less sincere, thank-you to everyone who's shared an idea, a critique, a resource, or a message of support at any time throughout this process. If you wonder whether I might be thinking of you, I am.

Introduction

—

In July 2016, the Los Angeles Tenants Union and the Yucca-Argyle Tenants Association held a protest. Their target: the proposed redevelopment of the 40-unit rent-stabilized Yucca-Argyle Apartments into a new luxury tower. Located in the heart of Hollywood, the project would include approximately 200 homes, including 39 units reserved for low-income households, along with a hotel, restaurants, and retail shops.

Railing against the developer, Champion Real Estate Company, activists and Yucca-Argyle residents shared stories of displacement and gentrification, hoisting signs with the slogans "Affordable for who?" and "Stop evictions! ¡Alto al desalojo!"[1] Many tenants had lived at the Yucca-Argyle for decades, subsisting on fixed incomes and paying stable rents limited to increases of 3 percent each year. If the residents couldn't stay in their homes at the Yucca-Argyle, where would they live?

A sizable share of the new apartments would be reserved for lower-income residents, but there was no guarantee that the units would go to the current residents. The market-rate homes, likely to rent for upward of $2,500 per month for the smallest units, would be far out of reach for most LA residents, to say nothing of those living at the Yucca-Argyle, many of whom were paying less than $1,000 per month. Sejal Patel, a five-year resident of the building, noted that she earned too much to qualify for the low-income units but too little to afford a market-rate home in the new development.[2]

To compensate residents for their displacement, the City of Los Angeles requires developers to pay each household up to $21,200 in relocation fees, depending on their age, disability status, and income and how long they've lived in the building.[3] But that money wouldn't go far in the Hollywood housing market. Most apartments in the area rent for at least $1,500 per month, even in older and less well maintained buildings.

For those threatened by displacement, this was devastating. Their options included renting a similar apartment at a much higher cost, finding a worse-quality apartment at a similar rent, or leaving the neighborhood or city that they'd spent years or decades making their home. Homelessness, which had increased by 17 percent in the past three years,[4] and would surge by another 17 percent in 2017,[5] may have also been a risk for some who lacked a support network of nearby family or friends. The outlook was grim. Sasha Ali, a resident of the Yucca-Argyle and an unofficial spokesperson for the residents, commented, "We're really most concerned about the elders and the low-income families. Where are they going to go?"[6]

Seen from another angle, the Yucca-Argyle project was a model for redevelopment done right. Just a few blocks from LA's busiest subway line, it would take 40 vulnerable homes in a rapidly gentrifying area and redevelop them into roughly 200 apartments and a variety of useful amenities. The 40 existing rent-stabilized units, which could revert to market rate at any time, would be replaced with genuinely affordable, long-term income-restricted homes on a nearly one-for-one basis.[7]

In Los Angeles County, a region with an accumulated housing shortage of 1 million homes and skyrocketing rents,[8] the Champion redevelopment would add much-needed housing and affordable units at no cost to the city. It would establish a windfall of new property and hotel tax revenues to fund other government priorities. And it would create hundreds of construction jobs, most of them well-paying union work. If development didn't make sense here, where would it?

For the region as a whole, and especially for the future residents of those 39 new income-restricted homes, the project was an unquestionable win. But for the current residents of the Yucca-Argyle Apartments, it was a nearly unmitigated loss. Whatever the supporters and opponents might have to say, the outcome of the project wasn't entirely good, nor was it entirely bad—it was both. It just depended on who you asked.

Champion Real Estate didn't fit the "greedy developer" stereotype. In response to the Yucca-Argyle protests, Champion worked proactively to come up with a variety of possible mitigations to make sure that existing residents could benefit from the project.

One proposal—the one the development team and residents ultimately settled on—would allow all the tenants to move into apartments in the new development when construction was complete, at the same rents they'd paid in the older building. They would also place rent stabilization restrictions on all of the approximately 200 units so that once a household moved into an apartment, their rent could increase by only 3 percent annually in most years. *And* Champion would pay for the temporary relocation of the tenants, including any rental costs that exceeded their rents at the old Yucca-Argyle, for the duration of construction.

For the tenants of the Yucca-Argyle this was a huge victory, worthy of praise for the residents and the groups who helped them organize and demand more. Not only would the residents be allowed to stay in their neighborhood, they would also enjoy vastly higher quality apartments at no additional expense. If every displacement looked like this one, some renters might be asking developers to come tear down their buildings, too.

But this wasn't such an obvious win for the entire Los Angeles region. The balance of costs and benefits was complicated. Yes, the 40 existing households got to stay in their community,[9] and there's a strong case to be made that the needs of existing tenants should take precedence over those of future residents. The cost, though, was the loss of 39 low-income units.

What started as 39 long-term affordable units and more than 150 market-rate units were now approximately 200 rent-stabilized units. Up to 39 of those rent-stabilized apartments would start out at very low below-market rates, assuming all of the existing tenants moved into the new building when it was completed, but the remaining units would mostly start at $2,500 per month or more. The rents for those remaining units would be rent stabilized, yes, but they wouldn't be "affordable." And even the below-market units—the ones that the Yucca-Argyle tenants moved into—would revert to market rate as soon as the tenants moved out, so most would be unaffordable within a few years or, at best, a few decades.

Does the immediate benefit to the Yucca-Argyle tenants out-weigh the loss of 39 affordable apartments—homes that would re-main restricted to low-income households for a full fifty-five years? Or does stabilizing the rents of 100 percent of the apartments also have some meaningful value, even if they're stabilized at $3,500 or even $5,000 per month? What is the social value of stabilized rents for 200 high-income households weighed against the affordable rents of 39 low-income households?

There are no easy answers to any of these questions, and yet we must answer them all the same. Like-minded people will assign dif-ferent values to stability versus affordability, short-term versus long-term benefits, and existing versus future residents. These differences are why housing is such a contentious and divisive place to be an ad-vocate, elected official, or planning professional. Well-meaning peo-ple will disagree, and those disagreements have real consequences for people's lives.

The response of Champion Real Estate is instructive, but the trade-offs described here are rarely discussed openly. They should be. No matter what field you work in—city planning or urban pol-icy, for-profit or nonprofit development, academia or finance, or as a volunteer who supports new housing options or tenants' rights—it's vital that these questions be discussed openly and transparently. If they aren't, we'll continue to muddle our way through, with predict-ably poor results. To this day, it's still not clear if advocates or policy makers believe the outcome of the Yucca-Argyle negotiation was the best-case scenario or simply the most politically expedient.

We need to have a conversation about what good outcomes look like, and then we need to create rules that guarantee those outcomes in the future—not through project-by-project negotiations and highly publicized battles between tenants, developers, and elected officials, but by mandate, by default: no intervention required. Not every developer will be obligated to negotiate as Champion did, and some will be less generous. Many developers who would like to do more will be unable to make such large concessions and still earn a profit. Not every residents' group will have the resources to organize successfully and demand better for themselves and their community.

The outcome of the Yucca-Argyle protest and negotiation was acceptable, perhaps even good. But it could have been better, and similar proposals often end up much worse. Our cities—and we as practitioners, activists, and voters—must do more to explore these trade-offs and decide how best to balance them. We desperately need more homes, but how do we provide them so that the greatest benefit and the least harm are conveyed to existing residents? We need affordable housing, but how do we require it of developers without killing the goose that lays the golden egg? We need stronger protections for renters, but how do we design protections that complement new housing construction rather than undermine it? Fundamentally, how do we ensure that our cities have a place for everyone, now and into the future?

The answers to these questions can't be left to ad hoc negotiations in which tenants win in some cases and lose in others, or in which we make one demand without realizing in hindsight that another would have been better. We need thoughtful, consistent, and effective rules that apply to everyone. Without these things, renters will continue to wonder if they'll be the next to lose their place in their cities and communities. Without these things, the housing we need will continue to be feared as a threat, not celebrated as an opportunity.

Having It All

The conceit of this book is that when it comes to housing policy, we don't have to take the bad with the good. Tenants don't need to suffer in service of housing abundance, nor must housing abundance be threatened by strong tenant protections. We can build new homes that serve people at all income levels, we can stabilize rents and home prices for future generations, and we can address other vital priorities such as mobility, health, social connection, and environmental sustainability. And at the very same time, we can protect existing residents from harm and help them live better lives. This book's goal is to empower readers with the knowledge, tools, and context needed to achieve these goals.

So many of our fights over housing policy boil down to siloed, single-focus thinking. Supporters of the Yucca-Argyle project's original proposal, many who might identify as YIMBYs ("yes in my backyard" pro-housing advocates), make their case on the grounds of regional, long-term benefit. The region needs much more housing, and while the immediate outcome may not be ideal for every resident of the city, it's for the greater good. It's creative destruction for housing: yes, some people will pay the price of progress, but in the end we'll all (or most of us will) be better off.

Those who sometimes oppose new development, such as the Los Angeles Tenants Union, instead focus on individual, immediate impacts. If the core question of YIMBYs is "Who benefits?," for tenant advocates it's "Who is harmed?" Why *shouldn't* residents be outraged when they're forced from their homes, somewhere they may have lived for decades, with nothing to show for it but a $10,000 check that won't cover their increased rent for more than a year or two? The residents protesting this treatment aren't interested in an academic debate about the theoretical value of development in a constrained housing market. They don't care about what economists believe is most "efficient" for the market. And why should they? They're fighting for their lives, sometimes quite literally.

Both of these perspectives are correct in their own ways and on their own terms.

We go astray when we focus solely on one or the other—when we concern ourselves only with the long-term regional benefit or the immediate, individual harms. It's long past time for us to move beyond this false choice and begin to take both concerns seriously. Our communities can't keep waiting, and many of our neighbors will be left behind if only one side gets its way.

This book draws from the advocacy and arguments of groups often at odds with one another, and it makes the case that those groups are not as incompatible as their rhetoric may sometimes imply.

On one side are pro-housing advocates who are responding to decades of political dominance by NIMBYs ("not in my backyard" activists), both described in more detail later in the book.[10] On the other side are pro-tenant advocates whose emphasis is on protecting existing residents and preserving affordable homes, whether they're privately owned or publicly subsidized. Despite their battles, the great majority of pro-housing and pro-tenant advocates are sincere in their desire for more affordable and accessible cities. Theirs is a difference not of goals but of emphasis.

There are many people who are both pro-housing *and* pro-tenant. They are this book's inspiration and its aspiration. My goal is to convince readers to join that big tent and acknowledge that policies from both the pro-supply and pro-tenant camps are essential. With careful design and forethought, they can work together more successfully than either approach by itself. We'll need everyone rowing in the same direction to finally deliver the affordable, accessible communities that we deserve.

The Housing Crisis

If affordable and accessible communities are the goal, we have a long way to go. Cities across the country are grappling with out-of-control housing costs, a worsening homelessness crisis, and a sense that young people today don't have the same opportunities for the "good life" enjoyed by their parents and grandparents.

Renters are falling further behind: between 2000 and 2016, income fell slightly for the median renter household while median rents increased by more than 50 percent. The share of households that are cost-burdened, paying over 30 percent of their income on rent, increased from 38.5 percent to 47.5 percent over that same period.[11]

Low-income renters are especially vulnerable. Shockingly, over 80 percent of households earning under $15,000 a year are cost-burdened, with approximately 71 percent paying over half their income on rent (defined as severe rent burden). The numbers are only slightly better for those earning $15,000 to $30,000 per year, with over 75 percent cost-burdened and nearly 40 percent severely cost-burdened.

Households led by racial and ethnic minorities have not shared in the benefits of rising home prices. In 2013, median net worth was $134,230 for white households and just $11,030 for black households. Similarly, more than one-quarter of black households have zero or negative net worth, compared with less than 10 percent of white households.[12]

More than a million affordable rental homes are at risk. Between 2017 and 2027, affordability restrictions on at least 1.1 million publicly subsidized homes will expire.[13] This will require governments to pay more money to keep those units affordable, diverting resources needed to grow the stock of affordable homes. Those that don't have their affordability covenants extended will revert to market rate and, in many cases, will no longer be affordable to low-income households.

Many vulnerable renters receive no assistance whatsoever. Fewer than one-quarter of households eligible for housing assistance actually receive any.[14] Whereas food stamps, health care, unemployment insurance, and other social services are guaranteed entitlements to those who meet eligibility conditions, housing is not.

The cost of construction is rising rapidly. The prices of land, labor, and materials are all growing faster than inflation, and this is increasing development costs for affordable housing and limiting the number of households that can afford market-rate homes.[15] In California, the cost of subsidized affordable housing had risen to $425,000 per unit by 2016. Today, new affordable apartments can cost upward of $450,000 per unit in places such as New York and Illinois and $600,000 to $700,000 or more in the most expensive California markets.[16]

In terms of housing production, the boom years of today are worse than the bust years of the past. The country's worst home-building year from 1993 to 2007 (1.292 million homes) was better than the best home-building year from 2008 to 2018 (1.250 million homes).[17] The United States simply isn't building much housing anymore, though it's become more visible as a larger share has moved into urban centers.

Student loan debt and other failures of the social safety net are compounding the housing crisis. Among households headed by someone aged 30 to 39, 17 percent held some amount of student debt in 1995; only about 15 percent of those had more than $25,000 in debt. By 2016, the share with student debt had ballooned to 40 percent, and nearly half held balances over $25,000. For the cohort aged 20 to 29, the numbers are even higher.[18] These debt levels put further strain on young householders' ability to afford a home, whether rented or owned.

Perhaps worst of all, homelessness is on the rise. The number of people experiencing homelessness in the United States fell from nearly 650,000 in 2007 to 550,000 in 2016, but it is now increasing once again.[19] Cities are spending more than ever on efforts to reduce homelessness and help rehouse record-breaking numbers of residents, but they can't keep up with the increasing rate of families and individuals falling into homelessness.[20]

Taken together, this is nothing less than a human and moral tragedy. It demands action that is equal to the task. The time for half measures has long since passed.

This is not a book about the stories of those affected by the housing crisis, but those stories are powerful, important, and far too commonplace. As a complement to this book, I would recommend *Generation Priced Out*, in which Randy Shaw documents the stories of dozens of families and individuals and the trials they've endured simply trying to stay in their homes. Discussions of housing policy often veer into the abstract and economic, but never forget that there are real human lives behind every statistic.

Difficult Choices, No Simple Answers

How do we resolve the housing crisis? From Los Angeles to Boston and from Seattle to Miami, cities across the country are struggling to answer this question, with various degrees of success. There have been many different approaches, but they can really all be reduced to two factors: (1) treatment of tenants and the protections they're afforded and (2) openness to the development and redevelopment of housing. While it's possible—and indeed admirable—to be both pro-tenant and pro-housing, most cities have chosen only one or the other at best, or neither at worst.

Pro-Tenant, Yet Anti-Housing

San Francisco is notorious for its emphasis on tenant protections and rental housing preservation and, along with the rest of the Bay

Area, for its severe restriction of the construction of new homes. San Francisco has stronger tenant protections than the vast majority of US cities, including a rent stabilization program that limits annual rent increases to 60 percent of inflation once a tenant has moved into a unit. Tenants are protected from eviction by "just-cause" eviction rules, and landlords must go through a formal, transparent buyout process if they want their renters to vacate a unit, even if the lease has expired—and renters are free to refuse. In most cases, disabled and elderly tenants may not be evicted even if the owners themselves want to move into their unit. There are many ways in which San Francisco's protections could (and should) go further, but they lead the nation in many respects.

Meanwhile, San Francisco trails nearly all its peers in housing production, especially relative to job growth. The city added a whopping 8.2 jobs for every new housing permit from 2010 to 2015, and the entire metropolitan area did only marginally better, at 6.8 jobs per new home. Since 2005, San Francisco has added 3.0 jobs per housing permit,[21] but this is still far too few new homes. Even if we assume that every new resident has a job, we would still hope for a ratio closer to 1.5. About 36 percent of San Francisco is made up of one-person households, and approximately 70 percent is one- or two-person households.[22] If the city wanted to also make room for nonworking residents, such as children and retired people, the target ratio should be closer to 1.0 jobs per home. From 2005 to 2017, the city added approximately 42,000 units, an annual growth rate of less than 1 percent during one of the biggest localized economic booms in world history.[23] By any measure, San Francisco has built too few homes for its growing job and population base.

The end result of San Francisco's experiment has been to produce one of the most expensive cities in America, with an average rent of $4,348 per month in May 2019; a one-bedroom apartment in the city went for more than $3,800 per month.[24] San Francisco has become a city of and for the rich, with more than one-quarter of its households earning $200,000 per year or more; 11.1 percent of California households and just 6.9 percent of US households make as much in a year. Over half of San Francisco households (53.9 percent) earn over $100,000 per year, versus 35.9 percent and 27.8 percent, respectively, for California and the United States. Reflecting the positive impact of its tenant and rental housing protections, however, San Francisco has also held on to an impressive number of very low income households, with 16.1 percent earning $25,000 or less, much more aligned with the share of California and US households (17.3 percent and 20.3 percent, respectively).[25]

San Francisco's pro-tenant, anti-housing approach protects many vulnerable families and individuals, but the city is no longer a place that the middle class can afford, and kids who grow up there have few prospects for forming their own households in the region. Despite many people benefiting from the city's protections, San Francisco's approach has not led to broad-based affordability by any reasonable measure.

Pro-Housing, Yet Anti-Tenant

Austin, Texas, takes the opposite approach, with policies that are very pro-housing and anti-renter (or, perhaps more accurately, pro-landlord). Austin increased its housing supply by a whopping 31.6 percent from 2005 to 2017, three times the pace of San Francisco, despite a cooler job market.[26] From 2005 to 2015, Austin added 1.4 new jobs for every permitted housing unit, a decent balance for a fast-growing city.[27] Rents are much more affordable in Austin, at $1,875 per month for all homes and $1,485 for one-bedroom apartments,[28] and as a result Austin has largely retained its middle-class character, with 43 percent of households earning between $35,000 and $100,000 per year, the same as the rest of the nation.[29]

But despite relatively affordable housing prices, rents have increased very significantly since 2011, by roughly 35 percent.[30] A quickly growing supply of homes has helped keep prices lower than they otherwise might be (San Francisco's rents increased by 55 percent over the same period),[31] but supply alone has not stopped rents from outpacing incomes in Austin—nor in virtually any other popular city.

Austin has not complemented a robust housing supply with strong tenant protections. In fact, not a single city in Texas has rent control or rent stabilization; such regulations are prohibited by state law. Texas also bans mandatory affordability requirements[32] and fees on new development used to fund affordable housing.[33] The consequences of these decisions are partially reflected in Austin's eviction rate of 0.98 percent (98 evictions for every 1,000 households) in 2016, approximately four times San Francisco's eviction rate of 0.25 percent.[34] (Notably though, Austin's eviction rate has fallen dramatically from its 2012 peak of 2.25 percent.) The consequences of landlord-friendly policies are also evident in the availability of housing options for low-income households: the Houston, Dallas, and Austin metropolitan areas rank third, sixth, and ninth, respectively, for the lowest share of rental homes available to those earning 30 percent of area median income or less.[35]

Austin's approach—and that of Texas in general—hasn't proven dramatically more successful than San Francisco's, especially when the environment is taken into consideration. Since 2005, 46 percent of new homes in Austin have been in the form of sprawling detached single-family homes.[36] This is better than the Austin metro area as a whole, where 62 percent of new homes have been single-family homes,[37] or the Dallas metro, where it is more than 70 percent,[38] but maintaining affordability through excessive destruction of wilderness and farmland isn't a strategy worthy of emulation. Austin traded away some environmental sustainability in exchange for affordability, but ultimately it hasn't done well on either metric.

Every US City Falling Short

If we look to other cities across the country, we see similar stories. Seattle has built more than virtually any big city in America, growing its housing stock by 28 percent from 2005 to 2017, with more than 80 percent of new homes taking the form of sustainable townhomes or multifamily buildings.[39] But Washington, like Texas, is prohibited by state law from enacting rent stabilization and other tenant protections. And despite Seattle's building boom, rents climbed by 51 percent over the past eight years.[40]

Denver tells a similar story, having grown by nearly 20 percent in the twelve years leading up to 2017,[41] but Colorado ranks forty-third in the nation for renters' rights by one measure.[42] Rent in the city has gone up by 56 percent since 2011.[43]

Minneapolis, Minnesota, voted to abolish single-family zoning at the end of 2018, allowing triplexes in all residential areas and abolishing parking minimums across the city.[44] This will lead to more housing in the urban center, more affordable new homes, and more transit-accessible and environmentally sustainable land use, but it remains to be seen whether it will produce a truly affordable city. Minneapolis also has the benefit of starting early, before its prices have gotten out of control—median home values are still well under $300,000—but it, too, has seen rents rise considerably, up by 30 percent since 2011.[45]

New York City has one of the strongest traditions of tenant protection and rental housing preservation in the United States. In June 2019, New York's state legislature passed a sweeping set of tenant protection reforms, most notably eliminating many of the loopholes that allowed landlords to remove units from the rent stabilization program or to raise rents by unmanageable amounts for renter households.[46] These reforms will help preserve New York's rent-stabilized housing stock, which declined by nearly 300,000 units between 1994 and 2017,[47] but they won't bring rents down from their current eye-popping levels.

While New York has more than a million apartments covered by rent stabilization or rent control[48] and 176,000 units of public housing, the city has done little to build new homes for the next generation of residents, adding just 6.8 percent to its housing stock between 2005 and 2017. Rents in New York have climbed less than in many other big cities, by 30 percent since 2011, but they also began the decade higher than in almost every other big city.

Among the country's booming metropolitan areas, there are few, if any, examples of cities with both strong tenant protections and a responsive, fast-growing housing stock. There are also, not coincidentally, no examples of cities that have maintained true affordability in the face of rapid job and population growth. Something is happening to cities in America—and around the world—that simple theories can't explain. The scale and breadth of the housing crisis are too great for there to be a silver bullet. There is no BuzzFeed-style "One Cool Trick for Fixing Your City's Housing Crisis." If it were easy, someone would have already done it.

International Examples

Advocates will sometimes point to international examples as proof that their One True Answer is the only solution that's needed. For supply advocates, that city is Tokyo. At 37.5 million people, Tokyo is the most populous metropolitan area in the world. But despite a consistently growing population, home prices have stayed roughly flat for twenty years, from 1995 to 2015. During that time, prices in San Francisco more than doubled, and in London they more than tripled. Even in Tokyo's booming Minato ward, where the population rose by 66 percent over a twenty-year period, from 145,000 to 241,000, rents increased by just 45 percent.[49]

It is exponentially easier to build housing in Tokyo than in virtually any US city; in 2014, with similar rates of population growth, Tokyo built housing at a rate five times greater than California per capita.[50] This can largely be attributed to Japan's deference to the rights of property owners: so long as new developments adhere to zoning rules, property owners can build whatever they like with very little fuss. Neighbors have no say in the matter, so opposition from nearby residents is not such an obstacle as it is in the United States.

The Japanese approach is a result of several factors, including a housing bubble in the 1980s that catalyzed nationwide changes to make development easier, and the country's earthquake-prone geography, which necessitates the demolition and redevelopment of buildings that don't meet modern structural standards.[51] Housing in Japan is less an investment than a consumable good: whereas in the United States and the United Kingdom approximately 90 percent of homes are sold secondhand, the same is true of just 15 percent of Japanese home sales.[52] The constant redevelopment of housing in Tokyo has also allowed for a rapid increase in living standards, with the amount of space per resident more than doubling from 1963 to 2013.[53]

The upshot of these policies has been dramatically more afford-able housing prices than in other world-class cities, with the median home costing 4.8 times the median household income in Tokyo. This measure of affordability ranks Hong Kong as the least affordable market in the world, with a "median multiple" of 19.4, followed by Sydney, Australia, at 12.9 and Vancouver, British Columbia, at 12.6. The worst US markets are San Jose, California (10.3); Los Angeles (9.4); Honolulu (9.2); and San Francisco (9.1). Even Sacramento, California, and Denver, Colorado, rank worse than Tokyo.[54] Thanks to Tokyo's abundant housing and low inflation rate, a family can afford a $300,000 mortgage for just $850 per month.[55]

However, affordable housing prices aren't guaranteed even in Tokyo. While the metropolis has remained relatively inexpensive compared with peer cities, prices have begun to rise more dramat-ically in recent years. Secondhand apartments sold for 36 percent more in 2018 than in 2012—given Japan's almost nonexistent infla-tion, this would be equivalent to nominal US home prices rising by closer to 50 percent over the same period. In Tokyo's central three wards, Chiyoda, Chuo, and Minato, prices per square meter also increased by approximately 50 percent during this time.[56] Even if US cities adopted pro-growth policies in line with Tokyo's, count-less households would still be impacted by price increases of this magnitude.

On the other end of the spectrum is Vienna, Austria, a social housing utopia for those who support strong tenant protections and heavy government intervention in the housing market. In Vienna, a whopping 62 percent of the population lives in social housing, which is government subsidized and run either by the city or by non-profits.

Unlike public housing in the United States, which is reserved for the very poor, Vienna's serves residents from diverse socioeconomic backgrounds; those earning up to about double the city's median in-come are eligible to live in subsidized homes. Vienna's social housing residents pay an average of $600 per month or less for their housing, about 27 percent of their income on average.[57] Incredibly, Vienna achieves this while being one of the most desirable places on the planet, regularly earning the top spot in worldwide quality-of-life rankings.[58] Vienna is exceedingly rare among major cities in its ability to blend extreme affordability with very high quality of life.

Vienna's appeal to socialists and social democrats is more than just rhetorical. The Viennese approach to housing has its roots in Red Vienna, an early-twentieth-century effort to bring socialist values to a capitalist state. It was, in the words of one writer, "a project to change society by changing the city."[59] By 1924, the municipal government had become the largest property owner in the city, and it built 60,000 new homes from 1923 to 1934, before the takeover of the fascist Austrian government. The government charged rents sufficient to cover operating costs but nothing more, leaving tenants to pay an average of just 4 percent of a worker's monthly wage for housing.[60]

While much has changed in the intervening years, Vienna remains committed to stable, affordable, quality housing for its residents. In a city of 1.8 million residents, about 13,000 new homes are built each year, with roughly one-third subsidized by the government. (This means that privately financed construction is still the dominant development type; there's a place for both the public and the private even in socialist Vienna.) Today, the city owns or indirectly controls about half of Vienna's housing stock, with 220,000 housing units directly owned and another 200,000 controlled through regulated limited-profit private owners.[61] The city spends approximately $700 million each year on refurbishing older buildings and developing new ones, and the revenues are raised through broadly shared sources such as income and corporate taxes.

Vienna's social housing program is heavily reliant on federal funding and may be threatened by the recent rise of a right-wing government. Similarly, anti-immigrant and anti-refugee rhetoric from nationalist politicians may undermine the city's image as a place where people of different socioeconomic classes freely mix. Perhaps most importantly, Vienna today is home to approximately 1.9 million people, about 140,000 fewer than its historical peak of 2.03 million in 1910.[62] This excess of supply likely provided a buffer against rising prices as the city grew again in recent decades, but demand will eventually catch up without continued housing production. Nonetheless, Vienna remains the gold standard for affordability achieved through heavy government intervention and delivering on the promise of housing as a fundamental right regardless of income or background.

Leadership in the United States

A combination of Tokyo's housing abundance and Vienna's tenant protections and egalitarianism might be the vision to which the United States should aspire, but we have a long, long way to go if we want to get there.

The American tradition of property rights is not nearly as laissez-faire as Tokyo's, and the role of the federal government in the housing market—especially rental housing—is far weaker here than in either Japan or Austria. Because of how expensive housing in US cities has become, unfettered development in the style of Tokyo would lead to large-scale displacement, with few new homes affordable to lower-income or working-class households; the cost of new development is simply too high. And a revolutionary shift toward socialist housing policy, in a country where most people own a home and have much of their wealth tied up in it, is also unrealistic—both politically and economically.

That doesn't mean that housing abundance, tenant protections, and egalitarianism are out of reach. Achieving them will just require an approach that fits within the American context.

Oregon is now leading the nation in this regard. In 2019, its state legislature scored a housing affordability hat trick: rent stabilization, just-cause eviction protections,[63] and a near ban on single-family zoning.[64] The new rules will apply statewide, a first-in-the-nation achievement for each of the laws. Henry Kraemer of Data for Progress described the kitchen-sink approach taken by Oregon and why it's so important.

> Like climate change, the $22 trillion American real estate system is too sprawling, and the crisis it created has too many tendrils to be tackled in a single thrust. Controlling rents will not address the desperation and constriction born of the housing shortage. Reforming zoning will not provide housing for truly low-income

families or give much-needed security to renters. Injecting even many billions of dollars into affordable housing will not provide enough homes to meet the full need. None of those will adequately unmake real estate speculation.

Recognizing the breadth of the crisis, we celebrate Oregon's approach to throwing everything and the kitchen sink at it. . . .

By adopting robust statewide protections for renters and legalizing workforce housing in the same session, Oregon shows that not only is it possible to safeguard current tenants and create more space for newcomers but also that these strategies are mutually beneficial and reinforcing. In addition to the individual benefits of each policy, tenant protections mitigate the possible displacement effects of new development, while expanding the universe of legal housing options undermines the charge that tenant protections will discourage new construction.[65]

Oregon has taken the first steps toward a truly pro-housing and pro-tenant solution to the housing crisis. It has shown that a strong enough alliance—one composed of environmentalists, tenant- and community-based organizations, leftists, urbanists, transportation advocates, housing builders, and equity groups, among others—can break the status quo to enact real reform. Without the buy-in of all these factions, that alliance might not have formed. And without policies that addressed both the short- and long-term needs of the state's residents, buy-in may not have been possible.

Even in Oregon, there's much more to be done. The state's newly approved policies will avert the direst housing shortages and prevent the worst landlord abuses, and that is more than any other state has achieved thus far. But they won't be enough to fully accommodate future population growth, assist all of those earning working- or middle-class wages, or keep all low-income households in their homes at stable and affordable prices. They will tip the balance of power toward tenants and away from landlords, though not far enough. The policies will begin to transition rental housing from a profit-oriented, often exploitative investment into something more humane and people centered, but the process of reform must continue.

The Three S's: Supply, Stability, and Subsidy

How can more cities adopt pro-tenant, pro-housing reforms like those passed in Oregon, and how can we build upon that foundation to make our communities affordable, accessible, stable, and welcoming to all? How do we take slogans like "Housing Is a Human Right" and make them a reality, with concrete policies designed to create abundance and equity? How do we build coalitions with those who share our goal of affordable neighborhoods but who differ in their approach?

In this book, I argue that the solution to America's housing crisis, both politically and technically, comes down to three coequal priorities that I call the Three S's: Supply, Stability, and Subsidy.

Supply is about having enough homes for everyone. When housing is hard to come by, all other obstacles to affordability and accessibility become exponentially more difficult to overcome. Rents and home prices rise as a result of scarcity, the cost of construction balloons as land and labor grow more expensive, landlords gain leverage over renters (and sellers over buyers), and poorer tenants are replaced by higher-earning households, with the less fortunate pushed to areas with fewer amenities and limited access to jobs, education, and community. Many cities have limited land available for development, but housing can always be built *up* rather than *out*. Oregon's ban on single-family zoning is one example of how we can make more space on already developed land, though more aggressive tactics will also be required. Providing an abundant supply of homes is about growing the pie for everyone's benefit rather than dividing it into smaller and smaller slices as a population grows. Supply is about recognizing the economic and physical realities of housing and making the most of both.

Stability is about recognizing the dignity of housing—that it's more than an investment vehicle and a means of creating personal wealth, as it is often treated today. It relates to tenant protections and rental housing preservation, two overarching programs that ensure all residents have access to safe, clean, affordable housing without fear that the rug might someday be pulled out from under them.

Just-cause eviction protections and rent stabilization programs, found in Oregon, California, and elsewhere, are a few examples of stabilizing policy. Providing stability to those who want it, to renters in particular, is how we turn housing into homes. The people who most depend on this stability are neither wealthy nor politically connected, but their well-being is the barometer against which we measure our commitment to basic human rights and dignity. If supply is about the economic and physical realities of housing, stability is about our moral obligations to those who live in it.

Subsidy is about ensuring that everyone enjoys the benefits of abundant housing and stable communities. A well-regulated private housing market can serve a large portion of our population, and tenant protections paired with rental housing preservation can assist even more. But there will always be people who are left behind by these efforts—sometimes temporarily, sometimes permanently. Acting through the collective will of our local, state, and federal governments, we have a responsibility to provide support to those who need it and to live up to our professed belief that housing is a human right. This may take the form of rental assistance, publicly subsidized housing construction and acquisition, and a host of other programs. Local efforts, such as Los Angeles's $1.2 billion measure to fund homeless housing and Durham, North Carolina's $95 million housing bond, exemplify such programs,[66] and proposals such as US Representative Ilhan Omar's $1 trillion Homes for All Act would expand such programs to national scope.[67] Supply and stability are our goals, and subsidy is an essential tool to ensure that they're delivered to every member of society regardless of income or background.

Supply, Stability, and Subsidy are all indispensable ingredients in the affordable city recipe book, and each is discussed in much greater detail in the sections that follow. One without the others will not bring true affordability and stability to a community—certainly not to all who need and deserve it. Nor can we simply enact the strongest possible intervention for one goal without considering its impacts on the others. Often, the most aggressive solution to one problem will undermine the best response to another.

Without the support of tenant protections and public subsidies, unfettered development may keep prices from rising but also may raise concerns about displacement and community disruption. It may stabilize rents but by itself be unlikely to dramatically *lower* them. And it almost certainly won't create housing that's affordable to those subsisting on poverty-level or working-class wages. Supply may depend on the market, but advocates for supply should not be solely and slavishly devoted to the "free market." Pro-supply housing policies are essential, but they're not enough by themselves.

Without supply to stave off scarcity and public funds to support those with the greatest need, the benefits of tenant protections and rental housing preservation will be unnecessarily constrained. Policies such as rent control help existing residents stay in their homes, but they do little to accommodate future growth from native-born children, new residents from other cities and states, and immigrants. They may keep things from getting worse for many renters, but they have little power to make things better. Designed poorly, price controls may also replace income-based discrimination with other, more insidious forms of discrimination, such as those based on race, gender, family composition, or other perceived markers of "good" tenants. Tenant protections and rental housing preservation are essential, but they're not enough by themselves.

Without an adequate supply of housing and robust tenant protections, additional public funding will mostly be absorbed into higher rents and construction costs. We'll end up pouring huge sums of money into assistance for people who, if not for poor policy decisions relating to supply and tenant protections, would never have needed assistance in the first place. And we'll have less money left over to assist the people who truly need it. Public subsidies are essential, but they're not enough by themselves.

The Three S's framework, despite drawing inspiration from groups at different ends of the housing advocacy spectrum, is not a moderate approach. Admittedly, it doesn't call for unfettered deregulation or a socialist revolution; in that sense, it doesn't go as far as some would hope (or demand). By any other standard, though, the proposals discussed here are bold, proven to be effective, and unquestionably controversial. They won't remove all barriers to housing construction, protect every tenant in every conceivable circumstance, or make our public sector the primary supplier of housing. But they can absolutely set us on that course.

A Vision for Affordable, Accessible Cities of the Future

The short- and medium-term goals of a Three-S policy framework are ambitious: more affordable housing for all, stability and protection for those who desire it, and abundant resources to assist the most vulnerable among us. The long-term goals of this comprehensive policy set are much grander, however. These grand ambitions are important not just for the positive impacts they'll have on renters and on society more broadly but also because successful advocacy requires a vision that inspires collective action on a massive scale.

The vision embodied by these policies looks something like this.

It's a nation in which renters, not landlords, wield the most power in the market—and where public- and nonprofit-owned housing is so abundant that private property owners must keep their rents affordable in order to compete.

It's a place where renting is safe, clean, and stable, where tenants needn't worry that they might someday lose their homes because of circumstances outside their control. It's a place where existing residents get to enjoy and continue contributing to the fruits of a thriving community.

It's a country where homeownership is available—and affordable—for those who desire it, but it is not the only path to stability and is not the primary means of wealth creation. It's a place where housing is inexpensive and we're free to invest our money in new and growing ventures that improve society rather than aging structures that become less affordable year after year.

It's a future of abundance, not scarcity, in which new neighbors, new jobs, and new homes are welcomed rather than feared. A future in which residents don't need to worry that changing demographics or gentrification may cost them their livelihoods, their homes, or both.

It's a national commitment to housing for all, in which we don't limit the provision of shelter to those who "deserve it" or those who win a lottery, because everyone deserves a place to call home regardless of income or ability or background.

At its core, it's a vision for America in which affordability and stability are guaranteed no matter where, or how, we choose to live. Renters and owners, wealthy and poor, families and groups and individuals—all should live without fear of losing their home, sleeping on the street or in their vehicle, or making the impossible choice to sacrifice food, utilities, or medicine in order to pay their rent.

This may sound utopian, and in a sense it is: politically, we are very far from achieving this vision. But when we look at the actions and funding needed to realize this apparent utopia, it's not as distant as it might seem.

During the three-year period from 2016 to 2019, the value of residential real estate in America increased by an average of $1.27 trillion per year.[68] Much more than half of that amount was due to appreciation of existing structures, not the development of new ones.[69] Currently, most of that wealth is accruing to those fortunate enough to own property, and among homeowners the lion's share of appreciation is going to residents of higher-cost states. Since 2012, fully one-third of the value of home appreciation has gone to one state, California, which represents just 12 percent of the country's population. Barely more than half of California households own their homes,[70] so the actual number of beneficiaries is even smaller. Meanwhile, the nation's renters face higher rents and ever-dimmer prospects of owning a home themselves.

If the fruits of our growing economy weren't captured by an increasingly unaffordable housing stock, how might we spend that money instead? At least $800 billion worth of growth in the residential real estate market is due to appreciation (on the basis of Zillow and Black Knight estimates), which would be enough to fully subsidize the construction of 2–3 million new homes each year. Assuming the tenants in these homes paid an average of $1,000 per month in rent, this number might climb to 4 million or more.[71] (There were approximately 137 million housing units in the United States as of 2017.) This would be in addition to market-rate and mixed-income housing that's already built privately, without public subsidies.

In ten years, this would be enough to build, improve, or

permanently subsidize the rents of 40–50 million homes, one-third of the entire US housing stock. This is investment on par with the New Deal and similar in scope to the vision outlined by the Green New Deal. Every renter in America would benefit enormously from it. All would be free to spend their income on goods, services, and activities that enrich their lives and to invest their savings in productive ventures rather than a plot of dirt and a slowly deteriorating box of lumber, copper, and drywall. It would be enough to provide a home for every homeless person in the country within just a few months (once new homes began opening up), for every severely cost-burdened renter within three to four years (approximately 11 million households as of 2017), and every severely cost-burdened homeowner in another two to three years (approximately 7 million).[72] Existing rental units would become less scarce, forcing landlords to lower their prices as well.

Home value appreciation would no longer outpace income growth, and to many homeowners that would feel like a loss. Relative to the status quo, it would be. But plans to build millions of new homes would require changes to local zoning rules that would increase the "development value" of many properties even as the "existing use value" fell (see the appendix for a discussion of these terms), mitigating potential losses and producing large profits for some homeowners even as tenants and future buyers benefited from lower prices. Single-family homes in desirable and transit-accessible areas would also become less abundant, increasing the value of those that remained.

Property owners could no longer expect annual appreciation of 5 percent or more, but many or most would maintain their equity and have many housing options available to them, at much more affordable prices. As with renters, they could then invest their savings into retirement funds, stocks and bonds, new businesses, or any number of options more desirable than a $4,000 monthly mortgage payment. It would be sensible, and affordable, for the federal government to backstop losses for those homeowners whose equity was negatively impacted by these changes.

This is a vision worth fighting for—and, with an approach to housing policy that prioritizes Supply, Stability, and Subsidy, it is achievable. But without all three we will never achieve a truly just and equitable housing market, and renters will continue to be treated as second-class citizens.

The Urgent Need for Comprehensive Solutions

The discourse around housing has been polarized and siloed for far too long. Even those who acknowledge the complex, interconnected nature of housing policy tend to focus too much on just one of the three key elements, Supply, Stability, or Subsidy. (I include myself in that assessment.) Policies to resolve one issue are proposed with little consideration for how they'll affect the others, and the net effect can leave us worse off than we were when we started. Because we haven't come together, we've struggled to permit more new homes in our cities: tenant advocates rightly argue that renters need protections before we start redeveloping neighborhoods and risking displacement of the most vulnerable. Because we haven't come together, tenant protections have languished: supply-side advocates argue that rent control and housing preservation will make things worse, not better. If we don't design our policies thoughtfully, they could be right. Because we haven't come together, the federal government has not prioritized renters or affordability: we've been too busy fighting each other locally to successfully advocate for ourselves at the federal level, where change is arguably most needed. It's time for the walls to come down and for us to adopt a comprehensive approach to housing affordability and tenants' rights.

My own journey into housing politics began with a focus on housing supply. Over time, my perspective shifted to include a greater appreciation for the importance of Stability and Subsidy. My blog, *Better Institutions*, reflects much of this transition, and my experience as a small-time landlord, living in one unit and managing the other with a below-market tenant, has also helped shape my views. (Not in the way you might expect: I've seen from the inside how landlords are incentivized to exploit their tenants, making me more critical of the entire system.) Wherever we started, more and more of us concerned with the future of our cities, and the people who live in them, are reaching the same conclusion: Supply, Stability, and Subsidy all have important roles to play, and creating more affordable, accessible communities will require an all-of-the-above approach. I hope this book helps more people reach the same conclusion.

This book is not a guidebook to utopia, but what it *can* help you do is make things better—better than they are today, and far better than they'll be if we don't change course soon. With concrete, actionable policy recommendations, this book will help advocates bring cities closer to the vision of the supply-focused market urbanist, the tenant-focused socialist, and the government reformers looking to spend public money more efficiently and effectively—and it can realize those visions with surprising harmony. For those whose primary goal is not ideological purity but real-world results, this is achievable. Affordable, inclusive, and welcoming cities are within our grasp.

I don't naively assume that achieving these goals will be easy, and you shouldn't, either. These recommendations are a serious challenge to the status quo in virtually every US city, and opposition by those who benefit from the current system will be fierce.

In part, it was recognition of the realities of housing politics that led to the writing of this book. I hope to convince readers that Supply, Stability, and Subsidy are all integral to creating affordable cities, but you needn't fully agree to find value in this framework. Decades-old political and economic structures stand in the way of affordable cities, and millions of people benefit from the status quo at the expense of everyone else. Those of us who seek change will need allies—a lot of them. If you finish this book unconvinced that Supply, Stability, and Subsidy are all essential, you will at least, I hope, understand that *your* priority won't get far without the support of allies whose perspectives may differ. There are too many bona fide opponents out there for us to waste our energy arguing with potential allies.

We need advocates of affordable cities to come together, not tear each other down.

This book is about bringing together the people who should have been allies all along, and it's about giving them a framework to organize around and shape to their own unique needs and contexts. We need everyone in. NIMBYs are powerful opponents, and they'll remain unbeatable until we put an end to the vicious infighting among those who ultimately want the same thing: affordable, stable, accessible, thriving communities. The set of policies described in this book will help you bridge the ideological divide and build the powerful coalitions needed to achieve that goal.

How to Use This Book

Most of the book is devoted to concrete, actionable policy recommendations for achieving the goal of more affordable communities. It will arm policy makers, advocates, and professional city planners with specific recommendations and policies, as well as general principles, to improve affordability and increase accessibility through local action. It may be read from start to finish, but it is also intended to function as a handbook or "field guide" for advocates and others to use as needed, whether to create their own advocacy plans or to respond to proposals from their state or local governments and elected officials.

In a spirit of togetherness and shared values, the book begins with a set of principles and general recommendations that should apply to all housing policy. These principles and general recommendations help us establish a common language around housing affordability and stability, and they provide guidance for developing policies that can deliver affordable, accessible cities. The values that we bring into housing advocacy often go unspoken.

Part I presents principles and general recommendations to make those values explicit and provide readers with a framework for implementing policies such as those found in this book, as well as other goals and policies not discussed here, such as strategies for reducing chronic homelessness with supportive housing and for reforming federal programs such as the Community Development Block Grant.

The policy sections follow, starting with "Supply" and followed by "Stability" and "Subsidy." Part II includes approximately a dozen recommendations for each policy section. As appropriate, each recommendation describes what the policy is intended to achieve, background and context, arguments for and against, considerations for when and how a policy should be pursued, and real-life examples of implementation, including what not to do. In accordance with the book's goal of equipping professionals and advocates with the information they need to enact affordable housing policy and bridge ideological divides in housing advocacy, the recommendations are written to complement one another across policy categories. This complementarity is an ongoing theme throughout the book.

Part III presents a policy blueprint that includes a concise implementation plan for each policy, including whether it should be pursued as an immediate, medium-term, or long-term priority. This is intended for professionals and public officials to use as a starting point in developing their own affordability strategies and to help advocates create their own plans and challenge their elected officials' plans against a publicly available standard.

Finally, the appendix offers a primer on real estate and development economics. This book seeks to be accessible to readers regardless of their background, but a basic understanding of the decision-making process of developers, how land and property are valued, and similar concepts is useful—essential, even—for smart and effective policy making in the complex world of housing. The primer is not required reading, but it's recommended for readers who don't have a background in urban economics or real estate.

Part I

Principles and General Recommendations

Before introducing specific policies, I begin with a set of principles and general recommendations intended to guide the policy-making process. They are considerations and values to carry with you into that process. Many of them do double duty by providing tactics and strategies for successful political messaging, meaning they are both motive and method. For example, the recommendation to focus on institutional reform is important for addressing the root causes of housing unaffordability and instability, but it also helps advocates avoid demonizing potential allies such as progressive-minded home-owners and home builders.

Creating stable and affordable cities is about much more than good policy; it's also about making the moral and economic case for action, building broad and effective coalitions, establishing shared values to fall back on when difficult trade-offs must be made, and elevating community knowledge for solutions that are responsive to local conditions. The recommendations that follow will help you navigate this process as you seek to design and implement effective policy.

01   Pursue the Three S's (Supply, Stability, and Subsidy) Simultaneously

—

Identify win-win solutions where you can; then let your values guide you when trade-offs are necessary.

Policies that support abundant housing, strong tenant protections, and increased funding are often driven by different constituencies, whether they're YIMBYs ("yes in my backyard" pro-housing advocates), tenant advocates, affordable housing developers, or one of dozens of other interest groups and coalitions. These constituencies must improve their collaboration and begin working to simultaneously pursue the Three S's: Supply, Stability, and Subsidy.

The Three S's are sometimes in tension: Will new supply lead to more displacement? Will tenant protections stop development? Will rental assistance lead to higher rents, enriching landlords rather than improving affordability? We are primed to see the potential weaknesses of someone else's plan and to be dismissive of the flaws in our own. It is plainly true that there are many beneficiaries of new housing construction, and it's equally true that there are some who are harmed. The same can be said of tenant protections and rental housing preservation, and even public spending can be harmful if it is not done effectively.

These concerns, paired with what are typically siloed, single-issue approaches to the many facets of housing policy, hinder progress. The concerns are legitimate, so the solution must involve breaking down the silos and applying a broad spectrum of programs and policies to improve affordability and accessibility. We must design pro-housing policies that target development where it will benefit the most people (such as where housing costs are highest or job concentration is greatest) and that discourage it where it may do the most harm (such as on sites where dense concentrations of renters already live, especially in lower-income communities and communities of color). We must design pro-tenant policies that protect renters living in affordable homes while ensuring that development remains a profitable venture on sites where tenants aren't threatened and it can do the most good. We must increase spending on rental assistance and affordable housing construction, and complementary zoning reforms and renter protections must be in place to make sure those funds are spent effectively.

Pursuing each of these goals and balancing their tensions is not as hard as it sounds. In fact, it's arguably the easier approach. In making the Three S's coequal priorities, advocates and policy makers can address the complaints of those who want improved affordability but are concerned about unintended consequences, cleaving them away from the true NIMBYs ("not in my backyard" activists) who claim to want reform but are privately motivated only by self-interest and opposition to change. If some opponents remain unmoved even after their concerns are addressed, it's likely that an affordable, accessible city isn't their primary goal—you can move on. And in the process you'll have addressed real weaknesses and listened to critics, building support for a comprehensive plan and strengthening your coalition.

Seattle's Housing Affordability and Livability Agenda (HALA) is an excellent example of this approach in action. The plan was initiated in 2014 with a twenty-eight-member stakeholder advisory committee composed of renters and homeowners, nonprofit and for-profit developers, tenant groups, contractors, community-based organizations, academics, business groups, and more. A year later, the committee released its comprehensive agenda with sixty-five recommendations. Those strategies fell under five main categories, four of which hew closely to the Three S's: (1) promotion of efficient and innovative development (Supply); (2) preservation, equity, and anti-displacement (Stability); (3) mandatory housing affordability (Supply and Stability); and (4) more resources for affordable housing (Subsidy). Category 5 entailed reforms at the state legislature; Washington State doesn't currently permit rent control or inclusionary zoning policies, which limits its ability to provide stable housing for vulnerable households.

The HALA plan has been implemented progressively over several years, with significant victories including a doubling of the

Seattle Housing Levy that was approved by 70 percent of voters, stronger legal protections for renters, and adoption of a density bonus tied to affordability requirements that applies to twenty-seven urban villages throughout the city.[1] The effort also built a coalition of supporters that included "social justice, labor, and environmental groups and businesses" as well as for-profit and nonprofit housing developers.[2]

Seattle has done more than virtually any other booming US city to address housing affordability, building homes at a rate more than double that of many of its peer cities and expanding funding for affordable housing and protections for renters.[3] It can attribute its success to the work of public officials and advocates who assembled a broad coalition of supporters with a comprehensive approach to housing affordability and accessibility. Other cities would be smart to learn from Seattle's success—and then go even further.

02 Take Action Now

—

The more unaffordable your housing stock gets, the more challenging it is to fix.

All else being equal, places that build more housing remain more affordable than those that build less. That said, there's very little evidence that building more housing will, by itself, cause a dramatic decline in rents or home prices. This is especially true where most housing development is privately funded: if a surging supply of new homes causes prices to fall, developers and their investors will tend to pull back and wait for prices to recover before building more.

What having enough homes *can* do is stabilize prices, preventing things from getting worse while complementary policies work to create new deed-restricted units, protect existing tenants, and raise public funds to be used for affordable development, multifamily acquisition and preservation, and rental assistance. This is a worthy goal in its own right.

Cities almost never reverse course on affordability. Virtually nothing short of a natural disaster or economic catastrophe can bring prices to dramatically more affordable levels in the short or medium term. In the United States, this is partly a result of our use of real estate as an investment vehicle: any actions that reduce the cost of housing will also tend to negatively impact homeowners' nest eggs, generating forceful and well-funded opposition. The longer a city waits to take its affordability crisis seriously, the higher prices climb and the more challenging it becomes to enact effective solutions, from a technical as well as a political perspective.

Across the United States, there's a clear relationship between the cost of existing housing and the cost of new housing. In Dallas, Texas, where the median home value is $215,000, a new home costs $200,000 to $250,000 to build. In Los Angeles, where the median value is over $600,000, building a new home costs $600,000 to $800,000.[4] In San Francisco, the median home is valued at nearly $1.4 million, and the cost to build . . . you get the idea. If your city's housing costs are in Dallas's range, count your blessings and get to work before you end up with LA-size problems. If you're in LA, look three hundred miles north for the best cautionary tale on the planet.

In Los Angeles, as in many other cities, older and more affordable homes are "filtering up" to middle- and upper-income households.[5] A thirty-year drought in home building is pushing higher earners into homes built before the 1990s, largely because that's the only housing available. If this drought had never occurred, those same residents could instead be living in homes built in the 1990s and 2000s, relieving pressure on those residing in older housing.

A consistently growing housing supply would have moderated price increases over the past several decades and the cost of new homes wouldn't be so unattainable. If LA had stabilized prices such that a new home today cost only $300,000 to build—instead of double that—its housing challenges would be easier to solve.

There's a proverb that says, "The best time to plant a tree was twenty years ago. The second-best time is now." There are many cities whose current housing challenges are comparable to those of coastal US cities twenty years ago, and they should start planting. For those of us already in crisis . . . better late than never.

03   Focus on Institutional Reform

—

Participating in broken and inequitable institutions doesn't make someone a bad person. Perpetuating them does.

In his book *America, Compromised*, Lawrence Lessig stated, "My belief is that we have allowed core institutions of America's economic, social, and political life to become corrupted. Not by evil souls, but by good souls. Not through crime, but through compromise."[6]

Lessig's argument is that what ails America is the corruption of institutions that, by design, all but guarantee outcomes contrary to their stated goals. In an interview with Ezra Klein, cofounder of the explanatory journalism website Vox and host of the podcast *The Ezra Klein Show*, Lessig used the United States Congress as an example. Members of Congress often spend 30–50 percent of their time fundraising, which puts them in constant contact with wealthy residents, businesspeople, and lobbyists near the top of the socioeconomic ladder. Lessig does not believe most members of Congress are corrupt in any lawbreaking sense of the word. They are doing what's needed to stay in office, and most are complying with the law, and yet the outcome is that Congress hears disproportionately about the needs of the wealthy and connected, not the vulnerable and workaday. The institution itself demands it. That's institutional corruption.

Single-family zoning is somewhat similar, though with darker origins. Single-family zoning was explicitly designed to exclude poor people, people of color, and other disfavored groups from middle- and upper-class white communities, but living in a detached single-family home in the twenty-first century doesn't automatically make someone racist or classist. An overabundance of single-family housing has led to myriad social, environmental, and economic harms, but people need a place to live, and most owners of single-family homes played no part in the lawmaking that led to the proliferation of these homes. We should always ask ourselves, "What alternatives are available to the participants in this unjust system?" If the answer is "None" or something extremely personally costly, the problem is probably the institution and not the individuals within it. (To be clear, the individuals do still have a moral obligation to seek institutional reforms.) Single-family zoning has done great harm to our social order, our economy, and our planet, but it's an institutional problem, not an individual one. We have to tackle the institution if we're going to fix it.

Ownership of rental property is another example. Landlords have a bad reputation, much of it well deserved. There are also many good landlords trying to do right, not putting profits ahead of the people in their care. The problem is that our institutions convey the greatest rewards to the bad actors: the landlords willing to lie, harass, and abuse their tenants are also the ones who often earn the biggest returns on their investment.

Statements like "Single-family zoning is racist" may not be wrong, but they can easily be misinterpreted as "Owners of single-family homes are racist." The reality is that most owners of single-family homes have no sense of the history of zoning and its racist, exclusionary roots. Properly informed, they might very well become allies in the fight for zoning reforms and tenant protections that can help repair the harms done by these policies. Treating the institution and its participants as synonymous not only misses the mark in identifying the underlying problem but also alienates potential allies.

As advocates, we need to refocus our efforts toward reforming institutions, not simply attacking the "bad guys," so that the good guys and neutral parties aren't made complicit in a broken, inequitable system. If we do our work effectively, the bad guys will still get their just deserts through the workings of newly functional, incorruptible (or less easily corruptible) institutions.

04   Adapt Solutions to the Needs of Your Community

—

Although some policies will work just about anywhere, solutions must always be context sensitive.

The recommendations in this book were not handed down from the heavens, and they won't be equally applicable everywhere. Rust belt cities experiencing population decline and job loss have very different challenges from high-cost cities experiencing rapid job growth and struggling with housing prices. Declining cities are more likely to need more and better jobs than more homes (though tenant protections can still help).

Fast-growing, lower-cost cities such as Phoenix, Arizona, and Dallas have their own set of challenges. Housing affordability is not so severe a problem for them, yet, but as they shift toward more sustainable, higher-density development patterns, the salience of these recommendations will grow. Vacancy rates are higher in these locations, so stricter forms of rent control may not be necessary, but anti-gouging rules could help keep a lid on the worst forms of tenant abuse. New construction is more affordable, too, so inclusionary zoning mandates and development fees may inadvertently do more harm than good, driving up construction costs and constricting the supply of new homes. Where the price gap between affordable and market-rate housing is small, such requirements can widen the gap and leave middle-class households out in the cold. Subsidies go a lot further in lower-cost cities, so continued housing production and well-targeted public funds may be the best bet for cities in this position.

Individual communities also have unique and different needs. The purpose of this book is to set a framework for thinking about those needs and what to consider when devising solutions. This framework can serve as a starting point for a conversation, but the values and history of a community must shape it to fit local conditions.

Importantly, the recommendations and strategies in this book will also help individuals advocate more effectively on behalf of their communities. They provide the context needed to dispel false narratives that leave disadvantaged communities with less than they deserve, and to demand more of our elected officials and the exclusionary systems that helped create our present-day circumstances.

05 Center Voices of, and Outcomes for, the Disenfranchised and Most Vulnerable

—

We can't heal the damage done by housing policy without the input and leadership of those most affected by its harmful past and present.

The history of housing policy in America is rife with exploitation, exclusion, theft, and racism. It will require affirmative steps to right historical wrongs. It is not enough to say, "Things used to be bad, but now they're fair and equal; therefore no one deserves special treatment." It is not enough to bring housing costs down from $500,000 per unit to $300,000 per unit when white households, through deliberate government actions stretching back more than a century, have been the recipients of unprecedented wealth through the subsidization and appreciation of property—an opportunity that was explicitly denied to black households, and the repercussions of which persist into the present day via the transfer of intergenerational wealth. More *affirmative* action—that is, not only removing unfair barriers but actively creating conditions for the success of historically disfavored groups—is a moral necessity for any just housing policy.

At the end of his book *The Color of Law*, Richard Rothstein shared a question he's often asked: "When my family came to this country, segregation already existed; we had nothing to do with segregating African Americans. Why should we now have to sacrifice to correct it?" His response is instructive.

Sherrilyn Ifill, president of the NAACP Legal Defense Fund, once responded to a similar question, saying, "Your ancestors weren't here in 1776, but you eat hot dogs on the Fourth of July, don't you?" What she was trying to convey is that Americans who preceded us fought for our liberty, sometimes giving their lives for it, yet we benefit without making similar sacrifices. When we become Americans, we accept not only citizenship's privileges that we did not earn but also its responsibilities to correct wrongs that we did not commit. It was *our* government that segregated American neighborhoods, whether we or our ancestors bore witness to it, and it is *our* government that now must craft remedies.[7]

When crafting those remedies, the groups most negatively affected—and those likely to be impacted by future change—must be given not just a seat at the table but a lead role. *The* lead role or roles. We must prioritize the voices of women; people of color; indigenous communities; people with disabilities; individuals from lower socioeconomic classes and from lesbian, gay, bisexual, transgender, and queer/questioning (LGBTQ) communities; and others who have borne the brunt of segregation, discrimination, urban renewal, and disinvestment. Many are already leading the charge on issues of justice and equity, but their contributions are often undervalued and overlooked. That must change.

Saying these words is easy; making them real is not. Many cities and public officials express similar sentiments with very little to show for it. Advocacy organizations and local officials must be willing to actively seek participation from those who are often poorly represented in such circles—if they're represented at all—and be willing to make space for others' voices. Some cities have taken rather bold steps, such as Seattle, where public funding of neighborhood councils was revoked in 2017. The councils were extraordinarily unrepresentative of the broader community, and the city didn't want to give them the appearance of democratic legitimacy. It believed the funds could be used for outreach and engagement that was more representative of Seattle's increasingly diverse population.[8] Improving representation and centering the voices of the most vulnerable is not an end state. It is an ongoing and iterative process, one of continuous learning, adjustment, and improvement.

I acknowledge the potential irony of these statements being made in a book written by a straight cisgender white male—especially a book that purports to tell others what to do. It's a valid critique and one I won't shy away from. This book is not the final word on housing affordability, but I hope it can serve as a starting or middle point for many. Ideally it can provide tools to help readers become more fluent in "housing-speak" and help more people become comfortable engaging in this important debate. I may also be criticized for the historical wrongs I've left unaddressed in this section, the groups I've failed to include, or the way my language might inadvertently rob them of agency. This is always a risk in discussing sensitive issues such as race and class, and I can only say the following: My intent is to be inclusive, welcoming, and empowering. Or, better yet, in the words of Tamika Butler, "co-powering." Where I fail, I will try to learn and do better in the future. I hope our approaches to housing policy advocacy and reform can share a similar spirit.

06   Use a Mix of Mandates and Incentives

—

Incentives are safer than mandates, but some things are too important to make voluntary.

In housing policy, there's an eternal debate over mandates versus incentives. On the one hand, mandates guarantee an outcome for any program or development subject to them. If you have a 15 percent inclusionary zoning requirement for new housing, 15 percent of units that are built will be set aside for low-income households. On the other hand, if developers can't afford the cost of the 15 percent requirement and nothing gets built, your city will get no low-income *or* market-rate housing and you'll be in a worse situation than the one in which you started. Mandates have their place, but getting them wrong can carry a high cost.

Of course, sometimes mandates are necessary. We wouldn't want to merely incentivize building code requirements that protect residents during a serious earthquake or fire. Faced with the imminent threat of climate change, mandating stringent fuel efficiency standards and reduced industrial carbon emissions is probably better than hoping to incentivize the right behavior. Bringing it back to housing, tenant protections don't lend themselves to incentives, either. Whatever rules are in place should apply consistently and uniformly.

Generally speaking, incentives are preferable to mandates when we want to make a good thing even better. Housing is good and necessary, and affordable housing is even better, so incentives that encourage more housing to be affordable are smart. Very common housing incentive programs include density, height, and floor area bonuses. In such programs, developers are allowed to build more units if they set aside some for low- or moderate-income households. These incentive programs are beneficial not only because they produce more affordable homes (at no cost to the public) but also because they produce more market-rate housing and often lead to lower per-unit costs. It's a win-win.

Mandates are better suited to preventing bad things from happening, such as displacement or pollution. This is part of why they're risky when applied to otherwise positive activities, including housing production. Sometimes there's no way around them, as with building code requirements, but it should be noted that even strict building codes come at a cost and can depress housing development. That may be a worthwhile trade, depending on how much additional safety is conveyed by stronger regulation, or it might not.

Affordable housing incentive programs are in use throughout California[9] as well as in Seattle,[10] Chicago,[11] New York,[12] and many other cities. Because they're voluntary, they allow cities to test out new approaches, see if they're successful, and adjust accordingly, all without negatively affecting development while they work out the kinks. Incentives should usually be the first thing to try, especially when it comes to housing production. For tenant protections and rental housing preservation, mandates are generally more appropriate.

07 Know What You're Asking For

—

Slogans and arbitrary targets may win votes, but they won't deliver affordable, accessible communities.

Politicians and activists will often rally around an ambitious target without exploring whether it's truly achievable. In some cases, it's okay to set an ambitious target and figure out the details later. If you set a goal of 100 percent renewable energy and get to 80 percent, you may have failed, but you've still made great progress. That same logic doesn't always apply to housing policy. Inclusionary zoning (IZ) mandates, which require that new developments set aside a share of their units for low- or moderate-income households, and in contrast to the density bonuses discussed earlier, are an illustrative example.

A number of cities have IZ mandates, and in 2017 they were a topic of debate in the campaign for Seattle's mayor and council members. Nikkita Oliver and Jon Grant, two of the candidates that year, called for a 25 percent IZ requirement. Michael Maddux, a Seattle resident and former council candidate, wrote an insightful article about what this would mean for the city.[13]

In it, Maddux noted that Grant (whose policy platform he was critiquing) called for a 25 percent affordable requirement, yet Grant didn't define "affordable." Should 25 percent of new units be reserved for moderate-income households—those earning up to 120 percent of the area median income (AMI)? Or should 25 percent be set aside for low-income (80 percent of AMI or below) or even extremely low income households (30 percent of AMI)? Each of these choices would have vastly different consequences for the financial feasibility of housing development in Seattle.

If new homes cost an average of $400,000 per unit to build, market-rate units need to charge at least $2,300 to $2,500 per month merely to not *lose* money, never mind earning a profit. A moderate-income unit might be required to rent for $1,750, resulting in an effective monthly subsidy of around $600 or $700. An extremely low income unit, meanwhile, might rent for $600 or less, requiring an implicit subsidy of over $1,700 per month. The developer might be able to absorb the cost of providing moderate-income housing for 25 percent of the units, but not the more deeply subsidized low-income, very low income, or extremely low income units.

Grant's proposal was also unclear about whether developers would receive any incentives to offset the cost of IZ requirements. In other cities, projects subject to affordability requirements often receive bonuses allowing for greater density, height, or floor area or reductions to required parking, open space, or setbacks. They might also receive property tax reductions or exemptions. Without incentives, an IZ policy might significantly reduce overall housing production; with incentives, it might actually *increase* housing production, delivering more market-rate units *and* more affordable units. (The Transit Oriented Communities program in Los Angeles is an excellent example of the latter case,[14] and Seattle ultimately adopted a similar plan that links higher affordability requirements to bigger zoning changes.[15]) In some circumstances, depending on the income level that affordable units are restricted to, an IZ requirement greater than 25 percent might even be appropriate.

All of this is to say that details matter. When discussing policies such as IZ, or value capture, or impact fees, the question of what's *possible* is just as important as what's *desirable*. A 25 percent requirement for moderate-income housing might be possible, but a 25 percent requirement for low-income housing might not. A 25 percent requirement for low-income housing might work if the costs are offset with additional density and floor area, and it might even be increased to 35 percent if those offsets are combined with, say, a property tax rebate.

This book seeks to avoid proposing specific targets, except as examples, because targets are context sensitive. What works for Seattle may not work for San Francisco, and lessons from San Francisco, where housing costs are astronomical, will not necessarily apply elsewhere in the country. For that matter, what works in a specific neighborhood might not work in another neighborhood just a few miles down the road. The specifics have to be worked out locally, always with an eye toward feasibility. A 25 percent target may sound great, but if it severely depresses housing development, it will do very little good: 25 percent of nothing is still nothing.

08 Pick One: Housing Affordability or Rising Home Values

Housing can't be an incredible investment and remain affordable in the long run. We have to choose one or the other, and the choice should be affordability.

Homeownership is a cardinal virtue in American culture, promoted not just for its perceived impacts on "rootedness" and community engagement but also for its ability to create wealth in a country where the social safety net is very weak. More than one-quarter of homeowners in the United States over the age of fifty-five have no retirement savings,[16] and home equity accounts for nearly half of homeowner households' net worth.[17] This is even more pronounced for black and Hispanic households: about 40 percent of net worth for white homeowners over the age of sixty-five is in home equity, whereas for black and Hispanic households this figure jumps to 65–75 percent. Owning a home is integral to financial security for most families in the United States, and rising home values continue to give the government cover for skimping on retirement programs such as Social Security and pensions.

But in keeping with the previous recommendation, it's important to know what to ask for. This is especially true of policies that encourage homeownership and rising home values, because ever-growing property values are completely incompatible with long-term housing affordability. The two are mutually exclusive. For homes to be an outstanding investment, their values must appreciate faster than inflation, and that means incomes *will* trail behind home values over time, without fail. On this path, housing inevitably becomes less affordable for each successive generation. Elected officials often call for more affordable housing options while also celebrating the tradition of American homeownership and its wealth-building potential. We must abandon this fanciful notion. Either home values grow faster than inflation, thus making them increasingly unaffordable over time, or they grow slower than (or equal to) inflation, thus making housing more affordable but also a less attractive vehicle for investment.

Writing for City Observatory, Daniel Kay Hertz summarized how this tension is typically handled: "Mostly, American housing policy resolves this contradiction by quietly deciding that it really doesn't care that much about affordability after all. While funds for low-income subsidized housing languish, much larger pots of money are set aside for promoting homeownership through subsidies like the mortgage interest deduction and capital gains exemption, most of which goes to upper-middle- or upper-class households."[18]

In an earlier recommendation, "Take action now," I noted that the cost of new housing reflects the cost of existing housing. The more expensive existing homes become, the costlier it is to build new homes and the deeper are the subsidies required to make them affordable. This is reason enough to avoid the trap of promoting ever-increasing home values. Some homeowners will gain (though not as much as we think; more on that later), but renter households will be immiserated and find it increasingly difficult to grab a rung on the wealth-building homeownership ladder. Meanwhile, public spending will balloon to address rising rent burdens, evictions, homelessness, and all the social and economic costs that accrue to a housing market that prioritizes investment value over affordability.

It's also important to recognize that rising home prices aren't even very good for homeowners in the long run. On the one hand, when home values rapidly appreciate it can feel like your investment is really paying off, and in a sense that's true. Down payments are a highly leveraged investment, and when home values appreciate rapidly, the returns can be phenomenal. Home equity also provides a healthy cushion upon which homeowners can rely in tough times.

On the other hand, what do higher prices really mean? For one thing, they often lead to higher property tax payments, which can be a burden for lower-income households and those living on a fixed income. More importantly, when a home's value increases, it's not doing so in isolation: prices are probably going up across the entire region. It may feel good to buy a home for $400,000 and see it appreciate to $700,000, but what can someone actually do with that appreciated value when all the other homes of similar size, quality, and location are also worth $700,000? Ironically, the biggest beneficiaries of rapidly rising home prices aren't the people who want to stay in their community and preserve its "neighborhood character"—instead, rising prices most benefit those who want to eventually sell out and move somewhere cheaper. While there's nothing wrong with moving to another city, it's perverse for a city's policy to bestow the greatest rewards upon those who leave.

This also applies to future generations. Many people view homeownership and rising home values as something they can pass along to their children, but this is a dark and pessimistic view of the future. Wouldn't it be better to have a world where homes are abundant and affordable, where our children can afford a place to live without a financial endowment from their parents? The American Dream, imperfect as it was and still is, was supposed to be about hard work and personal achievement. The new American Dream seems to be to wait for our parents or grandparents to die, passing on the wealth and stability that we can no longer realistically secure for ourselves.

Imagine an alternative history in which our country focused on maintaining affordability for everyone instead of promoting wealth accumulation only for some: where the price of a home remained just a few multiples of the average household's annual wages, and families never paid more than 20 percent or 25 percent of their income on housing. What if we built wealth not by spending all our income on a down payment and a mortgage but instead by investing in new businesses, mutual funds, or small-scale housing developments to keep our neighborhoods affordable and inclusive? In that world, what is good for homeowners wouldn't have to come at the expense of renters and future generations. We're a long way from that reality, but it's one worth striving for.

09 Don't Reward Idle Money

—

The real estate industry is full of people making money but adding very little value. Don't try to accommodate them.

Developers have a bad reputation, but they put their time and money into creating something essential to society: places for people to live. Landlords invest money in existing property and collect rents based on their ownership of the land and structures (and, admittedly, labor). Homeowners invest and collect appreciation based in large part on neighborhood improvements, increasing scarcity, or both, not improvements to their home itself. Right now we reward the latter two groups far out of proportion to their contributions, and that needs to change.

This doesn't mean that being a landlord is easy or that homeowners don't work to improve their communities and their own property. They're also not bad people for participating in an economic system that makes homeownership nearly essential for success and financial security.

But the fact that individual landlords and homeowners aren't culpable doesn't mean the system we have is worth keeping. The profits of landlords and homeowners come directly at the expense of renters and future home buyers: landlords' income comes on the backs of renters, and homeowners' appreciation means higher prices for the next generation of buyers. Every successive generation is less able to participate in this form of wealth creation. This trajectory—where the rich get richer and the poor get left behind—isn't sustainable.

Buying and holding property simply shouldn't be competitive with other investments such as starting a business or building something new. Our favorable treatment of land acquisition draws investment away from other sectors of the economy that actually add value and grow the pie for everyone. Property ownership simply reallocates resources. In the case of landlords, resources are transferred directly from lower- and moderate-income renters to wealthier and higher-income property owners. Worse, that transfer restricts the financial prospects of tenants, leaving them more vulnerable and more likely to depend on public assistance. It leaves our society poorer even as it enriches those already doing well.

It doesn't make someone a bad person to invest in rental property or be a homeowner. Nearly every aspect of our financial system encourages it. The problem is that the system encourages predatory and self-serving behavior, in which owners take what they can from renters and are rewarded for making housing increasingly scarce. Even the good landlords don't live forever, and when their property is passed along, it will go to whoever is willing to pay top dollar. That person will often be the one most willing to harass, abuse, and evict because there's more upside potential for bad landlords than good ones—and that's a problem we can't let persist.

10 Don't Coddle Landlords

Deference to mom-and-pop landlords gets in the way of effective, consistently applied housing protections.

Landlords have one of the most important jobs in the world. When they screw up—by neglect, ignorance, or deliberate abuse—people's lives and livelihoods can be put at risk.

Bad landlords can put their tenants at risk by, for instance, allowing mold or vermin to propagate, failing to address earthquake or fire risks, not disclosing vital information about their units, serving illegal eviction notices or rent increases, and a whole host of other serious and harmful infractions.

Given the degree to which tenants rely on the good behavior of their landlords, it's incredible that in most cities virtually no training is required to become a landlord. Having enough money to buy a property is the only qualification required, followed (in some but not all cases) by sporadic inspections to ensure compliance with local building and safety codes. It takes one thousand hours of training to become an aesthetician, but absolutely no training is required to become the sole owner and manager of the homes in which people work, cook, clean, eat, study, sleep, play, and raise their children.

This isn't to say that landlords are inherently bad—although, as noted in the previous recommendation, they shouldn't be unduly rewarded simply for acquiring property. Many landlords do a fine job and care deeply for the safety and well-being of their tenants. But many do not, and to leave this to the luck of the draw is an unconscionable abrogation of societal responsibility.

As we seek to create stable communities through measures such as rent stabilization and eviction protections, we should also consider the training of those who manage rental homes and the ways we hold them accountable to act in the best interests of their tenants. Right now we do a very poor job of it, often in the name of protecting mom-and-pop landlords.

Small-time landlords are very frequently held to a lower

standard, including exemption from many tenant protections (such as rent control) that larger property owners are subject to. This must end. We wouldn't exempt small-time battery manufacturers from safe toxic waste disposal practices simply because those requirements placed a proportionately larger burden on them than on their bigger peers. Similarly, providing safe, stable housing is too important a job—too fundamental to the well-being of tenants—to allow some people to skirt the rules. If rent control, just-cause eviction, and regular reporting to local authorities are too great a burden for mom-and-pop landlords, they shouldn't be in the business of rental housing management.

By exempting mom-and-pops from certain standards, we are saying that the financial return on a rental housing investment is more important than the health, safety, and well-being of our neighbors. We need to reverse this dynamic and put the fundamental needs of renters above returns on investment for landlords, even the small ones. Tenants shouldn't receive different protections based simply on who happens to own the building in which they live.

11   Track Everything

___

"You can't manage what you can't measure." —*Peter Drucker*

Los Angeles recently created a registry of all rent-stabilized housing in the city, requiring landlords to report basic information about their rental units. This registry includes the amount charged for rent and the length of tenancy for residents. As the owner of a rent-stabilized duplex in which I occupy one unit and rent out the other to a below-market tenant, I too am subject to this requirement. Similar registries should be created for all rental housing in any city concerned with maintaining affordability and protecting tenants.

Rental registries keep landlords honest. They prevent less scrupulous landlords from raising rents beyond rates that may be permitted in a jurisdiction, and they create a public, but confidential, record of tenancy that can be invaluable in eviction cases, which can sometimes boil down to he-said, she-said accusations.

While administration can be a challenge, especially for smaller jurisdictions, such registries can pay for themselves. They can streamline enforcement activities through random sampling of units in the registry and help direct real-life staff toward the most likely offenders for follow-up. They can also reduce the costs associated with illegal evictions and rent hikes, which tend to fall on the public in the form of legal counsel support, housing assistance, and spending associated with addressing homelessness.

Another very significant benefit of a rental registry is data. Currently, the resources available for estimating rental rates, affordability, and rent burden are imprecise and unreliable. These typically depend on aggregator websites that include only on-the-market units in their estimates (which tends to exaggerate the price that existing tenants pay) or US Census Bureau surveys, such as the American Community Survey, that are at least one or two years out of date when published and are aggregated to such a high level that they lose most of their informative value. Rental registries can provide real-time data that allow cities to respond nimbly to changing conditions.

12 Strive for Objective, Consistent Rules

—

Requiring negotiations and discretionary approvals for every project increases costs and invites corruption.

Many of our fights over housing come down to the subjectivity of the development approval process. This includes design review boards, zoning administrators, planning commission and city council approvals, site plan review, and the like. When these processes are present, virtually every aspect of a project becomes negotiable, throwing open the door to backroom dealing and outright corruption. And even when the process is negotiated honestly, discretionary approvals can create an *appearance* of corruption that's nearly as corrosive as corruption itself.

Opponents of new housing have it both ways when it comes to discretionary approvals. On the one hand, these rules create uncertainty for potential developers, driving up risk and therefore costs. They also allow housing opponents—in addition to well-meaning community members—to impose additional, often arbitrary conditions on developments, further increasing costs and delay. On the other hand, these same rules promulgated by anti-housing activists are then held up as evidence of an unfair, opaque process that "greedy developers" and "shady politicians" use to enrich themselves at the community's expense.

The simple but politically challenging answer is to eliminate subjective decision making as much as possible. Community input should still be an important part of the process, but it should take place as early as possible, and it should be independent of individual project approvals. Input should be sought for community-wide plans and design guidelines, created by consensus building before new developments are even proposed. Once such plans and guidelines are established, projects that comply with the rules should proceed without delay and without the opportunity for discretionary, subjective (and therefore unreliable) review.

Clear and predictable rules lower the cost and expedite the

schedule of development, helping us deliver housing faster and more affordably. Just as importantly, they establish a process that is fair and transparent while maintaining the important role of community input.

13 Expand the Conversation around Gentrification

There's more to gentrification than rents and evictions.

Gentrification isn't just about higher rents and displaced households, although those are some of its most visible and pernicious consequences. Gentrification also involves social and cultural factors.

When a neighborhood is changing, the daily life of longtime residents can be seriously disrupted even if they own their homes or are protected from rent increases and evictions. One example of this is longtime neighborhood-serving outlets, such as grocery stores and restaurants, being replaced with upscale businesses that don't cater to the needs or incomes of existing residents. This may not be a crushing burden for most residents, but it's a cost borne by those with the fewest resources, with no clear offsetting benefit.

Even when residents of gentrifying communities can afford to live somewhere else, if they choose, displacement has social and emotional consequences. In Randy Shaw's book *Generation Priced Out*, Francisco Gonzalez speaks about what it would mean to be forced from his neighborhood: "When you live in a community for twelve years, you are emotionally connected. I feel safe and secure in Boyle Heights. When I walk my dog through the streets I know people by name and they know me. I know the neighbors in my building, on my block, and a lot of people within a one-mile radius. . . . I would lose all of this if I have to move far from the area."[19]

This isn't something we can just wave away as the price of progress. We want affordable and accessible cities for the benefit of the people who live in them and those who *would* live in them. It isn't about affordability for affordability's sake; it's about people. How do we ensure that affordable cities benefit everyone, not just financially but also socially and emotionally?

Gentrification is also about safety—residents feeling that they're secure, protected, and welcome in their own community. Many lower-income neighborhoods and communities of color are havens for their residents—places to be free from the discrimination and bias they're subjected to in other, whiter or more affluent spaces. When a neighborhood's demographics begin to shift, this feeling of safety can evaporate, and the consequences can be very real. This is exemplified by incidents such as those in which white women, later dubbed "Barbecue Becky" and "Permit Patty," called the cops on black people whose entirely legal, ordinary behavior troubled them. These women were rightly lampooned by the media and the public, but their actions are symptomatic of a real problem: when white people move into communities of color, they bring with them their own notions of acceptable public behavior. The worst among them may try to use the police to enforce those norms, ignorant of or uncaring about the potentially life-threatening consequences of their actions. Given the propensity for police interactions to lead to unprovoked violence toward black and brown residents, this is no laughing matter. Whites and other privileged groups bring their norms and their relationships with state authority into vulnerable communities, and this can literally put people of color at risk for their lives. Any conversation about gentrification that focuses solely on affordability and displacement is incomplete.

14 Align Local Votes with Presidential and Midterm Elections

Pro-tenant, pro-affordability policies require pro-tenant, pro-affordability elected officials.

Many US cities and counties hold "off-cycle" elections, separate from congressional and presidential elections: national elections occur in even years and local elections in odd years. As a result, the electorate for local elections skews older, wealthier, whiter, and more conservative than the median resident—or even the average registered voter. They are also disproportionately homeowners rather than renters. Advocates who want to see more action on housing policy should work to align their local elections with presidential and midterm ballots.

According to Zoltan Hajnal, professor of political science at the University of California, San Diego, the timing of elections plays a big role in turnout. Nationally, turnout for municipal elections is only 27 percent among eligible voters.[20] In some cities, including Fort Worth, Dallas, and Las Vegas, turnout for mayoral elections has fallen below 10 percent.[21] Meanwhile, national turnout for midterm elections averages around 40 percent, and during presidential years it is typically between 55 percent and 60 percent.[22] When Baltimore moved from off-cycle to on-cycle elections, its voter turnout jumped from 13 percent to 60 percent of registered voters. When San Diego, which normally holds on-cycle elections, held a special election in 2013 following a mayoral scandal, turnout dropped from 76 percent to 35 percent.[23]

Voter turnout among young residents, aged eighteen through twenty-nine, hit a record high in the 2018 midterms. Nearly 36 percent of registered voters in this age range cast a ballot, compared with 66 percent of those sixty-five or older.[24] A turnout rate barely half that of older voters may sound bad, and it *is* bad in comparison with what we should aspire to. Nonetheless, young voter turnout rates of this magnitude would be revolutionary at the local level. In many US cities, the turnout rate for voters over sixty-five is many multiples higher than that for voters aged eighteen through twenty-nine. In cities such as Louisville, Kentucky, and San Jose, California, the turnout rate was three times higher for older adults for elections held between 2011 and 2015; in Nashville, Tennessee, and Los Angeles, it was five to six times greater; in Fort Worth, Texas, the turnout ratio was more than twenty to one.[25]

In cities with the lowest turnout of young voters, the gap between the age of the median adult and the age of the median voter is massive, upward of fifteen or twenty years in some cities. In places with higher turnout and a better balance of turnout rates for older and younger voters, such as in Portland, Oregon, and Seattle, the gap is less than ten years.[26] These younger voters are far more likely to be renters, and as a result they're far more likely to be directly affected by the housing crisis. Homeowners currently dominate local elections, and until that changes, they'll continue to dominate local housing policy, too.

––––––––

As discussed in the introduction and in recommendation 1, each of the Three S's, Supply, Stability, and Subsidy, is indispensable for affordable cities. In the following sections I dig into the details of each of the Three S's with specific actions that can be taken to improve affordability and household stability. A careless approach to any of these goals may undermine the success of the others, so these policies are designed to complement one another—to take the best from each of the Three S's and combine them into a cohesive and effective whole.

Part II

Policies

___

The following sections include approximately a dozen recommendations for each of the Supply, Stability, and Subsidy policy categories. These policies, taken together, are designed to grow the supply of housing to meet current and future needs, protect tenant households and preserve existing rental housing options, and increase the quantity and effectiveness of public spending on housing programs, especially for those most in need. Taken together, they can help chart a course toward realizing housing as a true human right—a system that privileges the protection, safety, health, and dignity of people over excessive profit and exploitation.

Supply: Why Housing Matters

Housing supply, or lack thereof, is the main driver of increasing prices. For decades, employment and population growth in superstar cities has outpaced the supply of new homes, resulting in a self-imposed scarcity. It's made housing more expensive and led to displacement, directly and indirectly, as higher-income residents outbid their less affluent neighbors for a place to call home. The overflow from superstar cities is cascading down to merely exceptional cities and their suburbs, affecting an ever-growing share of the population. We must make it easier to build housing, and do so in a thoughtful and careful way, to have any hope of creating more affordable and accessible cities.

All else being equal, zoning for more housing capacity will lead to more housing being built, and having more homes available will help stabilize the price of housing. If housing is abundant, landlords must compete for renters; if housing is scarce, renters must compete for landlords—and landlords take advantage of this by charging higher prices. This is the core of the supply-side argument for housing affordability, and it's borne out by the evidence. Cities that build more housing relative to their population (and population growth) tend to be more affordable than those that build less,[1] and jurisdictions with the most restrictive land-use policies also tend to be the most expensive.[2] Cities with higher residential vacancy rates—a sign that housing growth is keeping up with, or exceeding, housing demand—also tend to be more affordable.[3]

At a high level, we can separate the supply argument into two components: the rate of new development and the vacancy rate.

The first component, the rate of new development and its impact on housing affordability, follows from the theory of supply and demand. When a market is open and competitive, suppliers will provide more housing (or any other good) to meet growing demand, and competing suppliers will keep adding units of that good until it's no longer profitable to do so—or, more accurately, until the expected return on investment falls below an acceptable threshold. If a city is able to match the supply of new housing to growing demand, the cost of building new housing shouldn't rise any faster than the overall rate of inflation, give or take. And while homes and land aren't interchangeable widgets in the same way as are commodities such as wheat and ball bearings, the concept still holds up with housing markets to a rough approximation.

A key qualifier: The supply-and-demand theory bears out at the level of the regional or metropolitan area, but it's less clear whether it accurately describes neighborhood-level effects. Further, compared with products that can be quickly produced on an assembly line, it takes an exceedingly long time for housing supply to respond to housing demand (which many cities make worse with years-long approval processes). From the time developers recognize increasing demand to when they've finished acquiring land, entitling it for development, and constructing new homes, many years may pass. A lot can happen to neighborhood residents in that time, which is part of why supply—while essential for preserving long-term affordability in growing cities—is not enough by itself.

Vacancy rates are the second component of the supply argument. Think of the vacancy rate as being like the unemployment rate: when unemployment is low, employers are desperate for workers and will pay top dollar to attract new talent, giving employees increased market power. As a result, periods of low unemployment correspond to higher wage growth. Similarly, when vacancy rates are low, it's *renters* who are desperate, giving landlords increased market power. Periods of low vacancy correspond to high *rent* growth. The immediate goal of new housing is to maintain or even increase the residential vacancy rate, reducing the market power of landlords and giving renters more leverage in negotiating fair leases (and home buyers more leverage in their purchase offers).

Another popular analogy, comparing housing to automobiles, further illustrates the importance of supply. Unlike new homes in expensive cities, new cars are offered at a wide range of price points. Taking Toyota as an example, there are the Yaris and the Corolla at the low end, starting at around $16,000 to $20,000, all the way up to the Avalon at $38,000 and the Mirai at nearly $60,000.[4] Per car, higher-end vehicles are more profitable, so why does Toyota bother building Yarises and Corollas? Automakers are just as profit motivated as developers, so why does one industry serve people across the income spectrum but the other not?

One important answer is supply constraints. Automakers are allowed to manufacture as many vehicles as they want, their only limitation being the number they think they can sell. Many will be luxury vehicles: Lexuses and Model S's and even the occasional Lamborghini. But most people can't afford those cars, so manufacturers need something to offer the middle class. Each individual low- and midrange car isn't as profitable, but they can sell many more of them, so it still makes sense to build them. Thus, we have a car market with seemingly endless choices.

In 2017, Toyota sold 387,081 units of the Camry, its most popular model in the United States.[5] It sold over 2.1 million vehicles across all models.[6] Toyota's luxury brand, Lexus, sold 302,132 vehicles across all models in the same year. Now imagine that the federal government decides it wants fewer cars on the road and places a cap on the combined total number of Toyota and Lexus vehicles that can be manufactured each year. If that cap is under 300,000, we can kiss the Camry—and the entire Toyota vehicle line—goodbye. The Lexus is more profitable, and there's demonstrated demand for at least 300,000 vehicles at that price point, so the automaker will justifiably focus its efforts there. To do otherwise would be poor business sense and a betrayal of Toyota and Lexus shareholders.

With the more affordable line of Toyota vehicles off the market, the average cost of new cars would rise significantly. Middle-class households would be angry that "greedy automakers" were producing vehicles only for the rich. Some elected official, forgetting the origin of the shortfall, might eventually demand that automakers set aside 20 percent of their Lexuses for low-income households.

This cap would also have longer-term effects. Having fewer new vehicles would result in a shortage of used vehicles for down-market buyers. Vehicles wouldn't fall in value, at least not quite so fast, because the number of would-be used car buyers would far exceed the available supply. Most middle- and upper-middle-class buyers would still be able to afford used vehicles, but these vehicles would never filter down to low-income households. There simply wouldn't be enough to go around. Is this beginning to sound familiar?

As bad as this scenario is for cars, it's worse for housing. Cars, for all their usefulness, have serious negative impacts on the environment, urban design, safety, public health, and social cohesion. There's an argument to be made for limiting the proliferation of personal automobiles, though an arbitrary cap would be a ham-fisted way to do it. People can still get around in lieu of driving their own car, whether by carpooling, transit, walking, or bicycling. What people *can't* do is get by without homes, and the workarounds that people devise—overcrowding, illegal dwellings, tent and vehicle dwelling—are deeply harmful.

Filtering is another important concept in the housing supply debate. Looking at rental housing built in 1985, the California Legislative Analyst's Office found that when the units came onto the market, their lease rates were in the eightieth to ninetieth percentile for price. By 2011, rents for those same units had fallen to the fiftieth to sixtieth percentile.[7] Over a twenty-six-year period, these units had "filtered" down from the very top of the market to somewhere in the middle.

Filtering has its detractors. To some, it sounds like a rebranding of the supply-side "trickle-down economics" of the Ronald Reagan and George H. W. Bush era. When the value of filtering is over-stated, this assessment is not necessarily wrong. Filtering is real, and it really does help improve affordability, but it's easily observable only over multiple decades, and even homes that fall to the fiftieth rent percentile are unaffordable to a great many people.

When gung-ho advocates of housing deregulation claim that it is the sole solution to the affordability crisis (a claim, it should be noted, that is virtually never made by housing policy professionals), they are overstating the benefits of zoning liberalization. But anti-development and tenant advocates are also wrong when they argue that new market-rate housing doesn't benefit low- and middle-income households in the short term.

The theory behind the short-term benefits of new development, even when the homes are targeted at high earners, goes something like this. Housing will generally be allocated according to what peo-ple are willing and able to pay, and high-income households will lay claim to the highest-quality, best-located homes, while less desir-able housing will go to less affluent residents. If the highest-quality, best-located homes are in new developments, that's where many wealthy residents will live. If there are no new developments to move into, the wealthy will move to wherever the nicest housing already exists.

When a city's population is growing but its housing stock isn't, the wealthiest will bid up the prices of the most desirable homes, pushing families in the next income tier into less desirable neigh-borhoods. Those second-tier households are willing to pay more than the current residents of the less desirable neighborhoods, so the prices get bid up there, too. This cascades all the way down to the least desirable areas of the city, with the most tenuously housed residents eventually pushed into overcrowded conditions, onto the streets, or out of the city altogether. This has been aptly described as a game of cruel musical chairs. Replace chairs with homes, and allocate housing according to income rather than speed, and there you have our housing market in a nutshell.[8]

Filtering, even in the short term, turns this dynamic on its head. New homes are built for higher-income households (ideally without displacing any existing residents), and the cascade flows upward rather than down. In a simplified model city with just three income brackets—high, middle, and low—the high-income household vacates their existing home to move into a new development, creating an opportunity for the middle-income family to take their place. The middle-income family's former home is now available for the low-income household to move up into. In practice, households and housing stock both fall along infinitely divisible spectra, not such neatly separable categories, but the concept is the same.

Short-term filtering is difficult to measure empirically, but recent work from Evan Mast of the W. E. Upjohn Institute for Employment Research provides compelling evidence in support of this theory.[9]

Mast tracked the "migration chain" that results from new development, starting with the residents of 802 large new multifamily luxury buildings. Looking at the previous addresses of those luxury apartment dwellers, he determined who moved into their previous homes, and he repeated this tracking exercise for up to six rounds of previous tenants and addresses. Using estimates based on this empirical data, he found that "building 100 new market-rate units leads 45–70 and 17–39 people to move out of below-median and bottom-quintile income tracts, respectively, with almost all of the effect occurring within five years." That's up to 70 households who are able to "move up" to higher-income census tracts for every 100 new luxury units built; of those, up to 39 households are moving from the lowest-income, bottom-quintile tracts. Mast continues, "This suggests that new construction reduces demand and loosens the housing market in low- and middle-income areas, even in the short run." Creating a pathway for residents to move up from lower-income neighborhoods (if they choose) reduces pressure on those communities, benefiting them even when residents of the lower-income areas aren't able to move into the new homes directly.

The same study also found that people tend to move up as they migrate, from a census tract in the fourth income decile to one in the fifth, for example, or from the seventh to the eighth. This highlights an important fact: Individual households are not static. They change and evolve as careers advance, hardships are faced, relationships form, children are born, elders require support, and tastes change. A housing policy that doesn't address supply will never adequately respond to the ever-changing circumstances that are a natural part of all our lives.

Another study by Mast and colleagues Brian Asquith and Davin Reed found that rents in existing buildings were lowest near new luxury developments. Beyond two hundred meters from the site of the luxury project, rents increased.[10] This is strong evidence that new housing tends to dampen rather than increase rents for nearby homes, though more empirical research is certainly needed.

A last few points on supply.

First, increasing the availability of homes is about more than affordability. It gives cities endless opportunities to reshape their built environment in service of greater access to jobs, parks, educational facilities, shopping, and other vital amenities; improved public health and sustainability; economic development; infrastructure upgrades and resilience investments; community spaces and places for social connection; and more. These should be priorities for any city, and each of them will be easier to achieve when supplemented with private investment in housing and mixed-use development.

Second, once new housing is built, it provides ongoing funding for all of the efforts just noted. This is particularly true of jurisdictions that rely heavily on property taxes to fund their operations (as they should—this is discussed later). The discourse in big cities has turned against higher-income residents, especially those who work in the technology sector, but cities should be happy to spend those residents' money on local priorities that benefit the entire community.

And third: Scarcity isn't bad only for economic reasons. It also breeds social ills, bringing out the worst in society in the form of demagoguery and xenophobia. Anyone witness to the debates occurring in some of our most expensive regions, such as New York and San Francisco, has seen how ruthless these disagreements can become. When there's too little to go around, people begin to pull up the drawbridges to protect whatever they have. Any change becomes a threat. Some of our nation's most liberal, nominally pro-immigrant cities are also the most inaccessible, especially to low-income immigrants, because of their cost. Sanctuary cities mean very little if it is only the privileged who can afford to live in them.

Supply-side solutions tend to get a bad rap in housing debates, particularly in liberal and progressive circles. This can be explained partly by their connection, warranted or not, to trickle-down economics. Left-leaning groups are also often skeptical of deregulation, but it shouldn't be heresy to acknowledge that some industries are overregulated while others are underregulated, or regulated incorrectly. And further, it should be fair to acknowledge that allowing more housing in exchange for affordable units and community benefits is not necessarily *de*regulation but rather *different* regulation. Reforms should be evaluated on the basis of their projected outcomes, not on how neatly they hew to one ideology or another.

Some supply-side advocates also overpromise what zoning reforms can deliver, especially in markets where housing has already become unaffordable. It's one thing to reform your city's housing policy while the cost of a new home falls between $200,000 and $300,000. In that case, the price gap between affordable (in the subsidized, income-restricted sense of the word) and market-rate housing is quite small, and reform can ensure that even unsubsidized homes remain affordable to average families.

It's another thing entirely to say that deregulation will magically make a city affordable when it currently costs $700,000 to build a new home. That's a bridge too far. Done right, reform will absolutely make a difference, but it's just one essential component of a full-spectrum, long-term treatment. To argue otherwise makes pro-supply advocates appear ideological, uninformed, and unconcerned with impacts on individual households and communities. Fortunately, that isn't the position of most pro-supply advocates and policy professionals.

This section explores specific policies that can ensure your city provides enough homes for its existing and future residents. Supply is not a monolith, however, and supportive policies must be designed with consideration for their impacts on Stability and Subsidy. These tensions, where they exist, are discussed in the policies that follow.

15 Increased Zoning Capacity

—

The first step to getting more housing is allowing more housing to be built.

Upzoning is the process of changing the zoning designation of a parcel, or a group of parcels, or an entire neighborhood or city, to allow higher-intensity development. In this book, "upzoning" refers specifically to allowing more *residential* development—for example, allowing ten units on a parcel that previously allowed only two—though in other contexts it can also refer to increased capacity for other uses, such as office space or hotel rooms.

Upzoning increases the number of homes that can theoretically be built in a city, and that increased capacity means developers have more options for where they can build new homes and how many they can build on a given site. When residential capacity is low, there are fewer sites ripe for redevelopment. Those that exist command a premium, driving up the cost of land and, as a result, the overall cost of new housing.

Los Angeles exemplifies the impacts of scarcity. In 1960, LA had 2.5 million residents and a zoning capacity that would have permitted enough housing for 10 million people; by 2010, its population had grown to 4 million, but its zoned capacity had been reduced to 4.3 million.[11] Partly as a result of the artificial scarcity created by that process, the city went from a median home price that was 30 percent above the national average in 1970 to prices that were more than 250 percent above the national average today.

When upzones are enacted, they're usually neighborhood-by-neighborhood, piecemeal actions. In Los Angeles, they are done in manageable chunks through the community plan process: LA has thirty-five community plans that divide the approximately 470 square miles of the city. It also makes zoning changes through "specific plans," which tend to be smaller geographic areas that have fairly arbitrary boundaries and are located within community plan areas. Seattle similarly divides its neighborhoods into "urban centers" and "urban villages" that break down zoning plans into manageable chunks.

Los Angeles and many other cities have taken an overly cautious approach to reversing the downzoning of decades past, with development capacity and population growing at similar rates. While this has kept the scarcity problem from growing significantly worse, it hasn't improved the situation; just as was the case a decade ago, its development capacity is only marginally greater than the number of homes already in the city.

What cities need is a surge of upzoning to shift the balance of power away from current property owners—those who own the few sites where redevelopment is feasible. Where development capacity is limited, property owners can take their pick among developers desperate to find a viable building site. And when few sites are available, developers will build housing targeted at the very highest end of the income spectrum. They have no choice: the lack of viable sites means that the highest bidder will pay a great premium for the land, and the only way to earn a profit on that high bid is to build homes that can secure very high rents or sale prices. When development sites are more abundant, and competition for land less fierce, prices moderate and developers can serve residents at lower rungs of the income ladder.

Upzoning will frequently increase the value of affected parcels, but this should not be mistaken for making them less affordable. From a developer's perspective (and, ultimately, that of the future renters or buyers of the units they build), what matters is not the total value of the land but the value divided by the number of units. A parcel zoned for a single home might be worth $500,000, and upzoning it to allow ten units might increase its value to $1 million, but the land cost per unit will have fallen by 80 percent, to $100,000. This is an improvement to affordability that also happens to benefit the current property owner—which can be good politics as well as good economics.

Finally, multifamily housing is almost universally more affordable than single-family detached housing located in the same neighborhood. In the Desert View community of Phoenix, Arizona, the median condominium costs about 63 percent as much as the median single-family home ($278,000 versus $444,000). In Westwood, the neighborhood surrounding the campus of the University of California, Los Angeles (UCLA), condominiums are just one-third the price of single-family homes ($914,000 versus $2.7 million). In the Southwest Coconut Grove community of Miami, condos cost half as much as single-family homes ($439,000 versus $834,000).[12] Especially in high-demand urban areas, the cost of buying an entire plot of land—in addition to the home itself—will put single-family home-ownership out of reach for most households. Any policy that seeks to improve affordability in urban areas will require a much greater emphasis on multifamily housing, and large-scale zoning changes will be a necessary part of the equation.

16 Upzone Many Places at Once (Upzoning: Geographically Distributed)

—

Avoid overconcentration of investment (and gentrification) by spreading the zoning wealth.

Upzoning in just one neighborhood sends a signal that that specific neighborhood is a target for redevelopment and, potentially, gentrification and displacement. Especially when overall capacity is low (see the previous recommendation), investment is funneled into the few locations where higher-intensity development is permitted.

By enacting more geographically distributed upzones, either simultaneously or in quick succession, the impact on any given community can be diluted, with development happening in more modest quantities all across a city. Los Angeles's Transit Oriented Communities (TOC) program, a voter-initiated incentive program that created more housing capacity in transit-accessible areas throughout the city, is a fine example of this approach. It produced one of the greatest surges in market-rate and affordable housing development in the past thirty years, and it did so without any individual community bearing the brunt of the rapid uptick in construction. Minneapolis and the state of Oregon are also recent examples of geographically distributed upzoning, prohibiting single-family zoning and allowing duplexes or triplexes in nearly all residential areas. When you upzone everywhere, or in many neighborhoods at once, no particular neighborhood becomes the obvious choice for what Jane Jacobs called "cataclysmic redevelopment."

Among city planners, it's become almost axiomatic that the best place to build more housing is along major arterials and commercial corridors. These areas tend to have many retail and commercial destinations that residents will visit regularly, often have the best transit options in a city, rarely require the displacement of any existing residents in order to be redeveloped, and don't receive as much pushback from noisy NIMBY ("not in my backyard") neighbors.

This may all be true, to varying degrees, but it's debatable whether this is "good" planning that results in convenient and desirable communities. The parcels that line arterial and commercial corridors make up only a small share of the parcels in most cities, making it very challenging to achieve high capacity *or* sufficient geographic distribution. Designing walkable and transit-accessible communities is also severely hindered by this style of "corridor-based" planning.

Most parcels in a city are not on arterial streets but on the in-between sites, the "residential streets" that residents—especially homeowners—are most defensive of. If those areas remain low density, daily destinations will be stretched out along the corridors, and more trips will need to be made by car. Many trips that could otherwise be made on foot or bicycle will require residents to hop on a bus or train at best or into a car at worst. While not inherently problematic, this puts an unnecessary strain on resources and means fewer trips made using active transportation, the healthiest and most fun way to get around—and pretty great for the planet, too. It's also wrong to reserve quiet "residential" streets solely for single-family homeowners while locating more affordable multifamily housing only along noisier, more trafficked and polluted arterial corridors—places known to exacerbate childhood asthma and other illnesses.[13]

The places in the world that we most love to walk, the Parises and Barcelonas of the world, aren't dense only along their major corridors but in every direction. They bring everyone and everything closer together, allowing far more people to live near where they work and play. Despite its having become a popular approach by US city planners in recent decades, corridor-based upzoning is a policy born of fear of NIMBYs, not what's best for the city as a whole. None of the world's most beloved cities look like this, and the rest of our cities shouldn't aspire to.

17   Focus Upzones in Accessible and High-Opportunity Areas (Upzoning: Targeted)

Build housing where it will best support other economic, social, and environmental priorities.

Whatever ideology we bring to housing policy, we should be concerned about how development will affect low-income neighborhoods, people of color, and other vulnerable and disenfranchised populations. This doesn't mean buying into the idea that development is inherently bad. It *does* mean demonstrating genuine care for the welfare of others and recognizing that nothing in this world is black-and-white. Even if housing development is good and necessary, it can still have negative impacts. Even when something is good for a region, it may not be good for every individual in that region. How do we do what's good for the region *and* what does the most good and least harm for as many individuals as possible?

A simple rule of thumb is to start in high-opportunity areas. This can mean neighborhoods with a relatively affluent population, or particularly high-quality transit access, or an abundance of jobs. Because of their wealth and influence, these communities will often have a history of exclusion and a vested interest in maintaining the status quo. But those privileges are also attractive to the housing advocate because they're an excellent place to gain the benefits of more homes while minimizing potential negatives such as segregation and concentrated poverty, displacement, and social dislocation.

Development in areas that are transit accessible, wealthy, and rich in jobs has the smallest impact on congestion, allowing people to live in walkable and desirable neighborhoods and reducing gentrification pressure on lower-income communities. Every home built in a higher-opportunity area is a home that doesn't need to be built somewhere with greater potential for gentrifying impacts, as well as a home that doesn't need to be built in a more sprawling city, such as Phoenix or Dallas, where per capita greenhouse gas emissions are significantly higher.

As noted in the introduction to this section, research from the Upjohn Institute estimates that one hundred units of new "luxury" housing in higher-end census tracts makes available dozens of units in lower-income neighborhoods. This is the "migration chain" effect, in which a resident of a new home vacates a slightly down-market unit, which is in turn occupied by someone from a home slightly further down-market, and so forth. It points to an immediate affordability benefit when new market-rate housing is built, even to low-income residents in different neighborhoods. This doesn't abrogate the need for development incentives, mandates, and subsidies that create deed-restricted units reserved specifically for low-income households, but it makes an even stronger case for building lots of homes in desirable high-end neighborhoods.

Single-family neighborhoods are also a smart target for higher-density housing. Though perhaps not intuitive, allowing four-story apartment buildings in a single-family neighborhood is likely to do more good—in terms of increased affordability—and less harm— with respect to displacement—than the same change in a neighborhood full of small multifamily buildings. The *physical* changes resulting from upzoning are larger in single-family neighborhoods than in multifamily or commercial areas, but the social and economic impacts are least severe. Most single-family neighborhoods, though not all, are populated with homeowners who are free to choose whether they want to leave to make way for redevelopment, while renters living in the multifamily neighborhood generally are not. Because upzoning tends to increase property values, owners also receive a direct financial benefit when their property is rezoned and they choose to sell, while renters may only be at greater risk of displacement.

18 Find the Upzoning Sweet Spot: Not Too Big, Not Too Small (Upzoning: Rightsized)

—

Zone a parcel for too much density and no one may want to buy it. Zone for too little and it may not be worth redeveloping.

There are different theories about the optimal way to manage and shape neighborhood change. One theory we can call the Strong Towns approach, popularized by Charles Marohn, founder of the Strong Towns organization. This approach assumes that incremental change is best. Allow small-time property owners and investors to turn an empty parcel into a one-story Main Street commercial building, and over time, as the neighborhood grows, that building can evolve into a two- or three-story structure with housing above the ground floor, or perhaps turn the next-door parking lot into another two-story building. Maybe, decades later, it can be replaced with a six-story building, or perhaps it will remain as neighboring parcels grow into three- or four-story structures. This approach is slow and incremental and, most importantly, does not require massive, well-capitalized investors or public subsidies. It can be led and funded by people from within the community using their own resources and know-how.[14]

At the other end of the spectrum is the "go big" approach, which seeks to remove virtually all restrictions on land use. If someone wants to turn a surface parking lot into a fifty-story tower, feel free. If they want to build a church or a four-story bowling alley there instead, have at it. As long as no one is causing a nuisance (such as building a landfill or a rendering facility), just let people build what they want. Those looking to build the biggest—bringing a parcel to its "highest and best use"—will be willing to pay more for the land, and so their plans will typically win out. A selling point of this approach is that it is highly responsive to demand: when demand grows, supply can quickly follow.

These two approaches are about more than how communities

envision their future. They also have profoundly different impacts on the financial feasibility of development and the kind of community benefits that new development can provide. Neither approach is suitable in all circumstances, and most places will be best served by something between these two extremes.

Let's first look at our stylized version of the Strong Towns approach. Under this framework, the size and bulk of buildings might be held in check at a low level to ensure incremental change. If most of the buildings are one-story today, we might cap any future development at two or three stories. Similar restrictions would apply to setbacks, floor area ratio, and so on. The upside to this approach is that the kinds of investments you can make—adding a story or two, or replacing a one-story building with a slightly taller one—are within the financial and technical capacity of fairly typical residents. It's also less disruptive, and the physical character of the community will remain relatively harmonious.

A downside is that if demand grows beyond your expectations, prices may spike and money will flow into increasingly expensive *existing* real estate instead of consistent investment in *new* real estate. Further, in many places it is simply not financially feasible to replace a one-story building with a two-story building. The time and expense involved in vacating existing tenants (even commercial tenants), entitling a new development, demolishing the existing use and forgoing revenue for months or years of construction, and building a new structure simply aren't justified by the increased revenue from a slightly larger building. Los Angeles passed a ballot initiative in 1986, Proposition U, championed by former city council member and county supervisor Zev Yaroslavsky, which exemplifies this effect. The initiative reduced development capacity by 50 percent in commercial corridors throughout the city, effectively making redevelopment infeasible in all of these locations.[15] If you visit Los Angeles today and are shocked to see single-story strip malls lining major arterial corridors such as Wilshire Boulevard and Fairfax Avenue, now you know who to thank.

This form of incremental development may have worked well in centuries past, when a handyman could simply buy some materials and construct a second-floor living space above his ground-floor shop. However, modern bureaucratic processes and building codes don't lend themselves to such slapdash improvements. (Strong Towns advocates would probably argue that this bureaucracy and prescriptivism also needs to be reformed, but that's unlikely—beyond a certain point—in most jurisdictions.) Especially in faster-growing cities already struggling to maintain affordability, this approach does not seem appropriate. It's too little and much too late.

The "go big" approach resolves the flaws of Strong Towns while creating new challenges. Going big allows for projects that are much larger than what might exist today. One upside, as previously noted, is that development can be more responsive to increasing demand. Another benefit is that larger projects can more easily absorb the cost and forgone revenue of redevelopment, and a more dramatic upzoning creates more land value that can be captured for community benefit.

The risk of going big is that you can go *too* big in terms of zoning. Larger, taller projects are more expensive than smaller projects, not just overall but on a per-square-foot basis. They may require additional structural reinforcement, more expensive materials such as concrete or steel, more extensive fire safety equipment, elevators, deeper foundations, and other costly investments not required of smaller developments. Those additional costs narrow the range of tenants who can afford to live or work in the new housing, such that only a few parcels might be redeveloped. A neighborhood could end up with a few very expensive forty-story towers surrounded by surface parking lots and run-down strip malls, when it could have created a much more affordable (not to mention more walkable and pleasant) community with dozens of four- to six-story buildings.

This problem is compounded by landowners who determine the value of their land on the basis of the biggest, most profitable use for their site. If a community's zoning plans overestimate the demand for larger developments, landowners may hold out for top dollar while developers look elsewhere for more reasonably priced opportunities.

Unsurprisingly, the right approach for most cities and neighborhoods will fall somewhere between these two extremes. On the one hand, their zoning plans must accommodate future growth and be aggressive enough that redevelopment is financially feasible. On the other hand, they shouldn't be so aggressive that developers and property owners can't agree on the true value of land. If their incentives aren't aligned, the parties may find themselves at an impasse, with no new housing built until prices rise enough to justify the expense of much denser, taller development. Keeping rightsizing in mind while also following the three previous recommendations will help advocates and policy makers find the right balance.

19 Allow Housing in Commercial Zones (Mixed-Use Zoning)

—

Increase supply and reduce displacement by permitting housing in commercial zones.

Many cities unnecessarily limit the availability of new homes by prohibiting residential uses in commercial zones. This is an antiquated practice that should be abolished everywhere.

"Mixed-use" zoning and development have become buzzwords in planning circles. Although mixed use can include many typologies, including housing plus office, office plus hotel, hotel plus retail, and many other permutations, including three or more different uses, the most common form is housing paired with ground-floor commercial space (typically retail or services such as banks or nail salons). Mixed-use development can be highly sustainable, allowing people to make many of their daily trips with a short walk down the street—or even just a trip down the stairs or elevator. Commercial corridors also are usually more likely to be served by quality transit. There is certainly still a place for segregating housing away from noxious industrial uses, landfills, and the like, but there's no good reason to separate housing from jobs and daily needs.

Allowing housing in commercial zones has a few other benefits as well. For one, building homes in commercial areas, such as redeveloping strip malls, usually entails no direct displacement because no one lives there yet.

You may be reading this thinking that mixed-use zoning is in conflict with policy 16 ("Upzone many places at once"), which advocates against corridor-based planning. This is true to an extent. However, mixed use zoning should allow housing in many places *including* arterial corridors, whereas corridor-based planning tends to promote new housing *only* along arterial corridors. The latter is deeply problematic, but mixed-use zoning along arterial corridors is perfectly acceptable as one component of a broader housing plan.

Mixed-use zoning also encourages developers to make the highest and best use of their property. When demand for office space is limited but commercial and residential uses must be kept separate, property owners may have little incentive to redevelop. A parcel might be zoned for four stories of commercial and retail development, but the owner may be justifiably concerned that any above-ground space would go unoccupied. When housing is allowed, the developer might instead include office or retail space on the ground floor, where it is often easiest to find commercial tenants, and then fill the remaining floor space with multifamily homes. This flexibility allows developers to respond to whichever need is greatest—jobs or housing—on the basis of local circumstances. In most high-cost cities, housing is clearly the greater need.

Los Angeles's Adaptive Reuse Ordinance (ARO) is a good example of this. Prior to 2000, Downtown LA was packed with early-1900s high-rise commercial buildings that had been vacant for decades. The buildings, many of which were of beautiful design and stood twelve or thirteen stories tall, were empty except for ground-floor retail uses. In 1999, the city council passed the ARO, allowing these long-vacant structures to be converted to residential use—and, importantly, to do so without meeting current minimum parking requirements. After thirty years during which Downtown had added just 4,300 homes, the area added 7,300 new housing units in the decade following approval of the ARO, with most converted from these old commercial buildings.[16] The policy is widely credited with sparking Downtown's famous revitalization. The ARO is usually framed as a story about the harm caused by minimum parking requirements, and rightly so. But it's also a story of mixed-use zoning. There simply wasn't the demand for commercial space that there once had been, and by allowing the spaces to become housing, the city brought much-needed economic development to its central business district and added thousands of new, relatively affordable homes for its residents.

The fact that mixed-use zoning is good in many circumstances doesn't mean every development should be mixed use. Depending on the neighborhood and the amount of land zoned for commercial uses, it may make sense to allow 100 percent residential buildings in commercial zones. These may include projects with ground-floor lobbies and units accessed by internal stairs or elevators, or walk-up units that have separate entrances for individual units on lower levels.

In some jurisdictions the mixed-use dogma has arguably gone too far, to the point that every new apartment building must include ground-floor retail space. This can lead to a glut of commercial spaces that leave empty storefronts and reduce the financial viability of new development. Being required to provide space that's unlikely to lease up is an unnecessary drag on feasibility and bad urban planning. Better to turn those spaces into homes that are sure to be occupied—and to zone your city so that developers can make that choice where appropriate. A middle-ground position that policy makers might consider is requiring ground-floor spaces to be built for *potential* retail use, including high ceilings, but to allow developers to choose whether to use the space as commercial or residential.

20 Make It Expensive to Reduce the Supply of Homes (Home Sharing)

_____

Property owners should be discouraged from taking rental housing off the market to use as short-term vacation rentals.

Some skeptics don't believe that adding housing to the market can lower rents, but at the same time they believe very firmly that taking housing *off* the market can *raise* rents. Both cases are true, of course, and those who are serious about housing production should also be concerned about policies and programs—and businesses—that remove housing from the market.

Today's prototypical "housing remover" is Airbnb, which along with other vacation rental services encourages property owners to convert their long-term-lease units into short-term vacation rentals. Short-term rentals can often rent at upward of twice the daily rates of long-term rental housing, giving property owners a strong incentive to make the conversion. And even though short-term rentals require more hands-on care (fielding questions from guests, handing off keys, providing neighborhood information, cleaning and restocking materials after each stay), guests do not enjoy the same protections as long-term tenants, so landlords may prefer to operate as hotels in order to skirt the rules.

The most important impact of Airbnb-type services, though, is on housing prices and rental rates. CityLab reviewed research on the impact of Airbnb across multiple cities.

> In Boston, one working paper from the University of Massachusetts Boston Department of Economics found a causal relationship between Airbnb proliferation and housing prices: with every 12 Airbnb listings per census tract, asking rents increased by 0.4 percent. These findings were reinforced at the national level in another working paper in SSRN, which used American Community Survey data to find that with each 10 percent increase in Airbnb

listings in a U.S. ZIP code, there was a .42 percent increase in rental prices, and a .76 percent increase in house prices. Then, using that working paper's same regression model, David Wachsmuth, a professor of Urban Planning at McGill University, found that in New York City, Airbnb was associated with a 1.4 percent increase in NYC rents from 2015 to 2017.[17]

Pro-supply advocates often point out that if we simply allowed developers to build more housing (and hotels), we wouldn't need to regulate short-term rentals as heavily as we do. But that ignores a few issues, the first being similar to the argument behind tenant protections: a landlord can convert a long-term rental into a short-term vacation home almost immediately, whereas new housing takes years to come to market. Because of the cost of construction, new housing is also targeted at the higher end of the market, whereas many converted vacation rentals were once affordable to working- and middle-class families. Worse, those families are sometimes kicked out of their homes to make way for short-term rentals. Yes, we should allow more housing across the board, but there are also good reasons for enacting protections from "eviction by Airbnb." Finally, vacation rentals can also concentrate in specific neighborhoods, meaning the pain isn't shared equally: some may see a large share of their units converted over time, with a disproportionate impact on rents and home prices, while others remain relatively untouched.

Some cities have created regulations that permit vacation rentals only in a primary residence, meaning that property owners can share a room in their home, but they can't rent out an entire unit for visitors. This is an excellent start and is probably the only policy that most cities will need. They may also consider allowing full-unit short-term rentals under certain conditions, but they should establish clear and narrow guidelines for when this is permitted—for example, up to thirty days each year to allow residents to rent out their homes while away on vacation or business. The cost of participating in the regulated short-term rental market should be high enough to fully offset potential impacts on the overall housing market, and long-term tenants should be fully protected from displacement by short-term rental conversions.

21 Eliminate Density Limits in Most Places (Density Limits)

___

Don't fall into the trap of mixing up density with urban form or "neighborhood character."

Zoning exclusively for single-family detached homes has a racist and classist history in the United States. Dating back to the early 1900s, when the United States Supreme Court upheld the practice of zoning and described apartments as "mere parasites" preying upon single-family neighborhoods, and especially following the invalidation of racial covenants that prohibited Jewish people and people of color from living in specific neighborhoods, single-family zoning has served as a way to keep out "undesirable" groups by setting an insurmountably high bar for access: unless you can afford 5,000 or 10,000 square feet of land in this community, you're not welcome. The *New York Times* published a high-profile analysis of single-family zoning's prevalence in the United States, finding that major cities such as Los Angeles; Seattle; Charlotte, North Carolina; and San Jose have upward of 80 percent or even 90 percent of their residential land zoned exclusively for detached single-unit houses.[18]

Single-family zoning, which is more appropriately defined as a ban on multifamily housing options, should have no place in urban America. But that doesn't mean every part of cities should be zoned for twenty-story, or even five-story, buildings. In some neighborhoods, on some streets, cities may not want to allow buildings significantly larger than single-unit homes even if they include more than one household inside them. Eliminating density limits while maintaining restrictions on building size is a smart compromise for integrating "gentle density" or "missing middle" housing into such neighborhoods. This helps create more affordable housing options in communities that are often closed to working-class and middle-class households.

Density limits are usually set on the basis of parcel size. For example, a low-density neighborhood might require 2,500 square feet of parcel area for each home, such that a typical 5,000-square-foot parcel could host nothing denser than a duplex. Single-unit zones often require 5,000 square feet per home. Lower-density multifamily neighborhoods might allow one home for every 1,000 square feet of parcel area, so that same 5,000-square-foot parcel could accommodate up to five apartments or condominiums.

Other development standards can still apply, including maximum building heights; front, rear, and side yard setbacks; lot coverage requirements (the percentage of the parcel that can be covered with building structures); and maximum floor area ratio (FAR). FAR is the total amount of floor space that can be built on a parcel, expressed as a multiple of a parcel's lot area. A 5,000-square-foot lot with a maximum FAR of 0.5 would allow a building up to 2,500 square feet, whereas a 3.0 FAR would allow 15,000 square feet.

Eliminating density limits while retaining other development standards, including FAR, is a way of creating more homes—and a greater diversity of homes and households—without significantly changing the physical character of a neighborhood. In a neighborhood zoned for single-family homes and a maximum building size of 2,400 square feet, nothing except single-family homes will be built—most of them at or near the 2,400-square-foot limit. With density limits eliminated, the maximum building size is still 2,400 square feet, but it can shelter two households in a duplex of 1,200-square-foot units, three in 800-square-foot apartments, or four small households of 600 square feet each. The buildings look essentially the same, but they offer a wider range of prices and serve a wider range of household arrangements and phases in people's lives. It's estimated that more than half of owner-occupied homes in the United States have at least one spare bedroom, representing at least 44 million empty rooms.[19] Allowing homes that serve a wider range of household types—whether they be childless couples, single-parent households, college students, older adults, or otherwise—would keep prices lower and avoid much of this wasted space.

As a part of their reforms, policy makers might also consider identifying specific building forms that they wish to promote, with design guidelines offered to shepherd their development. These include classic, affordable residential designs such as row houses, bungalow courts, and courtyard apartments. Removing density limits can achieve a great deal, but bringing these kinds of well-loved forms back into production will require a more proactive approach.[20]

Minneapolis was the first city in the United States to eliminate single-family zoning, allowing triplexes citywide in addition to upzoning transit corridors and eliminating minimum parking requirements. The approved plan was intended to address housing affordability, but it also explicitly grappled with the racist history that had led to the development and promulgation of single-family zoning; Minneapolis's leaders view the change as a small step toward repairing that damage.[21] In July 2019, the Oregon legislature approved HB 2001, which will allow duplexes, triplexes, and four-plexes in single-family zones in cities with populations of 25,000 or more.[22] Eliminating density limits, especially single-unit density limits, is catching on across the country.

Allowing for accessory dwelling units (ADUs) is another variation on eliminating or reducing density limits. Also known as granny flats or in-law units, ADUs are secondary homes, often 1,000 square feet or less, built on the same lot as an existing home. They may be attached to or detached from the primary home, or designed as interior suites, though detached units are most common. They are more affordable than single-family homes because of their relatively small size and their ability to share the cost of land with another home; they are unobtrusive and compatible with existing buildings; and they help diversify housing options in lower-density neighborhoods. Vancouver, British Columbia, also has a long history with ADUs, which are known locally as laneway houses.[23]

US cities have begun to learn from Vancouver's success. California is the most dramatic example, with the state legislature legalizing ADUs statewide in 2016 and further streamlining the ADU development approval process in the following years. Applications spiked. In 2016, Los Angeles saw 254 ADU permit applications submitted; the new law went into effect on January 1, 2017, and applications grew to 3,821 by the end of that year—a fifteenfold increase.[24] ADU applications climbed even higher in 2018, to 5,429.[25] Other cities and states should explore a combination of legalizing ADUs and ending apartment bans to expand affordable and middle-income housing options in their own communities.

22 Eliminate Parking Requirements Everywhere (Parking Minimums)

—

Excess vehicle parking increases housing costs and encourages more driving. Find other ways to manage demand.

Concerns about the availability of parking are at the root of many anti-housing arguments. Residents may be concerned that a new development will increase the number of residents—and, more importantly, cars—in their neighborhood and believe this will reduce their access to free on-street parking (often while their own garages are used for storage or workshops).

But we know from decades of research by luminaries such as Donald Shoup, UCLA economics professor and author of *The High Cost of Free Parking*, that off-street parking is often oversupplied, that it dramatically increases the cost of new construction, and that its availability encourages more driving and congestion. When more parking is provided, more people drive, and they drive more. And when parking is *required* to be built in new housing and commercial developments, often more is built than is actually needed.

An overnight survey of parking garages in King County, Washington, found that approximately one-third of multifamily parking spaces were empty, an excess of 0.4 parking spaces per dwelling unit.[26] This is a shockingly consistent finding across metropolitan areas, and it's driven almost entirely by high parking requirements for new buildings. Even the Institute of Transportation Engineers, which is responsible for the original document upon which many local parking minimums are based—the *Parking Generation Manual*—has begun to acknowledge the harm its overestimates have done (and continue to do) to cities.[27]

Local residents are typically the driving force behind higher parking requirements, but no one really benefits when more parking is provided. Building parking in above- and belowground garages can cost $30,000 to $50,000 per space and can even approach

$100,000 per space in some buildings (the deeper you dig, the more expensive it gets). The additional cost guarantees that these homes will need high-income tenants, who are much more likely to drive. Car-free and car-lite households will be less interested because they won't want to pay such a high cost for a resource they won't end up using. The nearby residents who lobbied for more parking will experience more traffic as a result. Working- and middle-class residents, who travel by car less frequently, will not be able to afford housing in these new developments and instead will need to live farther from the city center, where driving is essential for most daily needs.

Developers certainly don't benefit, because the cost of parking means fewer projects will be financially feasible to build. The smaller number of new homes puts additional pressure on rents and home prices, worsening affordability for everyone. People who don't own a car—whether by choice or necessity—will overpay for homes in new developments because the cost of parking is very often wrapped up in the cost of the unit.

Even in cases in which parking charges are "unbundled" from rents, the unbundling is typically only partial. A parking space that costs $50,000 to build would need to charge nearly $300 per month to recoup its costs if it were separated from the dwelling unit rent, but few renters would be willing to pay so much for a single parking space. Instead, developers bundle most of that cost into their units and charge a more modest amount, often around $75 or $100 per month, for the parking itself. Renters are paying the full cost in either case, but those who own fewer cars end up subsidizing those who own more.

Where cities have come to their senses and reduced or eliminated parking requirements, the results are always positive. New buildings still provide parking in most cases, but they provide less. The homes in those buildings are considerably less expensive, on average, than "fully parked" developments,[28] and they provide options for car-free or car-lite households that wouldn't exist otherwise. Attracting those households is its own benefit because car-lite buildings are almost always located near transit, and households that own few or no cars are far more likely than their peers to rely on walking, bicycling, or transit for their daily transportation needs. We should be doing everything we can to encourage these households to live in our cities and continue to enjoy a sustainable, affordable, healthy car-free lifestyle.

23 Let Renters Decide What They Value (Micro-units)

—

Tenants can't assess a building's earthquake, fire, or electrical safety, but they can decide for themselves what kinds of amenities and unit features they want.

Many zoning and building code requirements are paternalistic preferences masquerading as consumer protections. Requirements such as minimum room sizes, building setbacks, common areas, and other shared facilities—and, yes, parking minimums—have no proven impact on the health or safety of residents, yet they're required all the same.

This isn't a harmless practice, because these requirements add significant cost. As a result, those who can't afford these well-appointed homes have no alternatives except to find older housing that's genuinely less safe (older wiring, earlier structural requirements, etc.) or move to another area entirely. It's like mandating that every car be a Lexus but offering no assistance to the people who can't afford to buy one.

Minimum unit sizes are a great example of this. Micro-units are small apartments, less than 200 square feet in some cases but often closer to 250 or 350, which rent at a lower cost than larger competitors.[29] Seattle experienced a boom in micro-unit construction in the early 2010s but subsequently changed its rules out of concern that the apartments were inappropriate for habitation. The thousands of units that were built remain extremely popular, much more affordable than larger units built at the same time and located in some of the most transit-accessible areas of the city.

There's no doubt that most people would prefer a bigger living space, all else equal. But all else isn't equal, and people make choices every day according to various constraints. Banning micro-units hasn't miraculously led to better housing options for the region's residents; instead, it's forced many to leave who would have preferred a small space in the city over a larger apartment twenty miles away, or to find roommates when they'd have preferred to live alone, or pay more money for a space that exceeds their needs or desires. There's nothing dangerous about micro-units, and if they weren't an appealing option—for some, not all—then they wouldn't all be leased up. Tenants can decide for themselves.

This is certainly *not* to say that zoning standards and building codes have no place in a modern, affordable city—obviously they do. Structural integrity, fire resistance, electrical safety: these are the types of building features that prospective tenants can't judge for themselves and that require effective standards and oversight. Cities should distinguish between what's required for the health and safety of residents and what is simply an aesthetic or paternalistic preference. As a general rule, they can do so by strictly regulating what the tenant can't see and leaving to individual preferences what they can.

24 Make Development Approvals "By Right" (By-Right Development)

To guide the development you want, create objective rules and then stick to them.

Even after public officials successfully upzone neighborhoods, develop the right incentives and mandates, and eliminate unnecessary regulations, building enough homes will still be difficult if project approvals remain slow and uncertain. Development applicants are frequently required to go through "discretionary" approvals, meaning that their project may be denied even if they do everything asked of them by local regulations. This practice is extremely common in some jurisdictions; in Los Angeles, for example, a whopping 93 percent of housing units proposed from 2014 to 2016 required discretionary approval.[30]

Rather than requiring a time-consuming, unpredictable discretionary approval process for each individual project, cities should invest time and resources into developing clear rules that apply equally to all projects and then automatically approve the projects that conform to those rules.

There are several reasons to rely on automatic, or "by-right," approvals. As the introduction to this book explains, supply is not enough by itself to create an affordable city because new supply can take years to catch up with increasing demand. The more time it takes for a project to receive its approvals, the greater the gap between growing demand (and upward pressure on prices) and the delivery of new homes. Discretionary approvals draw out this process by inserting more meetings and potential veto points.

Delay and uncertainty increase development costs, driving up the price of new homes and narrowing the spectrum of households that developers can profitably market their units to. The waiting period from project application to city approval can take years for some projects, with costs mounting as each day passes. This may seem like a minor issue. Sure, it's inconvenient, but if you're just waiting to receive a permit and not paying construction workers yet, what does it really matter? Because of the role of equity in real estate investment, it matters quite a lot.

Equity (as opposed to debt) is a relatively small share of the project, perhaps 15–30 percent of the total amount to be spent, but it can add significantly to the final project cost if approvals are slow. It's the first money invested in a project, and because it's at greatest risk it also demands the highest returns. Take, for example, a project that takes three years from start to finish and a $10 million equity investment with a minimum expected return of 15 percent. This investment would demand a 52 percent return (15 percent compounded three times), or $15.2 million including payback of the initial $10 million investment. If the total project cost is $40 million, a $5.2 million profit payback is a large amount but still just 13 percent above development cost. But extend the project duration to five years and this grows to $10.1 million, or 25 percent above cost. By seven years it has grown to $16.6 million—42 percent. If a city has a reputation for delay and inconsistency, investors might demand a 20 percent return instead. A seven-year project at that return rate would require $25.8 million in profit, and the development would be designed to target a higher income bracket to accommodate the additional expense—or, if those returns weren't possible, it wouldn't get built at all. (Please note that these assumptions and calculations are highly simplified and provided primarily for illustrative purposes.)

Slow approval processes generally don't reduce developer profits, at least not in the long run. In fact, by forcing them to require a higher risk premium, it makes their investments *more* profitable (though also riskier). There are few things simpler and more effective at reducing housing costs than cutting down on approval times and creating objective, consistently applied rules. Affordable cities are those where housing is a predictable, boring, low-yield investment, not a roll of the dice.

Discretionary approvals for individual projects also often lead to their being downsized, offering fewer homes than what is legally permitted in order to navigate the gauntlet of neighborhood engagement. There are many examples of downsized projects in

Los Angeles alone, amounting to hundreds, if not thousands, of lost homes, many of which would have been reserved for low-income households.[31]

This uncertainty doesn't benefit anyone—except, paradoxically, the developers whose investments ultimately pay off. (The ones whose projects are rejected lose big, of course.) Unlike parks fees or affordable housing requirements, there's no upside to the additional expense: it's higher cost only for the sake of higher cost. There is nominally a trade-off here, higher cost in exchange for increased "stakeholder engagement," but most of the time this engagement is little more than a few noisy, affluent, selfish neighbors using every available tactic to delay new homes in their community. Eliminating delay- and uncertainty-related costs should be among the highest priorities for any policy maker serious about improving affordability. It's far better to redirect those resources into investments that actually benefit the community.

There's one more problem with approving every project individually, on the basis of subjective judgments rather than objective standards: it invites backroom dealmaking and corruption, or at least the appearance of it. When developers can't be sure of what will be approved and what won't, neither can anyone else. And given the way that both politicians and developers are viewed by the general public, city leaders should do everything they can to eliminate the appearance of corruption vis-à-vis developers.

The time for subjective input is when zoning plans and design guidelines are written. After that, the vast majority of projects should be either approved or disapproved on the basis of compliance with those predetermined rules. This will significantly speed up the development of new housing and reduce the cost and risk premium associated with building homes.

It will also improve community engagement. Most local stakeholders do not have the time or resources (or interest) to attend multiple meetings for every single development project in their neighborhood. By consolidating feedback into community plan updates, planning departments can invest in robust outreach that gathers input from a broad cross section of the community. Where discretionary approvals are the norm, outreach dollars are diluted by dozens or hundreds of project-based meetings attended mostly by local busybodies who aren't representative of the community at large. Those resources would be much better spent on generating a vision for the future, in the form of community plans, rather than critiquing the facades, window sizes, setbacks, and landscaping decisions of individual projects.

25 Speed Up the Entitlement Process (Faster Approvals)

—

*Even when by-right development is possible, slow approval processes
raise the cost of new housing and delay its construction.*

Separate from discretionary approvals—which create unnecessary
uncertainty, increase delay, and raise costs—there is also the issue of
project approval durations regardless of their entitlement pathway.
Entitlements may be approved quickly, or they may move at a gla-
cial pace, depending on the jurisdiction. Even in jurisdictions where
most development is permitted by right, receiving final sign-off can
be a grueling process. And, as with uncertain discretionary processes,
slow approval timelines do great harm to housing affordability with
little or no offsetting benefit to the public.

A survey of planners in California cities found that over one-
third of jurisdictions required more than six months to approve multifamily developments that were fully compliant with local zoning
requirements. For projects requiring environmental review, which
automatically triggers discretionary approval in California, 95 percent of jurisdictions required more than six months for approval.[32]
Environmental review isn't addressed in any depth in this book, in
part because standards vary so dramatically among states. Suffice it
to say there is an important role for the review of potential environmental impacts, but its noble purpose is often co-opted merely to stop
or slow construction of new housing. The positive environmental
impacts of urban housing, including the reduction of sprawl development in truly environmentally sensitive areas, is well documented.
The fatal flaw of environmental review in places such as California
is that it treats the status quo as the optimal environmental outcome,
with any change regarded as negative, or neutral at best—even when
that change includes obviously environmentally beneficial projects
such as infill development on a surface parking lot or bus lanes designed to improve local transit service.

One simple policy goal that reformers should pursue is to exempt projects from most or all environmental review (except for truly essential work·such as soil testing and remediation) on any site that has been previously developed. In almost all cases, replacing a surface parking lot, single-unit residence, strip mall, or other small-scale existing use with higher-density housing is an inherently climate-protective action.[33] Subjecting such developments to months or years of environmental review and lawsuits achieves little except to drive up the cost of housing and incentivize more development on greenfield sites, such as former agriculture zones, where environmental destruction and climate impacts are much greater.

Further, insofar as individual projects adhere to existing community plans, they should be exempt from large-scale environmental review—again, except for genuinely necessary site-specific testing and remediation. Jurisdictions often must consider environmental impacts in their community planning process. If a site was part of a community planning process, and a proposed project is compliant with zoning on that site, it should be a given that the project is—by definition—meeting the environmental goals of that community.

Another analysis of four Southern California cities (Los Angeles, Long Beach, Pasadena, and Santa Monica) found that discretionary project approval times varied wildly among jurisdictions. Long Beach had the shortest approval period, averaging 10.5 months, whereas Santa Monica averaged a whopping *four years*—and that's just to reach the start of construction. Median approval times reflected a similar pattern, with Long Beach clocking in at 7.2 months compared with Santa Monica's 38.8. Although entitlement processing times are poorly reported in most jurisdictions, if they're reported at all, the experience of practitioners confirms that approval timelines are a large and growing problem across the country. This is especially true of high-cost cities where development is already more contentious and micromanaged.

Internal city processes have a big impact on timelines even when approval processes are similar across jurisdictions. For projects requiring the same level of environmental analysis, environmental impact reports (EIRs), approvals in Santa Monica took more than three times longer than in Long Beach (77 versus 23 months).[34] These are such long timelines that a developer could propose a project at the beginning of an economic cycle and not complete construction until the next recession had passed. This is another risk factor that leads developers to demand larger profit margins in high-cost cities and build only for the highest-income households.

Cities can reduce their approval times by making more development by right—and they should—but they must also act to reduce processing times for all cases, whether discretionary or ministerial. They have many options for doing so. They can increase staffing (including third-party consultants to handle spikes in demand); improve coordination among departments; establish centralized, web-accessible permitting processes; consolidate meetings in which review or approval is needed; eliminate redundant and unnecessary reviews, meetings, and approvals; set goals and mandates for approval timelines; and allow applicants to pay staff costs for expedited review, among other things. Most developers are willing to pay for any costs incurred by cities to speed up their approval process; local leadership just needs to prioritize it.

Using a mix of these approaches, Montgomery County, Maryland, eliminated its record plat application backlog and reduced processing times from 20–30 weeks to 8–12 weeks; developed ordinances requiring preliminary plans and site plans to be reviewed within 120 days (down from a year or more); and issued an executive order requiring building permits to be issued in 30 days or less (down from 8–12 weeks).[35] States including Massachusetts and Rhode Island have also assumed leadership roles in pushing their local jurisdictions to adopt more streamlined approval processes and speed up the delivery of desperately needed housing, an approach that was hailed as a model by the Barack Obama administration.[36]

26 Explore Other Ways to Bring Down Development Costs (Input Costs)

—

If we want the middle class to once again be able to afford privately built, unsubsidized housing, the cost of new development must come down.

More housing supply can keep prices from continuing to rise, and there's evidence that it can even bring rents down somewhat.[37] In theory, developers could keep building housing and we would see prices fall and fall and fall. But in reality, it's hard to imagine that prices could fall to the extent needed—say, from $2,500 to $1,500 per month—with abundant supply alone. Instead, many US cities are on a path to having a large supply of higher-end housing for the affluent, a decent stock of subsidized housing for the poor, and almost nothing in between.

There are several reasons why it will be hard for competition among privately financed developers to significantly cut costs. First, when rents begin to fall, there's suddenly less incentive for developers to provide more housing. If they keep building more, driving rents down even further, not only do their new buildings perform more poorly but their existing rental assets also do worse. Given how complex real estate development has become in the most punishing cities, there are also relatively few competitors left in the market. Second, if rents fall too significantly, residual land value (what the developer is willing to offer property owners for their land) will shrink as well. Property owners may be content to keep their property underdeveloped until the market rebounds. Developers and landowners are both disincentivized from taking action.

Third, and perhaps most importantly, some costs simply won't fall very significantly through competition alone. The Five L's of development cost are Labor, Land, Lumber, Laws, and Lending.

1. Labor costs go up in more expensive markets (the workers need
    to afford a place to live), and increased housing production
    will actually drive *up* demand for labor, raising costs further.
    Modular and prefabricated development have been put forth as
    ways to cut labor costs, but they can do only so much.
2. Land prices can adjust downward, but they can go only so far
    before property owners decide to wait for the next time there's a
    seller's market.
3. Lumber—all materials, really, including concrete and steel—
    could fall in price, and new materials might offer promising
    opportunities to reduce cost.
4. Laws are all about the process of development, especially proj-
    ect approval; the costs imposed by the approval process can and
    should fall precipitously.
5. Lending reforms could also bring down overall expenses, but it's
    unlikely that this can be done without public funding.

All that said, when you allow lower-cost housing to be built,
someone will build it. A case in point can be found in Los Angeles,
where a four-story, 111-unit modular development along Crenshaw
Boulevard was built by Universal Standard Housing. The project
includes zero car-parking spaces and was built in approximately ten
months—a blistering speed for a development of its size. The project
set aside thirteen units for extremely low income households,[38] and
the remaining units rent for around $1,400 to $1,800 per month,[39]
a significant discount relative to most new housing in the region.
Projects such as this are setting a new standard for what's possible in
high-cost cities.

Labor: Cities should promote modular and prefabricated construction to reduce costs, but they should also support job training in
the construction trades. The trades pay well, so labor policies should
focus just as heavily on increasing the supply of workers as on increasing their productivity.

Land: Not much can be done about land costs, but well-designed
property taxes can encourage property owners to redevelop their land
(read more about this in the "Subsidy" section). Well-targeted upzoning also allows cities to increase the total value of parcels—which

encourages property owners to sell or redevelop—while reducing the per-unit cost of land.

Lumber: Cities generally can't influence the cost of construction materials, but they can encourage the use of new and more affordable alternatives. Mass timber, including cross-laminated timber (CLT) and mass plywood panels (MPP), is one example. The 2021 International Building Code will permit the use of mass timber in buildings up to eighteen stories tall, competing with concrete and steel, which are currently required in structures of that size. While it is still a relatively expensive material, mass timber may become significantly more affordable as economies of scale are developed and as carbon taxes and tariffs add costs to concrete and steel.[40] Mass timber also has the benefit of being far more environmentally sustainable than concrete and steel, capturing carbon in its structure rather than emitting literal tons of it in the production process. Cities should be at the cutting edge of permitting new building materials and methodologies, helping to grow new and greener industries as they promote more options for affordable construction.

Laws: Laws refer to all of the earlier supply policies, and more, and their influence on housing affordability and accessibility.

Lending: Lending also adds costs, but government's influence over it is limited. We'll return to lending costs in the sections on stability and subsidy policies.

When housing is expensive to build, developers will be able to earn a profit only from homes targeted at a small, affluent subset of the population. If they begin to saturate the market for high-end housing, but nothing else can feasibly be built, development will slow and prices will again start to climb. Cities need policies that support a continuously growing supply of housing, balanced to meet or even slightly exceed rising demand as well as to catch up after years of underproduction. The most effective way to reach that goal is for housing development to be inexpensive enough that developers can market their homes to a broad swath of the population.

27   Promote Counter-cyclical Home Building (Counter-cyclical Development)

___

The best time for the government to build homes is when construction is cheap and unemployment is high.

One of the biggest challenges in home building is its cyclical boom-and-bust nature. When the economy is doing poorly and land and labor are cheap, no one's building anything. When the economy is strong and developers want to build (or, more to the point, when banks want to lend), everything is expensive.

This dynamic is obviously bad for the cost of new construction, but it also has negative impacts on the labor market. At the end of 2018, US construction employment was just shy of 7.5 million workers, about 250,000 fewer than its peak of 7.73 million in 2006–2007.[41] As of 2019, about 300,000 construction jobs were unfilled and nearly 80 percent of contractors reported that they were having a difficult time finding skilled workers.[42]

The industry is investing in worker training to fill these gaps, but the Great Recession left its mark. Between 2007 and 2010, the construction sector lost more than 2 million employees, nearly 30 percent of its worker base. Many never returned to construction after the experience. It's easy to see why: construction workers are extremely vulnerable to the whims of the economic cycle, and it can be hard to attract employees when they know a recession could put them out of steady work for years at a time. Facing that, a lower-paying but more stable job might be preferable. And even when times are good, the benefits of a boom don't necessarily flow to the workers themselves. The cost of new construction grew by an average of 4.8 percent from 2013 through 2018,[43] but the sector's average hourly wages increased at half that rate, about 2.5 percent per year.[44]

One way to fix both problems—the poor labor market for construction workers and the poor timing of construction—is to promote counter-cyclical home building. That is, to ramp up housing construction when the economy is *bad*, not good. Like the stimulus spending of the American Recovery and Reinvestment Act of 2009, counter-cyclical construction would support the economy when it's most in need and purchase public benefits when they're most affordable.

Counter-cyclical housing construction would smooth out the market for construction labor and materials, allowing contractors to employ a steady number of employees instead of enduring the peaks and troughs of the current employment structure. This would moderate prices across the economic cycle while keeping workers on the job when the economy is pushing more people into unemployment.

Making construction a more stable career would also help trade programs attract new apprentices to maintain a consistent supply of new workers. An adequate supply isn't good just for housing—it's good for workers, too.

But if counter-cyclical development were easy, it would have been done already. Counter-cyclical spending is difficult because it's required when government funds are in shortest supply. How can cities and states, which aren't permitted to operate with annual budget deficits, promote counter-cyclical housing construction?

One response is that the federal government should take the lead, not local governments. Only the federal government can run a deficit, and only it can print money. When recessions occur, the federal government should dramatically increase funding for project-based programs such as the Low-Income Housing Tax Credit (LIHTC) and the Housing Choice Voucher Program (also known as Section 8), both of which can fund affordable housing development and keep workers on the job. The federal government could also help cities purchase land with interest-only loans, which those cities could then sell at cost to affordable and mixed-income developers who want to redevelop the sites. The feds can provide loan guarantees (up to a certain value per new home) for developers who build in the middle of a downturn, offsetting the hardship of leasing new units during the early or middle stages of an economic recovery. They could also offer to cover loan interest costs under certain circumstances.

State and local governments have their role to play, too. As discussed further in the "Subsidy" section, better tax structures can help state and local governments weather recessions and leave money on hand for counter-cyclical investments. Specifically, those tax structures should be more dependent on property taxes, which are relatively stable, than on income taxes and other volatile revenue sources. Saving more money during boom times, while politically challenging, would also help. Not only would it mean more money available to spend during a downturn, it would also moderate spending when the economic cycle is at its peak. This would have the ancillary benefit of limiting construction demand (and therefore price inflation) during the economic upswing, so the public would get more for its money when times are bad *and* when they're good.

Stability: Why Tenant Protections and Rental Housing Preservation Matter

Strong tenant and rental housing protections are essential for cities to remain accessible to a wide range of families and individuals. Demand for a city or a specific neighborhood can change abruptly, much faster than even the most permissive development rules could ever respond to, and tenants get caught in the middle as rents rise but new homes remain years away from completion. Supply helps moderate prices at the city and regional levels, but only tenant protections will provide adequate security at the neighborhood and household levels. A reasonable median rent is not the sole measure of an affordable city; the experience of individual households—their stability, their fair treatment, and the safe, healthy upkeep of their homes—is at least as important.

Historically, renters in the United States were treated with benign neglect at best and outright contempt at worst.[1] Renting could be an unpleasant experience, subject to the whims of a landlord or property manager, but most (white) renters could eventually look forward to the independence and security of homeownership. Being a renter was just a phase of life that you had to endure. But homeownership is now out of reach for a large and growing share of our population, and many will be renting for the rest of their lives, whether they like it or not. It is no longer just a rite of passage. For many people it will be the only form of housing they ever know, and they deserve the same dignity and protections enjoyed by homeowners.

If the argument in favor of supply is economic, the argument for stability is moral. Landlords manage what is a fundamental human need—shelter—and thus shouldn't have the unconstrained ability to set prices and living conditions wherever they like. Housing is too important to leave purely to the whims of the market or to individual landlords. And when a community improves, it should be the people who live there who reap most of the benefits, not only the people who own property—many of whom might not even live nearby. There's an important public purpose served in ensuring household and community stability, and that implies a role for government to rein in the excesses of an unregulated rental market.

In cities where the rent gap between affordable housing and market-rate housing is greatest, building more homes is simply not an adequate solution for a large share of families. That goes double for places where new, denser housing will require the demolition of existing homes. As the previous section noted, supply is essential but rarely, by itself, sufficient. When the demands of economic efficiency and basic human dignity are in tension, there shouldn't be any question that human dignity wins out.

Rent control isn't the only means of promoting tenant and community stability, but it's probably the most discussed—and argued over. Economists take a dim view of rent control, yet empirical evidence of its costs and benefits has done little to change the minds of policy makers and advocates. Among the many academic papers evaluating rent control, few are as thorough as the 2018 paper by Stanford University researchers Rebecca Diamond, Tim McQuade, and Franklin Qian.[2] And few have been as hotly debated.

The study examines a change to San Francisco's rent control law made in 1994, which expanded the number of units covered under rent control to include multifamily buildings with two to four apartments. Previously, units in these buildings—which accounted for 44 percent of rental housing in the city—were exempt from rent control. The law's expansion included only buildings built before 1980, so the researchers were able to evaluate renters living in pre-1980 buildings as the treatment group and those living in buildings built between 1980 and 1990 as the control group.

Owners of rent-controlled units couldn't raise rents by more than a nominal 7 percent per year for existing tenants (later cut to 4 percent, then cut further to 60 percent of inflation), though owners could set rents at the market rate when existing tenants left and new tenants moved in. This "softer" form of rent control is often described as rent stabilization to distinguish it from stricter price controls (rent control) that carry over between tenancies.

The researchers found that tenants in the rent-stabilized housing were 3.5 percentage points more likely than control group residents (21.5 percent versus 18.0 percent) to live at the same address five to ten years after the law change and were 1.5 percentage points more likely to have remained after ten or more years (12.9 percent versus 11.4 percent). Tenants benefiting from rent stabilization were also 4.5 and 3.7 percentage points more likely to still live in San Francisco in the medium and long term, respectively.

Importantly, these effects were considerably stronger for black and Hispanic households. While white households in rent-stabilized housing were 2.1 percentage points more likely than the control group to remain at their address, black and Hispanic households were more likely to stay by 10.7 and 7.1 percentage points, respectively. They were also 10.7 and 10.1 percentage points, respectively, more likely to remain in San Francisco. This disproportionate benefit to black and brown households is often overlooked, yet it has important implications for racial justice in a deeply segregated US housing market.

An important feature of rent stabilization, and part of the reason it helps tenants stay in their homes, is that it smooths out the ups and downs of the market. Home prices might rise by 8–10 percent each year for a decade and then crash by 40 percent. If rents followed the same trajectory, America would see the displacement of millions of tenants as prices rose, only to revert to reasonably affordable rents when the crash arrived. Immeasurable and completely unnecessary harm would have been done in the interim. Better—and far more humane—to smooth out those peaks and valleys so that vulnerable residents can manage the change and stay in their homes.

One negative consequence of the San Francisco law was that rent-stabilized buildings were 8 percentage points more likely to be converted to tenancy in common or condominiums—two uses that were exempt from rent control. In a companion paper, Diamond, McQuade, and Qian estimated that the law resulted in a 15 percent reduction in the supply of homes subject to rent control—and in the supply of rental housing overall—and that this led to a 5.1 percent increase in citywide rents.[3]

Although the papers' findings are mixed, the authors took a negative view of the law.

> Incumbent tenants already living in San Francisco who get access to rent control as part of the law change are clearly made better off as indicated by their preference to remain in their rent-controlled apartment. However, this comes at the expense of future renters in San Francisco, who must bear higher rents due to the endogenous reductions in rental supply. In this way, the law served as a transfer from future renters in the city to renters in 1994, creating economic well-being inequality between incumbent and future renters of San Francisco.[4]

Diamond, McQuade, and Qian are economists, so their perspective is understandable when viewed through the lens of economic efficiency. At a human level, though, this is too dismissive. Putting aside the disproportionate benefits to black and Hispanic residents, which are quite profound and unfortunately rare in housing policy, the paper demonstrates that many people very significantly benefited from the expansion of rent control. Those who benefited most were existing renters, to whom city governments arguably have a greater responsibility than to future residents—though benefiting both groups should always be our aspiration. Tenants who moved into these homes after the study period also benefited from low, predictable annual rent increases, even if their base rent was quite high.

In their conclusion, the authors state that rent control may be counterproductive in the long run. They argue that more direct forms of assistance, such as government subsidies or tax credits, could be less distortionary (and presumably better targeted, too).

But in the context of a supply-constrained housing market, it's not clear why direct government assistance would be more effective than rent control. After all, prices are also likely to go up if the supply of housing is fixed but people suddenly have more money available to pay for rent.

The same critique applies to rent control. It enjoys many of the same benefits as direct rental assistance but also has many of the same drawbacks. If enacted in a context of limited supply, the unintended consequences might outweigh the positive impacts. The authors wrote that the benefits to existing renters come "at the expense of future renters in San Francisco, who must bear higher rents," but if rent control hadn't existed, then many of those benefits would have flowed to landlords at the expense of existing renters. How is that better? The lesson shouldn't be that rent control is inherently bad, but that it—like direct subsidies and other interventions—must be paired with complementary policies that address housing supply. Highlighting that fact is a core purpose of this book.

Opponents of rent control argue that if a community is building enough housing to meet demand, rent control isn't necessary; landlords won't have enough market power to raise rents much, so tenants needn't worry. Among other things, this claim ignores the delay between increased demand and the construction of new homes, the role of income inequality and jobs-housing imbalances on rental rates and home prices, and the varying price trajectories of individual neighborhoods within a city or region.

But let's assume none of those issues matter. It still follows that if an abundant supply of housing obviates the need for rent control, then rent control should do no harm in places with abundant housing. If plenty of housing is available, landlords will be limited in their ability to raise rents anyway. As long as we can design tenant protections to not meaningfully dampen housing production (and we can!), the brawls over which of these policies to prioritize are ultimately a distraction. We should prioritize both.

There are many other forms of tenant protection, including just-cause eviction requirements and right to counsel. These protections are important for reducing evictions and the negative impacts that accompany them, which include the education costs, juvenile justice costs, and welfare costs associated with homeless children; the negative impact of eviction on tenants' credit score, ability to re-rent, and the potential loss of a subsidized housing voucher; the cost of providing public benefits when jobs are lost due to eviction; the costs associated with homelessness, such as additional law enforcement and incarceration costs; the cost of family and community instability; preservation of financial and personal assets; preservation of affordable housing stock; enforcement of rent laws and regulations; and a reduction, over time, of the number of eviction cases filed resulting in improved use of city and court resources.[5]

Just-cause policies limit the circumstances in which landlords can evict tenants. These include "at-fault" evictions for reasons such as nonpayment of rent, violation of lease terms, or use of the unit for illegal purposes; they can also include "no-fault" causes such as plans to demolish or redevelop the property, owner or family member move-in, or a government-issued order to vacate. Right to counsel guarantees tenants legal representation in eviction proceedings, a practice that discourages underhanded or illegal tactics used by landlords to push tenants out. Both protections are included in the recommendations that follow.

An important loophole in many tenant and rental housing protections is the ability for landlords to "go out of business" with rent-stabilized housing, allowing them to take the units off the rental market. The owners may "go out of business" by moving themselves or a family member into a unit, converting a unit to another use (most often a for-sale condominium), or demolishing the existing structure to build something new. Whatever the reason, it always ends with tenants being evicted through no fault of their own.

The concept of going out of business as applied to rental housing is extraordinarily misguided and pernicious. When any other business closes shop, it may sell off its intellectual property or inventory, but it's still a financial blow. And why shouldn't it be? Going out of business doesn't happen because things are going well.

Only in the case of rental housing can going out of business result in windfall profits, far in excess of what the owner would make under business as usual. Apartment owners can use the excuse of going out of business to kick out longtime tenants, earning massive profits in the process. That profit is borne exclusively on the backs of the existing tenants, not from any value that the landlords have created for society, as most other businesses do.

There are valid reasons for governments to permit no-fault evictions. An obvious reason is for the safety of the tenants, such as when a building is deemed structurally unsafe. Another is to allow for higher-density redevelopment under certain circumstances—especially when that redevelopment increases the supply of affordable housing and provides for the needs of displaced residents. Ideally, residents should have the right to move back into these new buildings at their previous lease rates.

But the absurdity of the "going out of business" argument is apparent when a rent-stabilized apartment is purchased and, days later, the residents are served with eviction notices by the new owner. In what kind of world does someone purchase a business only to put it out of business so quickly afterward? The rules that allow this behavior have nothing to do with business; they're a tool of extraction for the rich and unscrupulous to wield against the poor, deliberately designed to undermine the goals of tenant protection policies. They're the corporate looting practices of the private equity industry applied to the housing sector, and they must be sharply curtailed.

Some landlords argue that if they can't go out of business, it will somehow affect the supply and affordability of housing. That's bunk. When a neighborhood convenience store goes out of business, it might not ever reopen. That can be a real loss for the community. When a landlord can't kick out existing tenants, the housing doesn't go anywhere; all that happens is the tenants get to stay and the landlord doesn't cash in.

Limiting apartment owners' opportunities to go out of business still leaves them with plenty of options. They can (1) continue operating the property "as is," (2) redevelop it into a higher-density property if the zoning permits, or (3) sell it to someone who is willing to do (1) or (2). We've chosen to prioritize the profit-seeking opportunities of landlords over the interests of tenants, and that needs to change. Those profits always come at the expense of renters. Investors can instead put their money into new development, stocks, or business ventures if they want above-average returns. There should be no place for windfall profits in the management of rental housing.

Another common claim made by the landlord lobby is that renter protections, including rent control, will penalize the "good" landlords and encourage them to raise rents annually by the maximum rate so they don't fall behind. No more "Uncle Landlord" living next door, giving you a great deal because he likes the cut of your jib.

But what we see, time and again, is that generous landlords are the most fragile of safety nets. Very frequently, evictions are precipitated after the death of a longtime landlord, whose property is passed along to the heirs or sold to an investor; at that point, the drawbacks of this approach become apparent. It's like saying that we shouldn't have Social Security or Medicare because churches and other community organizations should take care of their own. It's a nice idea, but in practice it's completely untenable. Too many people end up left behind, out in the cold without any support.

We can't let the kind acts of some landlords cover for the harm done by so many others. We need universal protections that everyone can rely on, regardless of background, age, social standing, race, religion, income, or other traits or characteristics. If that means fewer sweetheart deals and a more formal, businesslike relationship between tenant and landlord, then so be it.

Another rallying cry for tenant stability is the preservation of "naturally occurring affordable housing," also known by its acronym, NOAH. These are often smaller, older multifamily buildings that were built with private investment and are operated by private owners. They're affordable not because they were subsidized but because they were built at a time when building was inexpensive or because they lack the quality, location, or amenities of modern housing. In many places, they're threatened by demolition or upscale renovations as inequality rises and vacancy rates fall, so preserving them for the benefit of working- and middle-class residents has become a priority. Balanced with pro-housing policies that also allow for increasing density and a growing supply of homes, NOAH preservation is an important strategy for ensuring long-term stability with minimal cost and community disruption.

As with some of the more strident supply-side activists, some tenant advocates can overpromise on the benefits of tenant protections and undersell the importance of an elastic supply of homes. They're also often deeply distrustful of new development and of developers themselves. (This distrust is often mirrored in pro-supply advocates' feelings toward tenant advocates.) This antagonism makes comprehensive solutions very difficult to enact.

Without question, tenant protections and rental housing preservation help real people, in meaningful ways, and they're especially important for protecting residents who live in rapidly changing neighborhoods. But just like supply-side policies, renter protections are no panacea. They're difficult to target at those most in need, and they do relatively little for future residents—most of whom aren't newcomers from other cities and countries but are in fact the children of local residents. Tenant protections also won't increase the number of units affordable to low-income households; new development and subsidies are needed for that. In fact, tenant protections without a growing housing supply may make things worse in the long run: with more people able to stay in their homes, which is undoubtedly good, available housing will become even scarcer and new households may struggle to find a home.

Protections are also complicated and difficult to implement. Enforcing them costs time and money, and some people inevitably slip through the cracks. And after we implement one regulation (e.g., rent control), we often must layer on additional regulations to fix the fix (e.g., reforming "going out of business" provisions and enacting just-cause protections to close loopholes in rent control regulations). Programs such as right to counsel provide a great service, but tenants still must endure the stress of not knowing whether they'll keep their homes as they go through legal proceedings. In a world where there was enough to go around—where housing was in abundant supply—landlords wouldn't have the leverage to raise rents with impunity, and it would be easy to find a nearby replacement if your apartment was too expensive, managed poorly, or redeveloped. That's the world we should strive for, and it's why pro-supply policies are so important. But it's not the world we live in, not yet, which is part of why tenant protections are also essential.

One last note: stability needn't—and shouldn't—mean stasis. Communities can and must continue to evolve; it's in the nature of cities to constantly change, and those that focus on preserving the present will be poorly adapted to the future. "Community stability," as I use the phrase, means managing change, not by slowing or stopping it but by ensuring that anyone who wants to stay is able to and that everyone who chooses to stay feels welcome. It means that the benefits of change accrue to existing tenants as much as to future residents and to vulnerable and disenfranchised communities more than privileged ones. And it means that social connections grow and strengthen rather than fracture and decay. Done right, tenant and rental housing protections can strike that balance and ensure that communities are resilient now and into the future.

28 Place Moderate Restrictions on Rent Increases for Nearly All Housing (Anti-Gouging)

Reasonable limits on rent increases protect tenants and do nothing to slow down development.

There are vanishingly few reasons why a landlord should need to raise a person's rent by more than 10 percent in any given year. Such large rent increases are often used to legally evict a tenant when other means may be unavailable, but it's rarely a financial imperative on the part of the owner. It shouldn't be legally permitted under most circumstances.

Limits on rent increases in the range of 7–10 percent per year are often referred to as anti-gouging rules. Anti-gouging rules are technically a subset of rent stabilization or rent control regulations, but they serve a more limited purpose: preventing the kind of outrageous situations in which tenants have their rent increased by exorbitant amounts, sometimes 50–100 percent or more, all but ensuring their departure. Oregon passed a statewide anti-gouging law in early 2019 that prevents landlords from increasing rents for existing tenants by more than inflation plus 7 percent each year.[6] California passed a similar law later the same year that limits rent increases to inflation plus 5 percent annually.[7]

Unlike stricter forms of rent stabilization and rent control, anti-gouging regulations set at a reasonable rate—as in Oregon and California—would have no appreciable impact on new housing development. Even new developments that open in the midst of a recession could quickly catch up to market rates as the housing market rebounded, and developers themselves recognize this. Anti-gouging limits on rent increases apply to tenants only once they move into a unit; landlords are free to set rents wherever they like after a tenant leaves. This is known as "vacancy decontrol," a term that refers to rent restrictions being lifted ("decontrolled") when a unit becomes vacant. Vacancy decontrol and vacancy control are discussed further in the next two strategies.

Like many other price controls, anti-gouging rules should include a hardship exemption whereby property owners can argue that special circumstances make it necessary to raise rents to a higher rate. At times, these exemptions may be warranted, such as for structural repairs essential for the continued safety of the tenants, but such cases would be rare.

One argument against anti-gouging rules is that mom-and-pop landlords often give favorable deals to good tenants, keeping their rents below market rate to incentivize them to stay, or just to be good neighbors. If landlords know they'll be unable to raise their rent enough to "catch up" in the future (if the relationship goes sour, for example), then they're more likely to raise rents at a consistent rate year after year.

This may be true in some cases, but it's not reason enough to oppose anti-gouging rules. For one, any policy that relies on the goodwill of individual actors is going to be extraordinarily inconsistent in its application. Housing stability is too important to leave to the whims of individual landlords.

Second, landlords can still catch up as long as they're able to reset rents when a tenant leaves. Even if they give some residents a break on rent, they won't be locked into those rents forever.

In cities where housing is still relatively affordable, anti-gouging rules may be the only form of rent control needed. Where housing is already expensive and a more comprehensive approach is required, stronger restrictions may be appropriate.

29 Place Stronger Restrictions on Rent Increases for Older Housing (Rent Stabilization)

Rent stabilization helps households afford rent throughout their tenancies, and its negative consequences for housing supply can be minimized.

If anti-gouging rules are the weakest form of rent control, then rent stabilization, sometimes referred to as second-generation rent control, is the middle ground. Rent stabilization, as it's often practiced in the United States and elsewhere, limits how much a property owner can raise rents on tenants once they've moved in. The annual limit on rent increases is lower than for anti-gouging regulations—sometimes even below the rate of inflation—but as with anti-gouging rules, landlords are permitted to reset rents to market rates when tenants turn over.

Supply advocates are rightfully wary of rent stabilization because it can negatively impact new development and existing rental housing supply in ways that anti-gouging regulations do not. A city may end up securing short-term benefits for a portion of existing renters at the expense of an undersupplied, much less affordable housing market in the long run.

The outcomes are very dependent on how rent stabilization policies are drawn up. For example, if rent hikes are capped at the rate of inflation (or lower) and apply to all housing regardless of age, developers will be heavily disincentivized from taking the risk to build new housing. Projects take at least a few years to advance from concept to lease-up, sometimes seven to ten years or more in jurisdictions that are less friendly to new housing. Given those time frames, developers working on projects during good economic times may open their doors in the midst of a recession; if they're forced to lease their units at a loss for the first few years but rent stabilization rules prevent them from ever raising prices as the economy recovers, they may as well declare bankruptcy on opening day. Developers will understandably avoid cities where this is a possibility, and supply will stagnate. This is why rent stabilization doesn't apply to new housing virtually anywhere in the world.

If rent stabilization policies apply only to older units—say, those open for fifteen to twenty years or longer—then this is much less of a deterrent to home building. This approach is sometimes referred to as rolling rent control because it applies to more units each year on a rolling basis. Because of the time value of money (TVM), which is the principle that a dollar today is of greater value than a dollar tomorrow, developers and other investors don't worry much about maximizing financial prospects decades into the future; earning a good return in the near to medium term is far more important. By the time twenty years have passed, the success of the investment has been determined, and constraints on future profit are of less consequence.[8]

One argument made against rolling rent control is that it gives building owners an opportunity to either vacate their units or convert them to condominiums before rent stabilization takes effect. This is not a serious issue, for a few reasons. First, the owners are able to set rents at market rate from the building's opening to the day rent stabilization is applied, and in most cases they'll already be charging as much as they can before even considering how they'll respond to future limits on rent increases. Some landlords *may* choose to renovate their units before their nonstabilized term ends, but this is likely to be a niche activity and not very lucrative as long as new homes continue to be built and remain the most attractive option for people who can afford premium rates. The buildings will be only fifteen to twenty years old, so there'll be little need for renovations anyway.

Second, to the question of condo conversion—so what? Condos are also a great housing option, and they offer people a chance for homeownership, which is its own form of tenant stability. If much older, more affordable apartments are being renovated and converted to condos en masse, this can be a genuine threat to stability for local residents. Buildings in the fifteen- to twenty-year-old range, though, are still a relatively high-end product, and households who can afford to rent them will usually be capable of buying them, too.

That's good! Many cities underbuild for-sale multifamily housing for various reasons including onerous condo warranty laws,[9] so converting some newer rentals to ownership units would be a welcome development.

30 Be Careful with Vacancy Control

—

The strongest form of rent control can keep housing affordable for longer, but it's fraught with unintended consequences.

The third and strictest form of rent control is the type that includes vacancy control: rules that limit rent increases *even when old tenants move out and a new household moves in*. Supporting vacancy control may sound like a no-brainer. After all, if it's good to limit rent increases after a tenant moves in, wouldn't it be even better to also limit rent hikes for future tenants of the same unit?

All else equal, yes, it would. A legitimate issue with "vacancy decontrol"—rent stabilization rules that allow property owners to reset rents to market rates when new households move in—is that if a neighborhood's rents rapidly increase, even rent-stabilized apartments will become much less affordable over time because renters tend to move frequently. A rent-stabilized one-bedroom apartment that costs $3,500 per month may have predictable rents, but it's certainly no longer affordable in any commonly understood meaning of the word. Rent-stabilized housing, for all its benefits, is simply not synonymous with affordable housing.

Another problem with vacancy decontrol is that it gives landlords a strong incentive to evict their rent-stabilized tenants. The bigger the gap between the price-controlled rent and the market rate, the greater the incentive to push out the tenant, legally or otherwise. And, to put it mildly, landlords don't always strictly adhere to the law when large sums of money are at stake.

Finally, vacancy control could help resolve the "lock in" problem of rent stabilization. When rents can revert to market rate when a tenant leaves, renters often get stuck in place as the market outpaces their annual rent increases. Several years after moving in, they may be paying hundreds of dollars less per month than are renters in similar units who moved in more recently. While this is better than paying higher rents, these tenants often end up having to make a choice between staying in an affordable home that no longer suits their needs—whether because of a new job, a growing family, kids leaving home, a disability, or otherwise—or moving into a new unit that's outside their price range. This problem is at least partially resolved when all rentals are subject to the same price controls.

In practice, though, it's difficult to make vacancy control function successfully in a mixed housing market.

Imagine, for example, two equivalent units in the same rent-stabilized (decontrolled) apartment building, one with a long-term tenant renting for $800 per month and another with a new tenant paying $1,500. Now apply vacancy control. Whenever the units go back on the market, the $800 unit will be in much higher demand. Who among the applicants gets the cheaper apartment, and who gets the more expensive one?

One option is to ration vacancy-controlled rental housing, with long waiting lists for the most affordable units in the most desirable locations. In Stockholm, Sweden (population 965,000), for example, the waiting list for rent-controlled housing is 580,000 people long, with waits of over twenty years for apartments in some neighborhoods.[10] In a country where most housing is privately owned, as it is in the United States, managing city- or countywide waiting lists would be extremely challenging. Even if most housing were publicly owned, it would be a very difficult task. In the real world, where people have different and evolving household compositions, large variations in income, and different neighborhood preferences, operating such a system would be overwhelmingly complicated. Add to the equation apartments of equivalent quality that have their rents controlled at significantly different levels and it seems all but impossible.

Another option is to simply leave the tenant selection process to property owners, as we do today. But if landlords could no longer select tenants on the basis of their willingness to pay, they'd find other ways to pick their renters. In some cases, that would entail outright racial or ethnic bias, explicit or otherwise. More often, it might take the form of higher credit score or income requirements, preferred household composition (couples versus singles, childless versus families), or a whole range of subjective assessments about who seems like a "good fit." These forms of discrimination (meant in the descriptive, nonpejorative sense of the word) aren't all legal, but the laws prohibiting them are extraordinarily difficult to enforce. How can you prove that the reason a landlord selected a single man or a childless couple was that he doesn't want children in his units?

Property managers might take off-the-books monthly or lump-sum payments from potential tenants or might accept promises that tenants will invest their own money in apartment renovations. To be sure, the fact that some people might break the law is not always a good argument for why a law shouldn't exist. But the property management sector is so diffuse and difficult to monitor that widespread abuse seems inevitable under these conditions.

Vacancy control has become a rallying cry in progressive circles, but exactly how it would be implemented remains unclear. Cities such as New York, where a small number of units are still vacancy controlled, have become caricaturized for the lengths people will go to secure them, often fraudulently. Montreal has been hailed as a gold standard for North American rent control, with strong protections and decades of affordable rents, but this is more likely the result of weak demand and a surplus of housing than of the protections themselves. As demand has grown in recent years, the program (and the city's affordability) is buckling under the pressure.[11]

Advocates sometimes point to cities such as Vienna as examples to emulate, as described in the introduction to this book, but their success is based on heavy public investment and nonprofit or public ownership of housing—a completely different system from private ownership with government-mandated rent caps.

Cities such as Vienna are worthy of emulation, but they don't teach us much about how to implement vacancy control in the United States.

Berlin recently adopted rules limiting rents to no more than 10 percent above the average price for an apartment in a given community, with some limited success,[12] but it will be several years before the program can be properly assessed and its lasting impact determined. And, importantly, Berlin's rent control plans are accompanied by an ambitious effort to build two hundred thousand new homes by 2030.[13] These examples don't mean that vacancy control *can't* be implemented successfully, but the lack of clear success stories should give advocates pause and force us to ask how an effective program would actually work.

For cities that already have rent stabilization and want to adopt vacancy control but are concerned with negative unintended consequences, one option is to delay implementation of vacancy control on a unit-by-unit basis. That is, vacancy control could be applied to each affected unit *after* its next tenant moves in after the new rules are approved. This would allow all property owners to reset their rents to market rate before vacancy control goes into effect, setting all housing at the same baseline rent relative to its quality and desirability. This would prevent many of the problems described earlier, in which roughly equivalent units end up renting for vastly different rates, and the most desirable (and least needy) tenants receive the most deeply discounted rents. Over time, though, cities would still need to grapple with the inevitable challenges that arise as neighborhoods change. Rent-controlled housing in communities that became more desirable would be underpriced relative to other locations, leading to the same potential for discriminatory leasing practices that favor certain groups over others. Vacancy control has its benefits, but the consequences of a poorly designed program can be severe. Cities should tread lightly if they're considering adopting it.

31 Implement Inclusionary Zoning and Density Bonuses

Affordability requirements and incentives can deliver affordable, income-restricted housing at no cost to the public.

Requiring developments to set aside a share of new units for low- or moderate-income households is an increasingly common practice that may take a few different forms. One is inclusionary zoning mandates, which require all new development to provide some percentage of affordable housing on-site, occasionally allowing for an in-lieu fee to fund off-site affordable housing instead. Another is density bonuses, which offer development enhancements in exchange for affordable units. Incentives such as density bonuses are generally preferable to mandates, but sometimes both are appropriate. Remember from principle 6, "Use a mix of mandates and incentives," that incentives are best when we want to make a good thing better. Mandates are best when we want to discourage or prohibit something we consider bad.

There are two key distinctions between density bonuses and inclusionary zoning (IZ). One is that density bonuses are typically voluntary, while IZ usually is not. The second is that density bonuses offer something in exchange for affordable, income-restricted units, while IZ generally does not.

And when it comes to affordability requirements, density bonuses are generally preferred. This is for two reasons: First, housing is good, and density bonuses usually deliver more homes—both market-rate and affordable—than either baseline (unmodified) zoning or inclusionary zoning. Second, while density bonuses can be designed poorly such that they're not used by developers, they're rarely so poorly designed that they stop projects that would have otherwise gone forward. If density bonuses are not generous enough, developers may just build according to baseline zoning. If inclusionary zoning requirements are too high, developers may build nothing at all.

Density bonuses usually work as follows. Start with baseline zoning, for example, a 20,000-square-foot parcel that allows up to 50 units of housing. In exchange for restricting 15 percent of the units to low-income households, the developer may increase the number of units by 60 percent, increasing the project size to 80 multifamily homes. Because of the 15 percent affordability requirement, 12 of those homes must be rented to low-income households at a reduced rate. Instead of 50 market-rate units, which by themselves are good to have in a city with high costs and limited supply, we now have 68 market-rate units and 12 affordable units, which are *really* good to have.

It's important to include other bonuses to complement the density bonus, especially floor area ratio (FAR) and height. Without these bonuses, developers may technically be allowed to provide more units but in practice be unable to do so because they can't build a bulky or tall enough building to accommodate them all. Other incentives, such as reductions to setbacks, lot width, and lot coverage, as well as reduced minimum parking requirements (or no parking requirements whatsoever), are also helpful.

A valid concern with density bonuses is that they sometimes hold one good policy hostage against another. Parking minimums are a case in point. If we recognize that more affordable housing and less parking are both positive outcomes, why should we allow less parking only when affordable housing is also included? Why not simply eliminate parking minimums and mandate a minimum affordability requirement? In other words, why not go with inclusionary zoning?

In an ideal world, this would probably be the better approach. And, to be clear, parking minimums and other pernicious housing policies should still be abolished rather than being held hostage to density bonuses. But there's a significant risk of setting IZ targets too high, leading to reductions in housing supply at every income level. Furthermore, inclusionary zoning relies on high baseline densities to provide similar benefits to density bonuses, and most cities are not currently zoned for high baseline density. Even a well-designed IZ policy would require complementary reforms to citywide zoning, severely complicating the political and technical pathways to approval.

There is still a place for inclusionary zoning, however. Even though it's very easy to overshoot an IZ requirement, it would also be undesirable to have a rarely used density bonus in which the majority of development uses baseline zoning. To avoid this, cities might consider pairing their density bonus with a relatively low inclusionary requirement, perhaps 10 percent of units. This can serve as a backstop when the density bonus is not performing as desired, and cities can improve their density bonus program over time without losing out on large numbers of affordable homes.

32 Discourage Redevelopment That Requires Renter Displacement (Displacement Compensation and Right of Return)

Generous compensation for displaced renters can mitigate harm and direct development toward less vulnerable sites and communities.

One way to mitigate the impacts of redevelopment and ensure stability for vulnerable populations, including low-income communities of color, is to set different rules for development that impacts those populations. Such rules not only protect vulnerable groups but also have the effect of directing development toward locations where the same populations don't exist (or are less prevalent) and where the same rules don't apply.

This can be achieved by making developers pay relocation costs or rental assistance to tenants displaced by redevelopment and by offering displaced renters a "right of return."

Many cities have displacement compensation programs, including Los Angeles, the location of the Yucca-Argyle redevelopment discussed in the introduction to this book. In most cities that have such programs—perhaps all of them—the amount of required compensation is nowhere near enough. As of July 2019, Los Angeles tenants evicted via the state's Ellis Act program, which allows no-fault evictions for property owners seeking to convert or redevelop their buildings, must be compensated only a maximum of $21,200.[14] In a neighborhood where some rent-stabilized tenants are paying $500 to $1,000 below the market price for similar units, a $21,200 payment won't go very far at all. Within a few years the money will run out, and many residents will have to leave their neighborhood—assuming they can find an affordable home anywhere in the city.

Developers should be required to make much larger compensation payments to displaced households, and the value of those payments should be based on the tenant households' characteristics. The greater the gap between their current rents and the market rate for similar units in the same community, the larger the payment. The lower their household income, the larger the payment. The more children in the household, whose lives and educations may all be disrupted (and for whom suitable housing will be more difficult to find), the larger the payment. This is not a complete solution to the problem of displacement, but it's an obvious and essential first step.

For some households that are higher earning and are relatively new to their apartments, the payments might be quite small—perhaps $10,000 or less. For more vulnerable households, $50,000 or even $100,000 or more might be appropriate. These may sound like large sums, but even then they might not impart the same stability and protection as the rent-stabilized (or rent-controlled) home the tenants are losing.

Another option is to require rental assistance and right of return for displaced households. Right of return allows renters to return to a property once redevelopment is complete, typically in a similar unit and at the same rent as in their previous home. Rental assistance pays the difference between their existing rent and market-rate rent for a similar unit for the duration of construction, until they can "return" to the new building.

Generally, only one option should be required: a large compensation payment or a right of return paired with short-term rental assistance. Importantly, tenants should be given the choice of which they prefer to receive. Some will benefit more from the payment, and others will benefit more from right of return; the tenants themselves are in the best position to make that decision.

Some might read these proposals and argue that compensation at this scale would make some redevelopment projects financially infeasible. That's exactly the point. In urban settings, demolition will always be a precondition for sustainable growth, but all redevelopment is not created equal. Replacing a duplex with a twenty-unit apartment building, including three or four low-income units, is a worthwhile project in most circumstances. That same twenty-unit development replacing a twelve-unit rent-stabilized apartment building almost certainly is not. The purpose of these displacement compensation programs is not just to give tenants their due but also to direct development toward sites that have the least negative impact on existing residents—to align the financial cost of redevelopment with the human cost.

This is also why pro-supply policies are an essential complement to tenant protections, especially supply policies that increase density in high-opportunity neighborhoods dominated by low-density owner-occupied housing. With higher standards for redevelopment where renters already live, owner-occupied housing becomes favored for redevelopment because these mitigation costs do not apply: the sale of owner-occupied housing is voluntary, so no one is displaced who doesn't want to be. Renters who already live in the community can enjoy the amenities that accompany new development, and the region can still benefit from an abundant supply of mixed-income homes.

33 Make Affordability Requirements Permanent (Affordability Covenant Duration)

—

Subsidized housing covenants currently last thirty to fifty-five years in most jurisdictions. Those requirements should be made permanent or last for at least ninety-nine years.

For projects that use public funds, most commonly the federal government's Low-Income Housing Tax Credit (LIHTC), developers typically must agree to lease their income-restricted units at an affordable rate for at least thirty years. This requirement has been increased to fifty-five years for affordable housing projects in California, with no apparent effect on housing production and nary a peep from developers. The lesson from California is clear: cities can get much more out of their investments by making affordability requirements permanent—or for ninety-nine years, which is the longest term for a realty contract in many states.[15]

When developers consider the financial feasibility of a new project, they're most concerned with revenues and expenses shortly after opening. Look too far into the future and the numbers matter much less. For one thing, it's unrealistic to forecast more than a decade or two out; too many variables are at play to have confidence in any one possible future. Many developers build with the intent to sell very shortly after completing their building, once it is fully leased and stabilized, and these developers care even less about their buildings' long-term finances. They still must care somewhat, though, since they need to convince someone that the buildings are worth buying.

Inflationary pressures may be the most important consideration. Inflation, in its simplest distillation, means that a dollar received in the future is of less value than a dollar received today. In the parlance of the field, this is expressed as the discount rate—that is, how much less you'll value a dollar earned in the future, compounding year over year. A 10 percent discount rate would mean a dollar received one year from now would be valued the same as 90 cents today. Five years in, a dollar of income would be valued at just 59 cents.[16] Even assuming a modest 5 percent discount rate, a dollar received in year thirty is worth the equivalent of only 21 cents. By fifty-five years this falls to just 6 cents.

Virtually no one makes development decisions on the basis of their revenue expectations thirty years in the future. At fifty-five years it's even less relevant; many of the people involved in the project will be dead by the time the affordability covenant expires.

The cost of permanent affordability requirements is negligible from the perspective of developers, but the public cost of *failing* to make them permanent is very high. According to the US Department of Housing and Urban Development (HUD), approximately 424,000 units funded by LIHTC will reach the end of their thirty-year terms between 2025 and 2029. About 2.2 million homes were developed using LIHTC between 1987 and 2009, and the affordability covenants will expire on all of them before too long.

Cities can work with property owners to extend these affordability terms, or they can change the terms while maintaining some level of affordability, but that costs money. Especially in expensive cities, where LIHTC units are commonly found, the difference in value between an income-restricted unit and a market-rate unit can be hundreds of thousands of dollars. That may be an expense worth paying to maintain affordability, but it would be far better to avoid the cost altogether.

Many cities already have ninety-nine-year or permanent affordability covenants on rentals, for-sale housing, or both. These include Boulder, Colorado; Burlington, Vermont; Cambridge, Massachusetts; Chicago, Illinois (for-sale only); and Davis, California.[17] Every city concerned with housing affordability should adopt similar provisions. To learn more about this proposal, you can refer to a policy brief I wrote for the UCLA Lewis Center for Regional Policy Studies titled "Increasing the Duration of Affordability Requirements for New Affordable Housing."[18]

The prospect of permanent affordability restrictions raises at least one valid concern. If affordability requirements never expire, can the building ever be used for anything else? Ninety-nine or more-years from now we will live in a very different world, and it may be reasonable—necessary, even—to tear down some of these buildings, or change their use, or who knows what. Trying to make anything truly permanent, with no possibility of a different use in the future, is probably a fool's errand, with unpredictable consequences.

A fair compromise might allow property owners to buy their way out of affordability restrictions after a set time. Say, thirty or fifty years. The cost would need to be significant, roughly in proportion to the cost of subsidizing the construction or acquisition of a similar affordable unit elsewhere. In this way, a city could continue to accommodate necessary change while maintaining, and in fact continuously increasing, its stock of affordable homes.

34 Buy Naturally Occurring Affordable Housing with Public Funds

—

Most low- and moderate-income households already live in privately owned for-profit housing. We can keep those homes affordable at much lower cost than new construction.

The vast majority of spending on housing programs goes toward rental assistance and new construction, but this overlooks another important opportunity: acquiring existing housing with public funds.

Acquisition of existing housing is an idea that's grown in popularity in recent years. As mentioned earlier in this section, it even has its own acronym, NOAH, or naturally occurring affordable housing. This is housing that, while privately built and privately owned, is nonetheless serving working-class and lower-income households at affordable rents. This may be because the housing lacks modern amenities, has smaller than average unit sizes, doesn't include parking, houses long-term rent-stabilized tenants, or is in a less desirable area of a city, among other reasons. Acquiring NOAH is especially fruitful if it's located in a community on the brink (or in the midst) of gentrification or if a building requires significant upgrades to bring it to a proper state of livability. For those interested in community land trusts (CLTs), in which land is community owned and homes are sold and resold at affordable prices, the NOAH approach may also apply to land purchases.[19]

When it comes to the use of public funds, acquisition has many benefits in comparison with new development. First, it gets you much more bang for the buck: existing multifamily units can cost half as much as new ones, depending on their location and quality. Purchasing units also allows the buyer to make them permanently affordable, whereas most new subsidized construction is limited to thirty- or fifty-five-year affordability covenants.

New affordable housing developments often have 100 percent

of their units reserved for tenants who fall below a certain income threshold, physically separating the haves from the have-nots. Acquisition of existing buildings enables more flexibility and can promote better mixing of lower-income, working-class, and middle-income households. Mixing of different economic classes can also improve financial sustainability for affordable housing by allowing on-site market-rate (or even just moderate-income) units to cross-subsidize the expense of lower-income units. An acquired building might cost the government very little in up-front costs because it can rely on private debt; without a profit motive, the revenues from rents can be enough to pay off lending costs at little to no long-term cost to the public. After the building is paid off, surplus revenues can be funneled into deeper and wider affordability or be used to acquire more homes.

Acquisition also makes it easier to provide subsidized housing throughout a city—not just where opposition to new development is weakest or zoning is most permissive—and it protects at-risk rental housing from condo conversions and upscale renovations that push out lower-income tenants. Over the long term, it would safeguard a meaningful share of rental housing from speculative investment and predatory landlords.

Finally, acquisition acknowledges that there's no fundamental tension between supporters of market-rate housing and supporters of public housing and affordable housing. In practice, the cost of developing either is roughly the same; the question is not how much it costs but who pays. Acquiring existing multifamily housing and making it affordable over the long term breaks down the barriers between market-rate and affordable housing. Every building developed with private funding today could become a publicly owned apartment complex in the future. You can find more details about the benefits of acquiring housing with public funds at my blog, *Better Institutions*, in an article titled "Private Development, Public/Non-Profit Ownership: Recipe for Long-Term Housing Affordability."[20]

Acquisition has two main shortcomings. First, it doesn't increase the supply of housing, and supply is essential for the long-term affordability and widespread accessibility of housing. While it's true that not every solution needs to address every facet of the affordability crisis, this is a real drawback in a world where decisions must be made about where limited funds will be spent. It's absolutely critical that housing acquisition be paired with a pro-development policy approach. If new housing isn't being built, we'll run out of existing homes to acquire—and they'll only grow more expensive to purchase if demand continues to outstrip supply. Policies that promote housing growth also help keep acquisition affordable.

The second obstacle is how public housing has been portrayed in this country, especially in the past but even into the present day. Very visible failures have tainted the reputation of public housing, most notably the 1956 completion and subsequent 1972 demolition of the Pruitt-Igoe housing project in St. Louis, Missouri. The failure of Pruitt-Igoe, and other projects like it, has been used as an argument against public housing assistance, and its legacy remains with us today.

The reality of why public housing has failed in so many places (though not all of them) has much more to do with the early design of the program, undercut at every turn by legislators who never wanted to see it succeed—and who ultimately got their wish.[21] With appropriate funding for operations and maintenance, public housing and social housing have successful track records around the world, and that same success can be replicated here. New affordable housing developments, often funded by LIHTC and built and managed by nonprofits, have a much better reputation in the United States, and they're helping to shift the views people hold about government-supported housing. State and local governments might take a similar approach by handing nonprofits the responsibility for buying and maintaining existing multifamily housing.

How one implements an acquisition program is important; the details matter. It can be done in support of other goals, namely, housing production, or it can undermine them. Take, for example, the purchase of small-scale apartment buildings such as duplexes and triplexes. If acquired in areas zoned for lower density, there are no particular downsides. But in areas zoned for higher-density housing, where a duplex might eventually be redeveloped into a twenty-unit apartment building, preservation can do more harm than good. With the right incentives, that twenty-unit building might include three or four units permanently reserved for low-income households, helping more vulnerable families at deeper affordability levels and in safer, higher-quality units. Further, those affordable units would most likely be built at no cost to the government. If acquisition and preservation stands in the way of these kinds of outcomes—assuming strong displacement protections and mitigations are also in place—advocates and policy makers may make things worse, not better.

These nuances are important to consider and will determine the success or failure of a public acquisition program. Done right, acquisition, preservation, and stabilization of existing multifamily housing can be a powerful tool in the affordable housing toolbox. These activities should play a growing role in cities' approaches to housing policy, and state and federal programs should evolve to support their expansion.

35 Require Transparency from Voluntary Tenant Buyouts

—

Some people will benefit more from a bag of cash than the promise of a permanently affordable apartment.

Buyouts, in which property owners pay tenants to vacate their apartments, have a bad reputation. This is largely justified. In many cases, buyout offers are made "off the books" and don't meet minimum legal requirements; landlords make the offers hoping their tenants won't know their rights, and they're often rewarded for the deception. Many tenants believe their only options are either to (1) accept an inadequate payment and vacate their home or (2) delay, fight, and most likely lose their case—and then be forced to leave without even the initial buyout offer. Even if they ultimately win, the process can be torturous. Buyout offers may also be accompanied by intimidation or deliberately poor living conditions. Despite this, voluntary buyouts have a valid place in the housing market and should still be permitted in the right circumstances.

Lifetime access to a rent-stabilized unit is not the best option for every family and individual. Buyout offers in some cities can exceed $100,000, enough for a 20–50 percent down payment on a home in many US cities. If a tenant prefers to take the money and buy a home in a more affordable location—offering them more certainty and stability, to say nothing of wealth, than a rent-controlled home ever could—why should we stand in the way? Done right, voluntary buyouts can improve security and stability for those who choose to accept them.

Acknowledging this fact, San Francisco codified a voluntary buyout agreement process into law in 2015. Property owners must now go through a formal process to negotiate buyouts with tenants. First, they must provide tenants with a Pre-Buyout Negotiations Disclosure Form and then notify the city's Rent Board that the form has been sent. Finalized buyouts are reported publicly, including the address where the buyout took place, the total buyout amount, and the amount per tenant.[22]

This formalized process ensures that tenants are fully informed and are much less likely to be victimized by landlords, even going so far as to allow tenants to rescind their approval up to forty-five days after signing the buyout agreement. It also helps the city flag properties at higher risk of abuse to tenants, either during the buyout negotiation process or following a buyout rejection. Over 1,300 buyout agreements have been approved since the program's inception, with payments ranging from as little as $475 to as high as $310,000.[23]

San Francisco's Buyout Agreements program has created an open, transparent process that gives tenants the option to stay in their homes or take an appropriately sized, negotiated buyout payment. Some will take the buyout and some will not; the decision is truly up to them, not paternalistically made on their behalf. The program protects tenants who might otherwise feel compelled to accept an insufficient buyout as a result of lack of information about fair compensation or the alternatives available to them. It also gives property owners a clear and straightforward process for vacating their units, eliminating the threat of possible litigation or reneging on a deal. Other cities should adopt similar voluntary buyout agreement programs.

36 Prioritize Displaced Tenants for Affordable Housing Placement (Preferential Placement)

—

The benefits of redevelopment should accrue to existing residents as much as possible—especially those directly displaced to make way for more homes.

As a city grows its stock of affordable homes through new construction and acquisition, it should prioritize displaced tenants for placement into those units. The Yucca-Argyle case in this book's introduction illustrates a legitimate gripe: that displaced tenants are not usually the ones to benefit from the affordable or rent-stabilized housing that replaces their former homes. Despite the obvious appeal of providing affordable housing to those most impacted by redevelopment, this hasn't been a priority for most local governments.

Some will argue that if we simply stop displacement in all its forms, we won't have to worry about how to compensate those affected. We *should* acknowledge that displacement can have grave social and economic consequences for tenants, even if that displacement is accompanied by promises of a newer, better home at the same or lower rent (which today is rarely the case). Being displaced from one's home, especially when one's housing alternatives are bleak, can be a destabilizing and deeply harmful experience. Many of us also have an emotional connection to our homes and the memories we've created in them, such that no amount of money would be worth parting from them.

But we also can't freeze our cities in amber, and the decision to protect all housing in all circumstances has its own consequences: fewer new homes for a growing population, fewer affordable homes for low-income households, and higher costs for future generations burdened by scarcity. We need to build homes, and in urban environments that will always require the demolition of some existing housing. The question shouldn't be how to stop demolition altogether but rather what kinds of redevelopment we prioritize and what we do for those who are most directly impacted by it.

One reason why cities may struggle to identify affordable housing options for displaced tenants is that the demand for low-income housing is so great. Vacancies are rare, and especially so if the search is limited to a geographic area very close to a displaced tenant's former home. The problem becomes exponentially more difficult when a large number of people are displaced simultaneously, as with the Yucca-Argyle project.

One small way cities can make relocation easier is by requiring very early advance notice of impending eviction. With a year of notice, to the tenants as well as the city, the gears of government can begin their work of identifying housing alternatives for affected residents.

Acquisition of existing housing—an earlier recommendation—also gives cities much more flexibility with preferential placement. With publicly owned and nonprofit-managed apartments throughout the city, free of strict income qualifications on each individual unit, homes can be offered to displaced households at exactly the rents they previously paid, whatever those might be. With enough units under public and nonprofit ownership, some will always be available for new renters. And with a year of advance notice, cities could even identify new acquisitions before tenants are finally evicted.

Priority relocations could be made available to tenants regardless of their income, but the main beneficiaries should be lower-income and fixed-income households. In some cases, relocation of a low- or moderate-income household into an affordable unit—where tenants pay no more than 30 percent of their income—would actually mean a reduction in their monthly rent compared with their earlier tenancy. Positive outcomes like this should be the goal of any displacement mitigation plan, for as many renters as possible.

Zooming out to look at the big picture, a relatively small number of households are displaced to make way for new development each year. The cost of taking care of them would not be so great if our society cared to do so. We have the resources to make redevelopment-driven displacement something akin to winning the lottery for tenants, whereas today it's closer to spinning "Bankrupt" on the Wheel of Fortune. Residents should not have to live in fear that they, through sheer bad luck and no fault of their own, might be next on the chopping block. Strong protections, including priority placement and compensation for those affected, will give renters peace of mind and help reduce the fear of displacement that often accompanies new development.

37 Limit the Ability of Landlords to "Go Out of Business" (Rental Housing Preservation)

—

Loopholes have been written into law that allow landlords to earn huge profits by evicting tenants.

As discussed in the introduction to this section, owners of rent-stabilized housing are provided with numerous loopholes for evicting their tenants and reaping windfall profits in the process. This process is often described as "going out of the rental business," but, unlike virtually any other business closure, it can be massively profitable to the owner. Reasons for "going out of business" include conversion to another use, such as hotel rooms, condos, or tenancies in common; demolition; and redevelopment. Landlords can kick out all of their tenants, convert their buildings to condos, and sell for a profit of hundreds of thousands or millions of dollars. Meanwhile, renters are left out in the cold. This practice allows property owners to escape their obligations, and it should be ended under most circumstances.

A common response to proposals to end this loophole is, "Why shouldn't property owners have the right to do whatever they want with their property? Why should renters have more rights with respect to their apartment than the person or business that owns it?" The same question would apply to any requirements, really, including rent stabilization and just-cause protections (described here later). But here's another way to think about property rights: "Why shouldn't our rules regarding rental property be written with the basic needs of renters as the first priority, rather than the profits of property owners?" There's nothing forcing anyone to invest in rental property. If investors don't want to bother with a business model in which people come first, there are plenty of other places to invest their money.

Providing stronger protections might reduce the value of rental property, but at the right price, *someone* will be willing to buy and operate it. That price will reflect their new responsibilities and the cost of upholding them (see the appendix for an overview of how rental property is valued according to its revenues, costs, and regulations). That doesn't sound like such a terrible price for society to pay in exchange for stable housing for all our neighbors. This change in perspective, favoring renters over landlords, would be a huge shift and deeply controversial. Whenever I write about such proposals, the pushback from property owners is immediate and overwhelming. But when the dust settled, it would be hard to imagine how we ever accepted such arbitrary and unpredictable treatment of renters.

The ability to "go out of business" shouldn't be eliminated entirely. There are cases in which it should still be permitted, particularly when a property is to be redeveloped into higher-density housing. If a property owner wants to replace a rent-stabilized duplex with a forty-unit apartment building, including six units reserved for low-income households, apartment preservation rules shouldn't stand in the way. The tenants displaced from the duplex should still be fully compensated, as discussed in earlier policy recommendations, but that's a bearable cost for such a significant rise in density. Replacing a twenty-unit complex with that same forty-unit project, on the other hand, should almost certainly be disincentivized. If the property owner decides the cost of compensating all twenty households is worthwhile, then so be it, but in practice this will almost never be financially feasible. And that's the point.

Converting to nonresidential uses, condominiums, and tenancies in common (TICs) needn't be completely banned, but rules should be established to capture virtually all of the potential profit from such an effort. In theory, there's nothing particularly troubling about converting apartments to condos or TICs—it's still housing, after all. But converting $800-per-month rent-stabilized apartments to $500,000 condos is a win for no one except the property owner: the end result is the same amount of housing but vastly more expensive, with the original tenants unlikely to be able to stay. If the property owner can convince the renters to accept a voluntary buyout, they're welcome to do so, but there should be no legal means for compelling them to leave in such cases.

There are legitimate reasons for landlords to "go out of business," but they should almost never be accompanied by large profits (one exception being a successful redevelopment). Generous compensation requirements for displaced renters will discourage most of this behavior, but cities should also consider more direct prohibitions if these types of evictions remain commonplace. Another simple starting point for policy makers: prohibit "going out of business" within five years of purchasing a property except in order to build higher-density housing. The practice of buying, evicting, converting, and reselling at a massive profit becomes far less attractive when it requires a five-year waiting period to begin the process.

38 Use Just-Cause Protections to Discourage Evictions

Just-cause protections ensure that tenants who follow the rules won't have to worry about losing their homes.

There are plenty of legitimate reasons for a tenant to be evicted: ongoing failure to pay rent, repeated violation of the terms of a lease agreement, and substantial damage to the unit, among other things. "I want more rent from my tenants" should not be a valid reason for eviction, nor should "because I feel like it." Just-cause eviction rules protect renters from exactly this. Stable housing is too important to leave to the capriciousness of individual property owners. Again: if they don't appreciate the responsibility associated with being a landlord, they are free to invest their money elsewhere.

Just-cause protections, also called "good cause" protections in some cities, define the circumstances under which landlords can evict their tenants and prohibit evictions for any other reason. The permissible circumstances are divided into at-fault evictions—generally, those for which the tenant has in some way violated the lease agreement—and no-fault evictions, those for which the tenant is not to blame but still must vacate the unit.

At-fault evictions mostly fall into the categories described earlier: nonpayment of rent and other forms of rule breaking. No-fault evictions are a bit more complicated and include reasons such as the property owner (or one of the owner's family members) moving into the unit, conversion to a condo or co-op, demolition, or conversion to another use, such as a hotel or commercial building.

Just-cause eviction protections are especially important in cities with rent control and rent stabilization. Without these protections, the stability of annual rent hike caps means nothing; landlords can simply evict tenants for no reason and charge market-rate rents to the next tenants. Nearly every city in California with rent stabilization laws also has just-cause eviction protections for this reason.

Some cities, such as Santa Monica and West Hollywood, also apply these protections to housing that is not rent stabilized.[24]

Evicting tenants so that owners or their family members can move in is a permissible reason for no-fault evictions in most cases, but cities should consider restricting the practice more sharply. Why? In one sense, the same logic that applies to the "going out of business" cases (described in the previous recommendation) should also apply to owner move-ins: if you didn't want to be subject to the protections offered to renters, you shouldn't have rented your property in the first place. But this can get complicated. What if you own two units on a parcel and your family lives in one unit, but you plan for your elderly parents to move into the other—not today, but five or ten years in the future as their ability to live independently declines? It only makes sense that you should be able to rent it out in the meantime, but strong eviction protections might preclude your parents' ever moving in. No one benefits from rules that encourage property owners to keep homes empty.

A possible answer would be to permit owner or family move-ins under specific circumstances; in this case, a simple solution would be to allow owner or family move-ins only if the other unit is already owner-occupied. Even in such cases, evicted tenants should still be compensated at a level that will ensure that their eviction doesn't bestow a windfall profit on the property owner. This would strike a fair balance, allowing multigenerational, multi-unit households while eliminating the financial benefits that might be realized from gaming the system.

39 Require Government Notification for All Eviction Notices and Rent Hikes (Landlord Transparency)

Landlords will shy away from illegal and predatory tactics if they're unlikely to get away with them. Greater transparency would make consistent enforcement achievable.

The United States saw approximately 2.35 million formal eviction filings and just shy of 900,000 evictions in 2016. About 6.1 percent of renter households had an eviction filed against them in that year, and 2.34 percent were evicted.[25] Those are the cases we know about, anyway. A study of Milwaukee, Wisconsin, estimated that informal, off-the-books evictions were roughly twice as common as formal evictions.[26] Whether those results can be extrapolated across the entire renter population is impossible to know without further research, but it's clear that baseline eviction numbers are very high, and informal evictions push those numbers even higher.

Landlords have been known to baselessly threaten tenants with eviction and file illegal eviction notices to force them from their homes; this is an especially lucrative tactic in jurisdictions with rent-stabilized housing, where the gap between a tenant's rent and the prevailing market rate may be quite large. Landlords may also issue rent increases above the legally permissible rate, hoping that their tenants won't realize they're paying more than required. They may even throw away their tenants' rent checks to fabricate a legal basis for eviction (nonpayment). Such cases may be relatively rare (though data are hard to come by), but they do occur, and the harm to affected renter households is immeasurable. Cities must do more to prevent these kinds of abuse and severely punish bad-actor landlords.

Following the advice of recommendations 10 ("Don't coddle landlords") and 11 ("Track everything"), cities can reduce illegal and informal demands made by landlords by requiring them to submit all eviction and rent-related notifications to a centralized, public-facing database. This would not represent a significant imposition on landlords. It would only require that when landlords give their tenants notices relating to evictions or changes to their rent, they also submit the notices to a public database for record-keeping purposes. Landlords would also be required to include basic information about the actions, such as the reason for the eviction notice, the amount and percentage increase to rent, the buyout offer amount, and so forth. The action itself would not require government sign-off; the data would be collected purely for the purposes of transparency and accountability.

Under this system, when renters received an eviction or a rent hike notification, they would be able to cross-check it against the public database, confirming that it was formally submitted. If the notification was not uploaded to the database, the landlord would be fined for noncompliance.[27] Landlords guilty of repeated violations would be subject to escalating fines, up to and including seizure of the property for the protection of the tenants.

This approach would serve two purposes. First, it would discourage landlords from making illegal demands of tenants by requiring landlords to submit *all* demands to the centralized database. Bad landlords would be loath to submit proof of their own wrongdoing to the government, even if there were a chance they'd get away with it. The second purpose is self-enforcement on the part of tenants. Landlords attempting to evade the rules by making illegal demands and failing to submit notifications would put themselves at legal risk: if tenants check for the notice and don't find it in the database, they'll know something is fishy and can report it to the city's enforcement division. Though this system would largely be self-enforcing, city staff could also investigate a random selection of filings to ensure that the numbers line up and that tenants received the same notifications uploaded to the database. Enforcement staff already exist in many cities, and their work would be made more efficient with a tracking database of this nature.

Some cities have already begun to improve their tracking and monitoring systems. Los Angeles in 2016 established the Rent Registry Program, an online system that requires all rent-stabilized housing to be registered and have its rent recorded each year.[28] Among other things, this allows the city to automatically track rent increases to ensure they don't exceed the cap set by the Rent Adjustment Commission. Los Angeles should expand this to include other changes that affect renters' lives, especially eviction notices, and other cities should follow LA's lead and establish similar databases.

This can and should be part of a larger tracking effort. Cities need—but currently lack—real-time data on precisely how much their renter households are paying and how much rents are increasing for individual households each year. This database could provide it. With this system, cities also could easily connect eviction filings to specific addresses and households, track and appropriately monitor their worst landlords, and have a direct line to tenants to inform them of their legal rights and protections. Rental housing data management needs to enter the twenty-first century, and it will be up to local governments to lead the way.

40 Offer Free or Reduced-Cost Legal Counsel to Residents Facing Eviction (Right to Counsel)

—

Predatory landlords will have a harder time taking advantage of renters when they're backstopped by a right to legal counsel.

When renters face the threat of eviction, landlords almost always have the upper hand. In New York, upward of 90 percent of landlords show up to eviction court proceedings with a lawyer; only 1–10 percent of tenants do.[29] In Los Angeles, it's estimated that 85 percent of tenants have no legal representation.[30] This has major consequences for renters. In Philadelphia, Pennsylvania, unrepresented tenants end up with a "disruptive displacement" (i.e., eviction) 78 percent of the time, compared with just 5 percent of those with a lawyer.[31] A right to legal representation is guaranteed for defendants in criminal cases but not in eviction proceedings; however, some cities have begun to level the playing field with tenant "right to counsel" programs.

Right to counsel (RTC) programs offer lawyers or other forms of legal assistance to those facing eviction, especially low-income residents who cannot afford to pay for representation. In 2017, New York was the first city in the country to establish an RTC program. It set aside $15 million to help tenants with incomes below 200 percent of the federal poverty level, starting in twenty of the city's more than two hundred zip codes, hoping to expand the program to all city zip codes by 2022. Philadelphia is considering a similar program,[32] and Los Angeles is planning a trial with $3 million in funding, though it's estimated that at least ten times that amount would be needed to serve the whole city.[33]

The early results from New York are promising. In 2013, only 1 percent of tenants facing eviction in the city had an attorney. In the last quarter of fiscal year 2018, 56 percent of tenants in an RTC zip code had representation. From 2017 to 2018, evictions declined by 11 percent in RTC zip codes but by only 2 percent in non-RTC zip codes.[34]

In addition to the direct benefit to renters, there is a strong case that right to counsel can save cities money in the long run by reducing demand for publicly funded affordable housing and homelessness services. Los Angeles is a poignant example. The county spent $619 million to combat homelessness in 2018,[35] helping more than 21,600 people find homes, but the homeless population still increased by 12 percent that year, to nearly 59,000. Despite a concerted effort and hundreds of millions of dollars in new spending approved in the past few years, the county has been unable to keep up with the number of people falling into homelessness. In addition to the 21,600 people who were housed in 2018, the county prevented 5,600 from becoming homeless in the first place. All else being equal, doubling the number of people prevented from becoming homeless would have reduced the year's homelessness increase to just 1 percent; tripling it would have led to a 10 percent overall reduction in homelessness.[36] Cost-benefit analyses of proposed RTC programs in New York and Philadelphia estimated that each dollar spent on RTC would reduce costs elsewhere by between $1.60[37] and $13.00.[38]

As with the notification program discussed in the previous recommendation, RTC is likely to discourage predatory landlord behavior. Today, landlords can count on the vast majority of their tenants being unrepresented if they proceed with an eviction filing, and the mere threat of eviction will often be enough to oust a tenant because most renters know they lack the resources to win in court. When renters know they'll have representation—and, more importantly, when landlords know it—the incentive to make legally weak or baseless threats is greatly diminished. RTC is important for putting tenants on a level playing field when they go to court, but its greatest value may be in preventing them from ending up there in the first place.

41 Enforce Housing and Building Codes

—

Tenant protections have little value if rental housing isn't safe and habitable and if protections aren't enforced.

In a 143-page report published in 2019, the New York State Senate's Committee on Investigations and Government Operations had this to say about housing and building code enforcement.

> The enforcement of housing and building codes is fundamental to the safety and well-being of New York's residents and first responders. However, it is evident that a culture of poor compliance has spread, plaguing communities throughout the State. Lenient code enforcement and compliance endangers the quality of life of a neighborhood and gravely threatens the safety of residents and first responders. Exposed wiring, no means of egress, illegal conversions, absence of working smoke and carbon monoxide detectors, and rodent infestations are just the tip of the iceberg for egregious violations found in homes across New York State. It is the opinion of these Committees that government should be ensuring safe housing for its people.[39]

Every day, renters across the country face unlivable housing conditions, including broken or turned-off utilities, mold and water damage, rodent and other pest infestations, and more. These conditions are almost always illegal and the responsibility of property owners to resolve, yet a lack of enforcement and weak penalties lead many landlords to ignore their responsibilities at the expense of their tenants' health, safety, and quality of life—and sometimes their lives.[40] Tenants themselves have a right to report these violations, but local governments are often slow to act, and renters may face retribution from their landlords for filing a complaint. The threat of retribution is another reason that just-cause protections and right to counsel are so important: code compliance relies, at least partially, on tenants' confidence that reporting a violation won't result in harassment, eviction, or both.

The cost of poor code enforcement was tragically illustrated by the Ghost Ship, an Oakland, California, warehouse-turned-artist-collective that burned down in 2016, taking the lives of thirty-six residents and visitors. The building was leased by its master tenant, Derick Almena, who then illegally sublet portions of it for residential use. To be sure, the deaths were an indictment of the San Francisco Bay Area's housing crunch and the trade-offs residents sometimes make to find an affordable home. But it also represented a massive failure of government oversight and code enforcement. Despite receiving numerous complaints, including two made less than a month before the fire,[41] the Ghost Ship had not been formally inspected for over three decades.[42]

In New York, to make code enforcement more effective—and to prevent future injury and death to tenants whose homes are not adequately maintained by their landlords or are converted for illegal or unsafe uses—the New York State Senate's Committee recommended the following actions:

1. Increasing funding for code compliance inspectors to proactively identify violations and respond more quickly to complaints
2. Increasing penalties for code violation to discourage noncompliance, including escalating penalties for repeat offenders
3. Requiring limited liability companies (LLCs) that own residential property to reveal the identity or identities of their agents or owners, removing the veil of anonymity that allows LLCs to avoid accountability
4. Improving tenant protections, particularly those designed to prevent retaliatory evictions
5. Increasing standards for code enforcement personnel, including establishing a minimum standard for the ratio of code enforcement officials to housing units

All of these are excellent recommendations, especially the establishment of a minimum ratio of enforcement officials relative to rental homes. The committee found that current ratios vary widely, with one city, Mount Vernon, employing just one full-time inspector for a population of over 68,000 residents. Another city, Albany, employed thirteen full-time inspectors for a population of 97,300. Inspectors can do more than enforce codes: they can also serve as a liaison between tenants and their local governments, sharing important information about other tenant protections, such as rent stabilization and just-cause eviction protections.

When establishing a minimum standard, policy makers should be careful to acknowledge that cities with similar populations may have very different code enforcement needs. For example, a city with 20,000 renter-occupied homes and 5,000 owner-occupied homes will require considerably more personnel than a city of similar size where the majority of homes are owner-occupied.

The LLC transparency rule is also smart, and it complements financial crime reforms enacted during the Barack Obama administration that increase disclosure requirements for all-cash purchases in selected cities including New York, Los Angeles, and Miami.[43]

Cities should also explore programs to incentivize the legalization of unpermitted/unapproved dwelling units (UDUs).[44] Los Angeles adopted a UDU ordinance in 2017 to increase the availability of affordable housing and bring existing units into legal compliance— including compliance with codes intended to promote health and safety. The city requires that units brought into the legal housing stock through the UDU program be made affordable to low- and moderate-income households. This increases the supply of affordable homes while discouraging future illegal conversions: property owners can earn more money by going through the formal development process because it allows them to charge market rates for their units.

A well-staffed and proactive code enforcement program should not be expensive. Cities can fund these programs through relatively small fees on all rental property owners—Los Angeles's Systematic Code Enforcement Program (SCEP) costs landlords just $43.32 per year, or $3.61 per month—supplemented by hefty fines for violators, especially repeat offenders. Such programs are essential for ensuring safe and healthy housing for all tenants, and they can strengthen enforcement of other tenant protections, such as rent control. Every city must provide a well-funded, fully staffed, and effective code enforcement program for its rental housing stock.

42 Eliminate Discrimination against People with Housing Choice Vouchers

—

If tenants can pay the rent and follow the rules, they should be eligible to live wherever they choose.

The Housing Choice Voucher Program, also known as Section 8, assists 2.2 million households with their rent each year, filling the gap between market rents and what low-income households can afford to pay. For many, it is the difference between stable housing and homelessness. Unfortunately, the program is falling far short of what it could achieve, partly as a result of weak federal, state, and local laws relating to housing voucher use.

Across the country, landlords are allowed to discriminate against voucher holders and deny them housing, even when they can afford the asking rent. This discrimination has led to an overconcentration of voucher residents living in high-poverty neighborhoods[45] and unacceptably low utilization. In Texas, one in every four recipients are unable to use their vouchers because they can't find landlords who will accept them.[46] The problem is even more severe in housing-constrained cities. In 2019, the *Los Angeles Times* reported that "just under half the people who received a voucher in the city of Los Angeles had it expire in 2017 before they found a place, up from 18% in 2011."[47]

Los Angeles voted in 2019 to ban this form of discrimination, joining eleven states and over fifty cities and counties. As of 2018, it was estimated that only one-third of households with housing vouchers live in jurisdictions with nondiscrimination rules.[48] Cities, counties, and states that represent the remaining two-thirds—and the federal government itself—should quickly adopt similar provisions.

Studies have found that tenants with vouchers in jurisdictions that allow source-of-income discrimination are significantly less likely to have their vouchers accepted by landlords. One study estimated that voucher holders were more than twice as likely to be rejected in places that allowed this form of discrimination (35 percent in nondiscrimination locales versus 77 percent in places that allow discrimination).[49] It should be noted, however, that nondiscrimination rules may not be the only reason for the discrepancy. For example, limits on how much supplemental rent can be provided by vouchers may be too low in high-cost cities and neighborhoods. Even when the caps are not too low, landlords in housing markets with low vacancy rates have plenty of applicants and may choose to rent to those who do not hold vouchers because such renters require less government oversight or because of stigma associated with Section 8 renters—or both.

Nondiscrimination rules have the potential to save local and state governments large sums of money. Public housing agencies in nondiscrimination jurisdictions were found to have voucher utilization rates 5 to 12 percentage points higher than their peers.[50] The federal government picks up the tab, so leaving thousands of vouchers unused is extraordinarily wasteful from the perspective of local governments. In addition to the human cost to those unable to use their vouchers, when residents become homeless it's cities, counties, and states that are financially responsible for increased demands on the criminal justice system, hospital care and mental health services, affordable housing, and other downstream costs attributable to housing insecurity and homelessness. Better to let HUD pick up the tab.

A legitimate concern among landlords is that accepting Housing Choice Vouchers requires an inspection by the local housing authority, and this can be a cumbersome and time-consuming process. Cities should take this complaint seriously and work to reduce inspection turnaround times to no more than a few days. The local government's financial savings from increased utilization are reason enough to streamline the process and hire additional staff to ensure the program's smooth operation. Further, where cities already have strong tenant protections and rental housing habitability standards (including code enforcement), voucher program inspections should pose no unreasonable additional burden.

An ongoing challenge is improving voucher utilization in high-opportunity neighborhoods. In a 2019 analysis, the Center on Budget and Policy Priorities found that 18 percent of voucher-affordable homes were located in high-opportunity neighborhoods—already a low number—but just 5 percent of voucher holders lived in these communities. Meanwhile, 21 percent of voucher-affordable homes were in low-opportunity neighborhoods, but 40 percent of voucher users lived in them.[51]

A separate but related issue is the use of metropolitan area–wide Fair Market Rents (FMRs). FMRs set a maximum rent that HUD will subsidize for renters in a given metropolitan area, and this cap applies across the entire metro. For 2019, the FMR for a two-bedroom home in Denver, Colorado, was $1,508; in Cleveland, Ohio, it was $836; and in San Francisco, it was a jaw-dropping $3,170.[52] But rents at the neighborhood level can vary dramatically within each of these metro areas, with the end result that vouchers tend to further concentrate poverty by pushing voucher holders toward lower-opportunity communities. That's better than being homeless, but we should strive for more.

Small Area Fair Market Rents, which set higher subsidy limits in more expensive zip codes, have been used to increase access to high-opportunity neighborhoods.[53] In addition to lobbying for this program's expansion, advocates may consider using it to encourage smarter local land-use practices. For example, HUD could require cities to pay the cost difference between metro area and Small Area FMRs unless those cities upzone their high-opportunity neighborhoods to create more market-rate and affordable homes.

43 Prioritize Stability over Wealth Creation (Homeownership Assistance)

___

Homeownership assistance would help many more families if it focused on keeping prices stable for the long haul.

When governments design programs to help residents become homeowners, they need to first answer a fundamental question: Is this program's primary goal to increase stability and economic security for low- and moderate-income households, or is it to help them create wealth? Unfortunately, the answer can't be both (recommendation 8, "Pick one: rising home values or housing affordability"). The more a homeownership program focuses on generating household wealth, the fewer people it can assist with stable, affordable housing.

Homeownership assistance programs exist in many high-cost cities, including San Francisco[54] and Los Angeles.[55] Both cities offer zero-interest down payment assistance loans to help low- and moderate-income first-time buyers shoulder the high up-front cost of a home purchase.[56] In Los Angeles, the buyer is required to contribute a down payment of at least 1 percent of the purchase price; San Francisco requires 5 percent. Buyers do not need to make payments on the city loan, and it's repaid only when the home is eventually resold or rented or has its title transferred.

When the loan comes due, the local government collects the full principal in addition to a share of the home's appreciation. This is the point at which homeownership assistance programs favor either stability or wealth creation, and in the case of both Los Angeles and San Francisco, it's the latter. Each city currently captures appreciation based on the down payment loan value as a share of the original purchase price. So, for a $100,000 down payment loan on the purchase of a $500,000 house, the city would collect 20 percent of the appreciation. If the home was resold for $700,000, the original owner would pay back $140,000: $100,000 for the original loan and $40,000 of the appreciation.

Here's another way to look at that purchase and resale. Buyers in Los Angeles would need to come up with $5,000 for their share of the down payment to have it matched by $100,000 from the city. The buyers are putting down just shy of 5 percent of the total down payment of $105,000, but they receive 80 percent of the appreciation. (Remember, the city collects only the share of appreciation equal to its down payment loan divided by the total purchase price.) If the owners resell the home for $700,000 in five years, they'll keep $60,000 in profit (plus the mortgage principal that's been paid off) after paying back the city's loan and its share of appreciation. This is a nearly 30 percent annual return on investment for the homeowners. Should cities really be spending public funds to subsidize those impressive returns, especially when they could assist more households with homeownership if they collected a greater share of the appreciation?

It's fair to ask whether high-cost cities should spend any of their scarce resources on homeownership assistance when there are so many more pressing needs. A program like this will never be funded at a level that helps more than a token number of residents. San Francisco's Downpayment Assistance Loan Program assisted just ten households in 2018, at a cost of $2.8 million. That's in a city with 360,000 households, of which more than one-fifth earn less than $35,000 per year and the median rent for a one-bedroom apartment is $3,800 per month, or $45,600 per year. For those ten families, it's like winning the lottery—literally; the loans are allocated through a lottery system—but tens of thousands of equally worthy and eligible households receive no help whatsoever. That doesn't seem right.

If local governments wish to continue these programs, they should at least reconsider how they're designed. That begins with changes to how appreciation is shared. Loan programs should capture appreciation based on their share of the down payment, not the total purchase price. For a home purchase in which the down payment assistance program loaned $95,000 and the buyer added $5,000, the city would recapture 95 percent of the appreciation. That appreciation could then be turned around to support even more working-class households. This exact division of government versus home buyer appreciation may not be precisely the right model for every jurisdiction in the country, but it's far better than what most cities do today. Participating homeowners would still gain some appreciation, and they would gain all the principal paid off while living in the home. Most importantly, they would have a stable home with consistent monthly payments for as long as they chose to stay.

Some will take issue with this recommendation, arguing that poor and working-class households deserve the same opportunities for wealth creation as the rest of us. They're right. But we have nowhere near the resources needed to fulfill that promise right now, even for a small share of the population, and especially not through state or local action. Given that reality, we should be using what limited resources we have to help a much larger share of residents meet their basic needs. (As discussed in the "Subsidy" section, there are also many opportunities to increase the resources available to both rental and homeownership assistance programs.)

Some may also question why people would even want to own a home if they couldn't also enjoy the lion's share of appreciation. This is almost certainly a needless concern. There are plenty of other benefits to homeownership besides wealth creation (tax breaks, for one), and we had homeownership for centuries without explosive home value appreciation being the norm. Regardless, the best way to find out if there's demand is to redesign the programs and try it out. If no one bites, the money could probably be better spent on rental assistance or affordable housing anyway.

Fundamentally, cities need to ask themselves which is their greater obligation: to impart windfall profits on a small set of lucky home buyers or to provide decent and stable housing to as many residents as possible. Which do we prioritize: capital gains for ten people or stable shelter for one hundred? Clearly it must be the latter, and homeownership programs—to the extent they exist at all—should reflect that. We should also question whether homeownership should be the primary means of middle-class wealth building in the first place, but that's a much bigger question for another day.

Subsidy: Why Government Spending and Public Programs Matter

Market-rate housing can and should be able to serve *most* working- and middle-class households, but many people will never earn enough to afford unsubsidized housing. There is no realistic future in which the price of rental housing in high-demand cities—even low-quality housing—falls to $500 or less per month, and that's near the limit of what many can afford, especially seniors and people with disabilities who subsist on a fixed income. Tenant protections and rental housing preservation can help, but the poorest households mostly won't benefit from them because they can't afford privately owned housing in the first place. Direct assistance, in the form of either supplemental rent payments or subsidized affordable housing construction, is the only answer for these families and individuals.

We can afford to provide this support. In the United States, we lavish tens of billions of dollars on relatively well off homeowners, with only a pittance left over for renters. The federal government's housing programs should be laser-focused on those with the greatest need, and funds should be spent in ways that make the entire housing market more affordable.

In 2015, the federal government spent over $130 billion on home-ownership programs such as the mortgage interest and capital gains deductions, compared with just $55 billion on programs for renters. The mortgage interest deduction (MID) alone accounted for $70 billion, outspending all rental programs combined. Households with incomes over $200,000, mostly homeowners, received an average of $6,000 in federal housing benefits, four times the $1,500 received by households earning $20,000 or less, who mostly rent. Where income data were available, it was found that about 60 percent of federal housing spending went to families earning at least $100,000 per year. In fact, more was spent on homeowners with incomes over $100,000 than on renters at every income level.[1] This is despite the average renter in the United States being much poorer than the average homeowner.

Renters tend to receive more support at the state and local levels, though these jurisdictions also have a raft of wasteful homeowner subsidy programs. Even in liberal California, residents can deduct the mortgage interest from their second homes—homes that go empty most of the year as 130,000 state residents go without housing at all.[2] This program costs the state $300 million in revenue every year. In 2017, California State Assembly member David Chiu proposed a bill to end the second-home tax break; it was defeated by the powerful Realtor lobby a few months later.[3] Meanwhile, in Los Angeles alone, the waiting list for the Housing Choice Voucher Program (also known as Section 8) is approximately 600,000 people. Because of underfunding the list was closed for thirteen years, from 2004 to 2017, and once an applicant is on the list, the wait to receive a voucher can take years.

Arguably the most successful federal affordable housing program of the past few decades is the Low-Income Housing Tax Credit (LIHTC). Established in 1986, it has supported the development of approximately 2 million income-restricted units throughout the United States. About 100,000 new LIHTC units are built per year, but the affordability restrictions on many LIHTC-funded projects are reaching the end of their thirty-year terms and reverting to market rate.[4] About fifteen states also have their own LIHTC programs, which complement the federal tax credit.[5]

Federal spending on LIHTC was less than $10 billion in 2015, about 7 percent of the amount spent on homeowner programs. That amount should increase approximately tenfold. LIHTC funds often require local matching funds, so a federal boost of that size wouldn't necessarily lead to a tenfold increase in affordable housing development, but it would certainly make a big difference. If the program had been funded at that heightened level since its inception, there might be closer to 20 million low-income units rather than 2 million, enough to help every one of the approximately 19 million severely cost burdened renters and homeowners in the country.[6]

Raising funding to these levels isn't as crazy as it might sound. From the late 1970s to the early 1980s, the budget of the US Department of Housing and Urban Development (HUD) shrank from $83 billion to $18 billion in inflation-adjusted dollars, a nearly 80 percent cut.[7] By 2018, its budget had recovered to only $52.7 billion.[8] The peak

of US low-income home building came in the 1970s, with approximately 300,000 new homes each year (when the country had 100
million fewer residents); that had declined to 150,000 per year by the
1990s and about 100,000 per year in the past decade.[9] The number
of public housing units—homes not just subsidized by the federal
government but permanently owned by it—has been declining for
decades, from a peak of 1.4 million in 1991 to around 1.1 million
today. The affordability crisis is now affecting even middle-class
households, but this disinvestment has been hurting low-income
families for decades.

Subsidies aren't important only for new construction. HUD's
largest budget line item is Housing Choice Vouchers, which provide direct financial assistance to renters; this accounts for $21.4
billion (40.5 percent) of HUD's total budget. Vouchers supplement
the income of very low income, elderly, and disabled households to
help them afford rent in the private rental market. When voucher
holders move into an eligible rental, they're required to pay 30 percent of their income on rent and utilities, with the voucher covering
anything beyond that amount. A family earning $1,500 per month
would be required to pay $450 toward rent and utilities. If their rent
is $1,000, the government will cover the remaining $550 each month.
Note that the voucher payment is capped at a local maximum, based
on Fair Market Rent (FMR), so that it can't be used to subsidize
high-end rentals. There has been some moderately successful ex-
perimentation with raising the FMR in more expensive zip codes
to encourage low-income families to move to higher-opportunity
neighborhoods.

Direct rental assistance is important because it's flexible and responsive. It's not tied to a single location, allowing low-income renters to access neighborhoods where subsidized construction hasn't
taken place, and it doesn't require years of waiting for new homes to
be built. It also doesn't face the same NIMBY ("not in my backyard")
blowback that virtually all new development engenders—especially
when that development is for low-income residents.

There are drawbacks, however, to our shifting emphasis on rental
assistance over subsidized construction. When the government was
subsidizing the development of 300,000 low-income homes each

year, it was accomplishing two goals. First, it was directly assisting the families who would call those units home; in contrast, private landlords capture some share of the benefits of rental assistance. Second, it increased the supply of homes in a way that kept rents more affordable throughout the housing market, including privately owned rental housing. When funding for new construction declined and support for voucher-style rental assistance grew, more money flowed into a supply-constrained housing market, and prices likely climbed as a result.

To be clear, this isn't an argument against vouchers, pitting one subsidy against another. It's a question of short-term versus long-term solutions. Efforts to address homelessness face a similar conundrum: with a limited budget, do you invest in short-term measures, such as emergency shelters, or long-term solutions, such as permanent supportive housing? The correct answer is "Both": you must treat the symptoms and tackle the root causes at the same time. Exactly how much you allocate to each priority is a judgment call; there's no objectively correct answer. But the more money you have to work with, the more you can do. And the better your supply and stability policies, the fewer people who will need assistance.

The example of homelessness is also instructive because it demonstrates how spending more up front can reduce costs over the long haul. It's been well documented that providing homeless residents with housing and wraparound social services can be less expensive than treating problems associated with living on the street. The status quo is expensive. People experiencing homelessness accrue significant public costs in the form of policing, jails, courts, emergency rooms, ambulances, sanitation, and other services. When they're placed into supportive housing and stabilized, their use of public services often drops precipitously, reducing public expenses overall.[10] Homelessness is an extreme example, but there are almost certainly similar pro-social benefits to keeping residents stably housed, paying a reasonable share of their income on rent, and avoiding the stress of potential eviction and the impossible choice of whether to pay rent or put food on the table.

Diverting resources from homeownership programs would help affordability even if the funds weren't spent on renters (though they should be). Mortgage interest and property tax deductions, capital gains exclusions, and other homeowner subsidies all artificially inflate the cost of housing. If they were phased out, home prices would adjust downward to offset the increased monthly costs to homeowners. Research suggests that the benefit of tax subsidies is capitalized into the price of housing, most likely offsetting the increase in homeownership induced by lower taxes; this capitalization is strongest in regions where supply doesn't grow in response to demand.[11] We spend over $100 billion every year on homeowners who don't need any public assistance, and the money isn't even making them better off.

The federal government's retrenchment on affordable housing has left state and local governments holding the bag, with predictable consequences. Local governments have much smaller revenues to work with, meaning fewer resources are available for rental assistance and affordable housing development. In addition, local jurisdictions are often the least motivated to act on behalf of their lower-income constituents—particularly when action requires the construction of new apartments that nearby homeowners don't want. The federal government handed responsibility for affordable housing over to cities, and cities have proven themselves both financially and politically unfit for the job.

Subsidies aren't just about tax credits and direct spending; they're also about incentives. Take, for example, the federal Economic Recovery Tax Act of 1981, which cut the depreciation schedule for rental property by more than half, from thirty-two to fifteen years, and made changes to tax shelter provisions and capital gains taxes that were favorable to rentals. This led to a spike in multifamily construction, which vaulted from 390,000 new homes in 1981 to 670,000 in 1985. Many of these changes were reversed in the Deficit Reduction Act of 1984 and the Tax Reform Act of 1986, causing development to plummet to 175,000 multifamily homes per year by the early 1990s.[12]

Prior to 1981, the rental housing vacancy rate had stayed below 6.5 percent since the late 1960s. After the 1981 law change, the vacancy rate began a nearly decade-long climb to almost 8 percent. Among buildings with five units or more, which accounted for most multifamily construction in the 1980s, the vacancy rate was even higher:

10.4 percent in 1986. The apartments built during this era are still some of the most affordable unsubsidized homes on the market.

It's fair to ask whether changes to tax shelters, depreciation schedules, and capital gains are the most efficient and equitable means of improving housing affordability. Directly subsidizing low- and moderate-income housing construction could arguably be more efficient, with more immediate benefits and fewer middlemen. Or perhaps not: maybe leaving it to the market would lead to more immediate and widespread benefits with less bureaucracy and delay. Either way, it's clear that taxes and fiscal policy play a significant role in the housing market, even when those policies aren't centrally concerned with home building.

The "Supply" and "Stability" sections of this book focus primarily on state and local interventions, but this section places a somewhat greater emphasis on federal policy. In large part that's because of the federal government's power of the purse, expansive taxing authority, and unique ability to print money and operate with budget deficits. It can use those powers to fund a wave of construction and acquisition at prices with which the private market—and local governments—simply can't compete.

Interest rates on long-term loans, which the federal government has the power to support, can make a huge difference in the ongoing expense of owning and operating rental housing. Take, for example, a forty-unit apartment building worth $10 million, or $250,000 per unit. If an investor wished to buy the building with nothing but debt (which can't be done, but we'll make the assumption for simplicity's sake), a $10 million, thirty-year loan with a 5 percent interest rate would require a monthly payment of nearly $54,000. At an interest rate of 2 percent, the payment falls to $37,000, and at 0 percent, it's just $28,000, barely half the cost of the 5 percent loan. Assuming additional per-unit operating costs of around $600 per unit, the total monthly cost for the building with a 5 percent loan would be about $78,000, and for the 0 percent loan it would be $52,000. Assuming no profit, break-even rents on the 5 percent loan building would be $1,950 per month. The 0 percent interest buyer could rent at two-thirds the cost, just $1,300.

With low- or zero-interest loans, nonprofits could buy new or existing apartment buildings and freeze rents indefinitely, or even lower them over time. Those same nonprofits could also be exempted from the down payment requirements typically tied to acquisition loans. (Down payments help buyers avoid owing more than their property is worth if the housing market dips, but a low-interest loan would ensure that projected rental revenues far exceed costs at the time of purchase.) Private builders and operators could take part, too, in exchange for setting aside a share of the units for low- or moderate-income households. Reduced rates could also be offered on construction loans, decreasing carrying costs and enabling more affordable units to be provided at virtually no public cost. By lowering financing costs, reduced-interest loans could also spur additional home building as developers were able to market their units to residents further down the income ladder.

Subsidies, tax credits, and other government assistance will never be the entire solution. In our most expensive cities, more than half of households are cost-burdened. At a cost of hundreds of thousands of dollars per unit, the minority who are not cost-burdened will never be capable of fully subsidizing the housing costs of the cost-burdened majority. If housing supply is stagnant, pouring money into rental assistance will only drive up prices across the housing market; if more opportunities for development aren't created, the value of grants and subsidies will find its way into the pockets of property owners, not renters.

Market-rate and mixed-income construction should serve as many people as it possibly can, preserving public funds to help those with the greatest need. Tenant and rental housing protections should keep existing homes affordable for as many people as they possibly can, reducing the number of cost-burdened and homeless residents in need of government support. But for those who the market can't serve and who protections overlook, subsidies will be essential—and they'll need to be much more robust and better designed than they are today.

44 Institute a Progressive Tax on Home Sales (Real Estate Transfer Tax)

—

High-cost housing is a luxury good, and it should be treated as such.

From 2017 to 2018, the total assessed value of Los Angeles County real estate increased by $93 billion, to $1.51 trillion total.[13] Most of the increase, $82 billion, was attributable to home sales and annual 2 percent taxable value increases.[14] Eleven billion dollars was from new construction, and of that $11 billion, perhaps $1 billion was collected as profit by those new projects' investors and developers. In other words, for every $1 billion that developers earned from new construction, $82 billion was earned by existing property owners, most of whom made no substantive improvements to their homes or land. Our tax policies and community benefit programs are laser-focused on extracting maximal value from the small share of value created by new development, yet we ignore the unearned value conveyed to idle property owners, which is orders of magnitude greater.

Cities can and should change this practice by instituting a progressive tax on the sale of high-value homes, similar to the higher marginal income tax rates imposed on high earners. "Real estate transfer taxes," as such taxes are often called, function like a wealth tax, and they're more progressive than income taxes. Even when households earn the same amount of money, their backgrounds may differ such that their actual lifestyles and advantages are not equal. The racial wealth gap is a good example. Black families have dramatically less household wealth than white families, largely because of the lingering effects of redlining, racial plunder, and other discriminatory treatment of the past and present. Additionally, families and individuals who come from impoverished backgrounds are more likely to have greater demands on their income, such as family members who rely on their support, lack of family assistance with funding for higher education and a first home purchase, and the like.

In Los Angeles County there is already a "documentary transfer tax" of $1.10 for every $1,000 of property value, a shockingly low tax rate of just 0.11 percent. The cities of Los Angeles and nearby Culver City impose an additional 0.45 percent tax on property sales.[15] These taxes are important, but they're too low, and they're assessed at a flat rate whether a property is worth $100,000 or $100 million.

San Francisco goes further with a truly progressive tax on the sale of real property. The City and County of San Francisco assesses a 0.5 percent tax on the sale price of properties valued under $250,000, with the rate increasing to 0.75 percent for properties valued between $1 million and $5 million. The rate triples to 2.25 percent for properties worth $5 million to $10 million and peaks at 3.0 percent for properties valued over $25 million.[16] As a result, San Francisco collected $280 million in property transfer taxes in fiscal year 2018,[17] compared with Los Angeles's $209 million,[18] despite LA having a population that is 4.5 times higher.[19]

Progressive taxes on the sale of real estate will decrease property values, but only slightly. A high tax rate (at least compared with current practice) of 5 percent would most likely reduce the sale price of a property by 5 percent or less, which is less value than many homes gain in a single year. The cost to the property owner is not very significant, but, once again using Los Angeles as an example, a 5 percent tax rate could increase the city's transfer tax revenues manyfold, to billions of dollars per year. That would be a game-changing amount of money for the city to spend on affordable housing construction and acquisition, supportive housing and shelter for people experiencing homelessness, and rental assistance for the housing insecure. Los Angeles shouldn't adopt a 5 percent flat rate, nor should any other city. A progressive rate that increases for higher-value properties, like San Francisco's, would be much more appropriate.

San Francisco's plan still has room for improvement. For one, it is not currently a marginal rate, so a property that sells for $5,000,001 would be taxed at three times the rate of a property sold for $4,999,999. This shouldn't be the case; higher rates should be imposed marginally, like the federal income tax, only on the share of property value above a specified threshold. For example, dollar number 4,999,999 would be taxed at 0.75 percent, but dollar number 5,000,0001 would be taxed at 2.25 percent. The rates for each bracket might be raised slightly to offset the lost revenue. In its 2019 legislative session, Washington State adopted a progressive tax on home sales that uses marginal rates and is more aggressive than San Francisco's. It collects 1.1 percent of value below $500,000, 1.28 percent of the portion from $500,000 to $1.5 million, 2.75 percent for the portion between $1.5 million and $3 million, and 3.0 percent for the portion of sales over $3 million.[20]

Additionally, advocates should consider implementing tax rates for residential property based on the value *per unit* rather than the value of an entire building. Basing the tax on the value of the entire building imposes a larger tax on multifamily properties, even though individual units are typically more affordable than single-family and other low-density properties. Again, rates at each tax margin can be increased to offset the revenue loss from this change.

Finally, a note of caution: taxes on home sales may have the effect of reducing household mobility (the literal act of a household moving from one home to another). Property taxes achieve the same goals as a tax on home sales without dampening home buying and selling, and thus they are preferable wherever possible. Unfortunately, property taxes are more politically challenging to impose and increase, so a progressive tax on home sales may be the best politically viable option for many jurisdictions, at least in the short term.

45 Tax "Flipped" Houses at Higher Rates

—

House flipping decreases affordability and adds nothing to the housing stock.

House "flipping" is the practice of buying a home, quickly renovating it (typically in less than a year), and reselling it for a large profit. House flippers earned an average 49 percent return on investment in 2018,[21] far in excess of the profits earned in other industries, including real estate development from the ground up. They take a relatively affordable home, fix it up in both substantive and superficial ways, and turn it into a luxury product. This is a growing problem in cities that are struggling with affordability and a shortage of housing, and policy makers should take action to limit its impact.

One could argue that house flippers are providing a useful service and shouldn't be overregulated; after all, if their product weren't in demand, people wouldn't pay such high prices for it. There's some truth to this, but the drawbacks often outweigh the benefits. For one, when home flipping is easy and profitable, it diverts money that could otherwise be invested in new housing. On sites where zoning allows for more than one unit per parcel, flipping a single-family home makes the economics of future redevelopment (and higher density) less favorable. The discussion of "development value" versus "existing use value" in the appendix helps explain why this is the case.

New construction is expensive and has always been targeted at residents with relatively high incomes, though not to the degree experienced today in our most expensive and housing-scarce cities. An important upside to new construction is that it draws wealthier people away from existing housing, preventing them from bidding up prices and displacing existing residents. New construction is also often accompanied by community benefits, including low-income units, parks and open space, school funding, and more. Flipped homes provide none of these benefits, and because they compete with newly constructed housing, they also depress the market for new development.

Local taxes on the profits of flipped properties should be high, possibly upward of 50 percent. The exact percentage would depend on whether the goal is to generate revenue (in which case a moderate tax rate would be appropriate) or to discourage the activity altogether (where a high tax rate would be better). The policy could be designed in many ways—for example, with a tax rate that starts at 50 percent on the day a home is purchased and declines to 0 percent over a period of five years. It should include profits only *after* accounting for reasonable closing costs, labor, materials, and other verifiable renovation-related costs.

It's a pain to do a renovation yourself, and plenty of people genuinely find value in having the work done for them before they purchase their home. This is a difficult reality to square with the negative impacts to the overall housing market, and it means that there's no simple or obviously correct answer to the question of flipped homes. To start, cities might consider a house-flipping tax that's limited only to (1) parcels with single-family homes zoned for higher density and (2) single-family homes within a quarter mile of high-quality transit, such as a rail station or intersecting high-frequency bus lines. This, at the very least, would prevent renovations in areas that would be better served by redevelopment to a higher and better use. If they're flipped, then the economics of redevelopment look very bleak—even when higher density is permitted—and the properties are likely to stay low density for decades. This is a poor outcome where more housing is possible, especially in highly transit-accessible locations.

46 Utilize Property Taxes

—

Property taxes raise revenue and incentivize behavior that's beneficial to society, unlike many other major funding sources.

Property taxes are superior to other government revenue sources in many ways, including their ability to disincentivize passive real estate investment and land hoarding.

Unlike sales taxes, property taxes are naturally progressive and based on the value of someone's home, commercial property, or land. Unlike income and business taxes, both of which *can* be progressive, property taxes also discourage harmful behavior: hoarding of property and speculation. Excessive business taxes may genuinely force local businesses to close their doors, not to be replaced; the same can't be said for landlords, who can always sell to someone else willing to operate under a new regulatory regime. Income and business taxes, while still useful, represent a mild deterrent to positive behaviors such as work and entrepreneurship.

Property taxes deter behavior that leaves valuable land underutilized. They make it very expensive to hold property for speculative purposes because the year-to-year carrying costs are too great. Acquiring property—and this is distinguished from *developing* or *improving* property—doesn't create anything new, and if one person doesn't purchase a given property, someone else almost always will, for the right price. Higher property taxes ensure that underutilized property goes to buyers who actually want to do something useful with it.

Property taxes are also much more stable than other revenue sources because land and property values tend not to fluctuate dramatically (and because rates can be automatically adjusted to reach revenue targets).[22] This creates predictability and stability for state and local governments, something that is notably absent in states such as California and New York, which depend heavily on income tax.

Property taxes are capitalized into property values such that higher taxes are offset by reduced home values, resulting in more affordable housing.[23] Since home prices are ultimately based on what residents are willing and able to pay, a higher property tax payment necessitates a reduction in mortgage principal and interest—in other words, lower home prices. The monthly payment on a $400,000 home in Colorado (effective property tax rate 0.55 percent), including mortgage and property taxes, is approximately $2,330 per month. In Texas, where the effective tax rate is 1.83 percent, a $2,330 monthly payment would buy a $338,000 home. (This ignores the impact of the mortgage interest deduction and other tax policies, which offset some of this difference.)

Given two households with equivalent incomes, one in Colorado and one in Texas, the Texas buyer would need to save only $67,600 for a 20 percent down payment, while the Colorado buyer would need to save $80,000. If prices rise at the same rate in each state (e.g., 3 percent per year), homes in Colorado will fall out of reach to first-time buyers at a faster rate. It may seem desirable that you could purchase a more valuable home in Colorado than in Texas and pay the same monthly cost, but not if you can't save enough to get your foot in the door. And not if Colorado requires higher sales and income taxes to make up for less property tax revenue.

Even more than taxes on the sale of homes, property taxes function as a wealth tax. This is arguably what's needed in America today. Two households can have the same income but very different opportunities and burdens based on their family's wealth.[24] Those with affluent families may carry no student loan debt because their parents paid their tuition; they may have had help with rent while they saved up for a down payment; they may even have had a home gifted to them directly by their parents or grandparents; they almost certainly didn't need to help out a jobless or disabled parent with rent or electricity. Those from less privileged backgrounds who lack these advantages may carry significantly more student loan debt, have less savings because they support a family member, and be responsible for all their own housing, transportation, and other costs. Rather than treating these two individuals as equivalent with our income tax system, a greater reliance on property taxes helps level the playing field, offsetting the accumulated disadvantages that have accrued to the low-wealth individual—often through explicitly racist policies such as redlining and contract buying, or merely the bad luck of having bought a home in Cleveland, Ohio, rather than Palo Alto, California, in the 1970s.

There are still valid reasons to tax income, sales, business, and other activities, but property taxes generally do a better job of encouraging the kinds of behaviors most of us agree are desirable: more productive work and business investment, less hoarding of land and wealth. This also isn't necessarily an argument for raising people's overall tax burden. A revenue-neutral property tax increase and income tax reduction would significantly improve housing affordability and reduce wealth and income inequality—especially if the income tax reduction is targeted at the lower end of the income spectrum. This is a challenging policy to implement because it strikes directly at many families' most valuable asset—their home—but moving toward a funding structure more reliant on property taxes should be a long-term goal for cities and states across the country.

47 Tax Underutilized and Vacant Property

—

Discourage speculation, owner neglect, and blight with higher taxes on vacant and otherwise underutilized properties.

Developers and property owners—homeowners included—consider their tax burden when they make choices about how to use their land. In California, many vacant parcels, surface parking lots, and otherwise underutilized sites have remained stagnant for decades because Proposition 13 keeps taxes low even when the market value of a property rises dramatically. (Those who've met me know I wouldn't write a book without mentioning Prop. 13 and its multitudes of awfulness.) To discourage property owners from squatting on underutilized properties and to encourage redevelopment to a higher and better use, cities should ensure that taxes keep pace with actual property values. This is especially important because vacant and low-value parcels often represent the best opportunities for development without displacement.

Land value taxes (LVTs) are a more aggressive take on this principle, encouraging higher-density redevelopment by charging property taxes based purely on the value of land, not structures. Since property owners pay the same amount regardless of what's built on the site, they're incentivized to "go big": the larger their project, the smaller the impact of property taxes on their bottom line. LVTs are a parking lot killer.

A pure LVT would tax land exclusively, with no taxation of improvements (the structures on the land). In lieu of a pure LVT, which would be a major shift in most jurisdictions, a hybrid approach can be taken that taxes land value at a higher rate than improvements. The shift could be made gradually to reduce its impact—for example, by starting at a fifty-fifty ratio of land to improvement taxes in year one, sixty-forty in year two, seventy-thirty in year three, and continuing until the favored end point is reached. This hybrid approach may actually be more desirable than a pure LVT: even though an LVT does more to incentivize development, property taxes help pay for essential public services, and larger buildings often place greater demand on those services than lower-density uses. Whatever tax structure is selected, it can be done with or without increasing overall property tax burden.

Cities have also begun to target vacant homes, recognizing that prices are affected when housing stays off the market longer than necessary. Vacant homes have become a talking point among supply skeptics who argue that new development isn't actually providing homes for anyone and that these supposedly empty buildings are evidence we don't need more housing. Rationally, this makes no sense—especially for rental housing. Apartments make money only if they're leased, and there's no magical accounting trick that turns zero revenue into massive profits.

There is also empirical evidence that vacant apartments are not a serious problem. Downtown Los Angeles made the news in 2018 for its residential vacancy rate, which, as the real estate information company CoStar reported, hit more than 12 percent at the end of the previous year. This was three times the citywide rate and fodder for anti-housing advocates. It turned out to be nothing. Downtown Los Angeles has a small residential base and a booming development scene, and a few large buildings (each with hundreds of units) had opened very shortly before the report. Those buildings were empty when they first opened, of course, and this caused the vacancy rate to spike for a short time. The vacancy rate was just 4.7 percent for Downtown buildings open for at least one year, on par with the citywide rate for all housing regardless of its age. In fact, Downtown apartments were leasing up faster than expected, even with multiple buildings opening at the same time.[25] To read more about housing vacancies, with a Los Angeles focus but lessons for every city, you can find a working paper I wrote for the UCLA Lewis Center for Regional Policy Studies titled "Does the Los Angeles Region Have Too Many Vacant Homes?"[26]

Vacancy taxes may have more impact on condominiums and single-family homes because these, unlike apartments, can be profitable speculative investments even if they're unoccupied (though this depends on weak production to keep housing scarce). In 2018, the City of Vancouver, British Columbia, enacted a vacant homes tax that would charge owners 1 percent of their property's value if it was unoccupied for most of the year. With an average home sale price over $1 million, the fee would amount to over $10,000 annually for many property owners. The city saw vacancies decline by 15 percent over the following year. That said, the reduction was small in absolute terms, with reported vacancies falling from 1,085 in 2017 to 922 in 2018.[27] The overall impact of 163 additional homes on the market in a city of over 300,000 units was undoubtedly very small.

Vancouver's 1 percent tax is probably an appropriate amount. Some property owners may choose to keep their properties vacant even in the face of a $10,000 annual fee, and that's okay. $10,000 is enough to assist at least one household with rent for an entire year, so the fee is doing its job of offsetting the loss of a vacant unit.

While their ability to put more homes on the market may be limited, vacancy taxes are important, if nothing else, as an acknowledgment that housing supply matters. The growing interest in them represents a positive shift in perception. And if we adhere to the principle that housing data should be much more robust and better tracked by public agencies, a vacant home tax should be relatively simple to implement and manage.

48 Don't Sell Public Land; Lease It (Public Land and P3s)

Don't give away long-term value to make a quick buck.

Developers and investors are strongly incentivized to focus on the short term: through the magic of discount rates[28] and other investor-speak, a dollar of profits collected today is of greater value than that same dollar received a year or a decade in the future. Revenue earned twenty or thirty years in the future has almost no value to them. Governments are not limited in this way; they have an obligation to plan for the well-being of their residents many decades hence—centuries, even—and they shouldn't trade away long-term value for a short-term windfall. The differences between public and private planning horizons mean that governments should avoid selling their land, instead offering ground leases to interested developers whenever possible.

Marina del Rey, California, located just south of Venice in un-incorporated Los Angeles County, is one highly successful example of ground leasing of public land. The county built the marina in 1965 at a cost of $36.25 million, creating 550 acres of new land and storage space for thousands of boats. The county government retained ownership of the land and offered sixty-year ground leases to developers interested in building housing, hotels, shopping malls, and other projects on the site. It is now home to approximately ten thousand residents living in over six thousand homes and generates $27 million in annual revenue for Los Angeles County.[29]

Ground leases can lock in solid, consistent revenues for a local government without sacrificing the upside that accrues as land becomes more valuable over time. They can be used purely to maximize profits for the government (which can then be reinvested in important public services) or, as is often the case, lease agreements can include special requirements that reduce ongoing revenues but secure public benefits. For example, a city or county might accept a lower annual lease payment if a developer sets aside some apartments for low-income households, or the government may even donate the land to a community land trust[30]—though this is probably appropriate only for lower-density neighborhoods, given the cost and complexity of multifamily development. Maximizing long-term revenues may be more in keeping with the concept of long-term ground leases (because up-front requirements will devalue the land according to the developer's discount rate, not the government's), but it may not be politically realistic to forgo community benefit requirements in such deals. Local officials and advocates will need to find the right balance with the understanding that up-front requirements will have an outsize impact on long-term revenues.

Ground leases are a form of public-private partnership (P3), and P3s have a mixed reputation in the United States. Perhaps the most famous example of a P3 gone awry is the sale of parking meter operations in Chicago, Illinois, to private investors for a seventy-five-year lease period. Under former mayor Richard Daley, the right to operate the meters—and, more importantly, collect their revenue—was sold in 2008 at a price of just $1.15 billion. The buyers are expected to recoup their investment by 2020,[31] at which point they'll still have sixty-three years of profits to look forward to. Making a bad situation worse, the contract also locks Chicago into compensating the investors any time a meter is out of service, creating an ongoing drain on the city's finances and limiting its ability to implement streetscape improvements that require the removal of on-street parking. It has rightly been derided as "a lesson in worst practices" for public-private partnerships and for governance in general.[32]

Governments looking to pursue a ground lease deal with the private sector should be prepared to hire expert outside counsel to ensure they get a fair deal. The harm done by the Chicago contract could have been minimized by a much shorter contract duration (without severely lowering the value—again, investors don't care much about revenues so far in the future), but ground leases necessarily require leases of at least forty to fifty years because they include the development and maintenance of such a large capital investment: a building or buildings. With case studies such as Marina del Rey, effective counsel, and careful contractual language (that ensures the public sector can share in successes and unexpected windfalls), ground leases can be a smart way to deliver ongoing revenues and community benefits.

49 Minimize Impact Fees and Charge Them Equitably

There's a role for fees on new development, but they can't become the piggy bank for every city priority.

Many cities assess impact fees on new development to fund things such as parks, education, and transportation improvements. The rationale for the fees is that new homes—and the residents who occupy them—put additional strain on public facilities and that the developers (or the new residents themselves) should bear a greater share of that cost. This neglects a few important facts: new residents pay taxes just like everyone else; the residents of these new homes usually have already lived in the area before moving into the new home; and older homes weren't typically subject to similar fees when they were built. Impact fees serve a purpose, but they've grown out of control in many jurisdictions.

Impact fees are typically collected when a project begins construction or opens its doors, and they can run into tens of thousands of dollars per dwelling unit, or upward of $100,000 per home in some places. In Fremont, California, housing fees add up to $75,000 per unit for multifamily homes and $147,000 for single-family homes.[33] These costs add approximately $400 to $800 per month to the cost of housing before construction even begins.

These fees can have one of two impacts on housing prices and supply. One possibility is that they're absorbed into the residual land value, reducing what developers are willing to pay for land. This doesn't directly affect the cost of new homes, but it *does* reduce the incentive for property owners to sell—fees reduce the "development value" of land without affecting the "existing use value" (see the appendix for a discussion of these terms). As a result, fewer sites will be viable for redevelopment; competition among developers (and therefore the cost of the remaining developable land) will increase; and new homes must target higher rents or sale prices to offset the additional expense. In other words, new housing gets more expensive. The other scenario is more direct: fees are directly passed on to the tenant or owner. Either way, new housing costs more money. A mix of both effects is probably at play in most cases.

Using impact fees to fund public facilities and services is far from ideal. After all, if something is truly a public priority, shouldn't everyone share the burden? And, ideally, shouldn't that burden be determined according to people's ability to pay rather than when they arrived or the age of their home? And given the incontestable need for more housing and the fundamental role homes play in everyone's lives, is it even fair to treat housing as an "impact" in need of mitigation?

Impact fees probably aren't going to disappear entirely, but cities should strive to make them as low and equitable as possible. For example, impact fees should generally be assessed on the square footage of a building rather than the number of units, as is often the case. The latter perversely favors larger homes. A $10,000 park fee assessed on a per-unit basis, for example, would treat a 350-square-foot micro-unit the same as a 3,000-square-foot penthouse condominium; this is clearly unfair and creates incentives to oversupply larger, higher-end homes. Fees should also be assessed at issuance of the certificate of occupancy, when a building opens its doors, rather than at issuance of the building permit, as this will reduce project carrying costs.

Impact fees *may* be used to disincentivize lower-density detached housing that places a greater strain on government budgets and the environment, but policy makers should ensure that zoning actually permits homes in denser, more sustainable communities. There's little sense in discouraging one type of development if all others are effectively off-limits. If there's nowhere to build higher-density homes, larger impact fees will serve only to increase the cost of new housing or prevent it from being built altogether.

A Note on Linkage Fees

Linkage fees, sometimes referred to as development impact fees or affordable housing impact fees, have become a go-to funding source for affordable housing in cities across the United States. The fees are assessed on new development, including commercial and residential, and can cost a few dollars, or dozens, per square foot. A 100-unit, 100,000-square-foot apartment building might pay a linkage fee of $1 million to $2 million, for example. The idea behind the fee is that market-rate housing (as well as commercial development and other job-producing uses) attracts high-income residents, and those residents' day-to-day spending creates demand for low-wage jobs in the service and retail sectors. Those low-wage workers need places to live, and thus the linkage fee is charged to help offset the "impact" of new market-rate housing by funding affordable housing development. The market-rate housing is "linked" to greater affordable housing demand. If it sounds convoluted, that's because it is.

The logic behind this argument quickly falls apart under scrutiny. First, the analyses used to establish the need for linkage fees tend to assume that 100 percent of market-rate housing residents come from another city, state, or country. This is patently untrue. My analysis of the Los Angeles metropolitan area found that 68 percent of residents living in housing less than five years old moved from within fifty miles of their new home. For housing five to fifteen years old, 88 percent were locals.* Nationally, at least 70.9 percent of residents living in housing built in the past two years moved from somewhere less than fifty miles away.† Linkage fees are being assessed to offset the "impacts" of people who already lived in the area. They penalize the very housing supply that keeps high-income residents from moving into older, more affordable homes.

What about the residents who *did* move from more than fifty miles away? Are new market-rate homes *causing* those households to move into the city, creating new demand for low-wage jobs? This also seems unlikely. Let me pose a question to readers who have moved to a different city at some point in their lives: At what stage did finding a home to rent or buy enter into your decision to move? For most people, choosing exactly what home to rent or buy is one the last decisions in the difficult process of pulling up stakes and settling in a new city. We move away to take a great new job, or to go off to college, or to chase our dreams for reasons that have very little to do with housing availability. We take the leap, and we figure out the rest as we go.

To the extent that housing choices do factor into a moving decision, it's to figure out if we can afford to live in a new city. Most of the time, we first decide that we want to move and we then decide whether we actually can. The supply of new market-rate housing (or lack thereof) isn't going to be the thing that deters us. If we're price sensitive, we're not looking at new housing anyway. What *could* deter us is a housing shortage and out-of-reach prices even for low-quality, poorly located homes. High-income residents can come to the city whether new homes exist or not, so adding cost to development with no offsets (such as higher density or reduced parking) will only make matters worse. Linkage fees are likely to do more harm than good, and cities should find more responsible and broad-based funding approaches to support low-income residents—and those approaches, importantly, should avoid demonizing market-rate development and new residents.

*"Who Moves into New Housing, and Why?," *Abundant Housing Los Angeles* (blog), July 17, 2017, https://abundanthousingla.org/who-moves-into -new-housing-and-why/.

†US Census Bureau, "American Housing Survey (AHS)," https://www .census.gov/programs-surveys/ahs/data/interactive/ahstablecreator.html#?s _areas=a00000&s_year=n2017&s_tableName=Table6&s_byGroup1=a4&s _byGroup2=a1&s_filterGroup1=t1&s_filterGroup2=g1&s_show=S. Note that only 13.0 percent of respondents reported moving from more than fifty miles away. The remaining 16.1 percent did not report where they moved from.

50   Don't Let Small Buildings off the Hook (Missing Middle)

—

*Single-unit and small multifamily buildings often have
fewer community benefit requirements than larger buildings.
They shouldn't.*

When impact fees are assessed or community benefits are required
of new development, small buildings—especially single-unit detached homes—are frequently given a pass. They're often exempt
from stability-enhancing regulations such as rent control because of
our deference to mom-and-pop landlords, and they're rarely subject
to affordable housing or community benefit requirements because
their low densities make value capture difficult to implement. We
shouldn't let them off the hook.

When large multifamily projects are built in high-cost cities,
they're typically subject to a raft of fees and requirements: on-site
low-income units or affordable housing fees, park fees, school fees,
open space, common areas, tree requirements, and so forth. These
requirements are easier for larger projects to manage for a variety
of reasons, but, somewhat perversely, the end result is that some of
the most affordable housing on the market pays the most in fees
and provides the most community benefits. Condos that sell for
$600,000 end up providing significantly more public benefits than
$800,000 townhomes and $1.5 million single-family homes in the
same neighborhood.

There is no easy resolution to this problem, and it's important to
distinguish small multifamily buildings (between two and roughly
ten or twenty units) from single-family units. The former, often
known as "missing middle" for their size and their unfortunate rarity
in modern development, can be naturally affordable to middle-class
households, subsidy free. Adding excessive fees and requirements
may help some low-income households, but it can also bring about a
barbell distribution of new housing, with income-restricted housing

for poor households, market-rate housing for rich households, and nothing in between. And because land that allows duplexes or triplexes may be only marginally more valuable than land that bans multifamily units altogether, there's limited opportunity for value capture—set the fees too high and single-family buildings may never be redeveloped into denser, more affordable housing. Care must be taken when adding fees and requirements to missing middle development.

Single-family homes are another story. As discussed in the "Supply" section, single-family zoning is a driving force behind the housing crisis, and allowing—much less *requiring*—low-density housing in urban centers is extremely problematic. More than any other housing type, single-unit detached homes should be subject to the largest fees and community benefit requirements of any housing typology. They are the most expensive, car-oriented, energy-intensive, and environmentally destructive kind of housing that we build, and while that doesn't mean we need to ban them, we should certainly be charging them full freight for their negative impacts.

Many cities currently limit inclusionary zoning (mandatory affordable housing set-asides) and other public benefit requirements to buildings ten units or larger. A starting point would be to establish requirements for single-family homes that are greater than any other housing type, with significantly lesser requirements for missing middle housing. Single-family development can't accommodate on-site affordable units (it would be either 0 percent affordable or 100 percent affordable, making a 15 percent inclusionary requirement meaningless), so in-lieu fees would be more appropriate. These fees could help pay for affordable housing, parks, mobility improvements, and other investments that benefit the entire community. If the fees led to less low-density development and teardown-rebuilds, that would be viewed as a feature, not a bug. One important note: single-unit detached housing is sometimes built as relatively dense "small lot development." Because of its higher density, fees should be lower than for single-unit developments on larger parcels.

Even for teardowns, or perhaps *especially* for teardowns, fees in excess of $100,000 could be appropriate for single-unit development in some markets. When a home that is falling apart on a

5,000-square-foot lot sells for $1 million or more, and it was purchased decades ago for $200,000 or less, a $100,000 fee tacked on to support affordable housing would be easily absorbed by the seller.

Fees on small multifamily developments may also be considered but should be more carefully applied. For example, small multifamily projects might be exempted in high-cost, high-opportunity neighborhoods in order to direct more housing into these locations rather than lower-cost, lower-opportunity communities. Whether this is a reasonable approach, or just a giveaway to property owners in affluent neighborhoods, will depend on context. If the sites are already zoned for small multifamily development, removing or reducing fees may spur more activity in the area; if the sites are upzoned or benefiting from a density bonus incentive program, fees or other community benefit requirements are more likely to be appropriate.

51 Reform or Eliminate Most Homeowner Subsidies

Homeowner subsidies increase prices and mostly benefit high-income households who don't require public support.

The preceding recommendations in this section have focused on policies that can be enacted at the state and local levels, but federal reforms are also essential. As discussed in the introduction to this section, the United States provides far more financial assistance to homeowners than to renters. This is despite the median renter household's income being only half that of the median homeowner household: $37,300 and $73,100, respectively.[34] The three biggest culprits are as follows:

1. Mortgage interest deduction, which costs the government approximately $70 billion per year in forgone revenues
2. Property tax exclusion, which costs over $30 billion per year
3. Capital gains exclusion, which exempts homeowners from paying taxes on the first $250,000 of profits on the sale of their home (or $500,000 if married and filing jointly), which costs the US government another $25 billion per year

Together, these three programs account for over $125 billion in annual homeowner subsidies. More than $80 billion, or about two-thirds, goes to households earning over $100,000 per year. More than half of that $80 billion goes to households earning over $200,000.

This is a clear case of misplaced priorities, especially when three-quarters of renter households eligible for government housing assistance don't receive any: all households eligible for homeowner assistance automatically receive it through the tax code while most renters get nothing. This is worse than it appears, because homeowner subsidy programs don't even succeed at the goal they're nominally designed to achieve: supporting homeownership.

This is partly explained by who benefits from homeowner subsidies. In most of the country, households earning $100,000 or more—that is, those currently benefiting from the subsidies—don't require any extra incentive to purchase a home. The benefits are clear enough without the government throwing bags of money at them, so the subsidies are just a giveaway to people who would've made the same decision regardless.

The other part of the story is how homeowner subsidies drive up the price of housing, with deductions capitalized into home values. The subsidies don't reduce the cost of homeownership—rather, they enrich existing property owners, increasing the amount that buyers can spend on housing by returning a large share of the money as tax deductions. And it gets worse. Because of the way tax deductions work, higher-earning households actually receive larger subsidies than lower-earning households, even if they're purchasing the same home for the same price. For example, consider two households deciding whether to purchase a $300,000 home. One earns $50,000 per year; the other earns $200,000. Both have $60,000 on hand for a 20 percent down payment, and their mortgage and property taxes will cost about $1,540 per month, or about $18,500 per year. In a fairer world, this would be the end of the story, or perhaps the person earning $50,000 would receive a small amount of support to level the playing field. In reality, it's the exact opposite.

The high-income household most likely itemizes their deductions, so they will write off their mortgage interest and property tax payments. These add up to approximately $15,000 in the first year of homeownership. This household is in the 32 percent income tax bracket, so writing off $15,000 saves them $4,800 on their annual tax bill (32 percent × $15,000). They end up paying $13,700 per year for their home after deductions, or about $1,140 per month.

The household earning $50,000, meanwhile, is taking a standard deduction and therefore receives no direct subsidy for their housing costs. They pay approximately 26 percent more for the same home, despite earning only one-quarter as much as the higher-income household. This is the system we've designed.

Fixing this structure may be politically challenging, but it's technically simple. There are many ways to improve the mortgage interest deduction, including the following:

1. Make it a flat percentage (e.g., 20 percent) regardless of income so that households paying higher marginal income tax rates don't receive a greater benefit than others (ignoring that higher-income households are more likely to itemize their deductions).
2. Cap the amount a household can deduct each year (e.g., $5,000 to $10,000 per year).
3. Phase out the deduction as household income increases (e.g., the deduction is halved for income over $100,000 and falls to zero at $150,000 to $200,000 per year).
4. Reduce the mortgage value from which interest can be deducted (it was lowered from $1 million to $750,000 in 2017).
5. Use a combination of the four previous options.
6. Eliminate the deduction entirely.

The savings from any of these changes wouldn't have to come at the expense of middle-class homeowners who benefit from the mortgage interest deduction today. The funds could easily be redirected back to these households in a more direct fashion, with the two-thirds currently accruing to high-income households instead spent on lower- and moderate-income renters and homeowners.

Thankfully, the property tax deduction was neutered by the Tax Cuts and Jobs Act of 2017 alongside a lowering of the value of mortgages eligible for the mortgage interest deduction.[35] We can and should go much further in the coming years, adopting a mix of the foregoing options or eliminating the mortgage interest deduction altogether.

The capital gains exclusion on profits from home sales serves no public purpose whatsoever, and it should be eliminated. Sellers would typically be subject only to the capital gains tax rate of 15 percent, an entirely reasonable tax to pay on profits of tens or hundreds of thousands of dollars. This would also make home investment moderately less tax advantaged compared with other investments, reducing overconsumption and price inflation for existing housing. Importantly, sellers should be able to deduct the cost of home improvements from their profits.

Taken together, these reforms would save the US government tens of billions of dollars on subsidies that only make housing more expensive. These funds would be much better spent on affordable or public housing construction and rehabilitation, homelessness prevention and services, and direct rental assistance for low-income households. They could even promote homeownership for more low- and moderate-income households—people who actually need public support. The 2017 tax bill passed by the Donald Trump administration showed that you can reduce homeowners' subsidies without much backlash, even in the context of a trillion-dollar giveaway to wealthy families and international businesses. Imagine how it could be received if those funds were instead used to help everyday Americans.

52 Reform and Increase Funding for Affordable Housing Construction

—

The funding process for affordable housing is expensive, slow, and underfunded. It needs to once again become an American priority.

The US approach to affordable housing in the mid-twentieth century was focused on subsidized home building: we built approximately 300,000 low-income homes per year in the 1970s, and this has fallen steadily—yet dramatically—to around 100,000 per year over the past decade.[36] This is partly a result of the austerity-minded "Reagan Revolution" and a general retrenchment of support for low-income households, but it also occurred in the context of a shift toward direct rental assistance such as Section 8 Housing Choice Vouchers. Supplemental rent payments have also been touted as a more "efficient" and better-targeted form of housing assistance, which may explain some of their relative popularity.[37] While rental assistance is essential and should continue (and even grow), the reduction in subsidized home building was a massive mistake that should be reversed as quickly as possible.

There were countless problems with the design and implementation of public housing in the 1950s, 1960s, and 1970s, but the overall goal of providing affordable homes for low-income households of different backgrounds was 100 percent correct. A growing population requires a growing supply of homes, and subsidized housing construction was an effective way to provide it. It may have been hoped that direct rental assistance would spur more housing development, but that isn't what happened. This should have been (and perhaps was) foreseen. Rental assistance would not have been enough to help low-income households pay the full cost of new market-rate housing, so the supplemental payments would instead flow into the low-end housing market, driving up prices. Rental assistance absolutely helped the low-income renters who received it, but it was also

a boon to landlords and likely drove up costs for nonsubsidized renters in places where housing was undersupplied.

When we built large numbers of subsidized low-income homes,
we directly served many residents who would not have been able
to comfortably afford market-rate privately owned rental housing,
even if it was decades old. This was a benefit in itself, but it also had
two knock-on effects. First, it reduced competition between low-
and moderate-income households, helping to stabilize prices at the
lower end of the housing market; a relative abundance of housing
was available for people in these income brackets. This is in contrast
to today's housing market, in which market-rate construction is providing the greatest affordability benefit to households competing for
higher-end housing.[38]

Second, stabilized prices at the lower end of the market eased
upward pressure on prices at the higher end. In other words, the cost
of building market-rate housing was also stabilized, allowing developers to serve a wider market. (Remember: the cost of newly built
housing is closely related to the cost of existing housing in a given
market.) By having the public sector subsidize housing construction
for the lower end of the income distribution, market-rate developers
were able to provide housing for more people at the middle and the
upper end—a win-win.

This is the system we need to return to. It should start with a dramatic increase in funding for affordable housing of all types: low income and extremely low income, moderate income, mixed income,
public, nonprofit—all of it. The largest funding sources for affordable housing at the federal level are the Low-Income Housing Tax
Credit (LIHTC) and Section 8 project-based rental assistance. Each
program receives approximately $10 billion per year in funding,
with supplemental LIHTC programs in many states. An increase
in LIHTC spending to $50 billion per year would bring us back to
our peak subsidized home-building days, with construction of at
least 300,000 affordable homes per year. A goal of 400,000 to 500,000
would be more appropriate, given the country's population growth
over the past forty years, our decades-long housing backlog, and the
severity of the affordability crisis. A $50 billion program would also
cost only marginally more than the homeowner subsidies currently

accruing exclusively to households earning $200,000 or more. We have the money; all we lack is the political will to spend it more justly.

In the longer term, we should also consider replacing the LIHTC system altogether. The program is viewed as more politically stable than other affordable housing efforts because it's funded through the tax code rather than the federal budget, but this approach comes with its own costs. For one, changes to the tax code can cause inadvertent harm to LIHTC: cuts to the corporate tax rate in 2017 are expected to reduce the program's output by about 200,000 units, or roughly 20 percent, over the next decade.[39] Also, because the program relies on participation from private investors, it has multiple layers of middlemen, each with their own complex reporting requirements, deadlines, and cut of the profits. Syndicators, who work to find investors on behalf of affordable housing developers, collected $300 million in 2016.[40]

Replacing LIHTC would be a big lift and is unlikely to happen in the near term. A smart compromise would be to increase funding for LIHTC but also begin to dedicate a larger share of federal housing spending to non-LIHTC development subsidy programs. These non-LIHTC programs should operate much more simply, preferably as grants rather than tax credits. This approach could also support LIHTC projects by filling funding gaps for projects that use the tax credit. For example, LIHTC can't be used to pay for the land on which a project will be built.

Finally, the federal government should increase the flexibility with which local governments can implement LIHTC and other development subsidy programs. It is currently highly prescriptive, narrowly defining the share of units that must be affordable, what income levels they must be affordable to, utility allowances, and more. While well intentioned, these rules make it challenging to, for example, include market-rate units in affordable developments when there is insufficient funding to max out a site's development capacity with exclusively subsidized units. A site's zoning might allow seventy-five homes, but an affordable housing developer has funding for only fifty. Under current rules, the developer would have little choice but to proceed with the fifty-unit project. With greater flexibility, the developer might be able to add twenty market-rate units and use the "profits" to cross-subsidize five additional affordable homes.

What about Public Housing?

There are 1.1 million public housing units in the United States today, housing about 2.1 million residents. This is approximately 250,000 fewer public housing units than there were two decades ago—most were demolished or otherwise removed from the housing stock, often because of poor upkeep. Like LIHTC and Section 8 project-based voucher units, public housing is limited to low-income households. Unlike these other programs, public housing is owned and administered by local public housing agencies.

Public housing has become a rallying cry for some on the left, even spurring its own acronym, PHIMBY ("public housing in my back-yard"), as a counter to YIMBYs ("yes in my backyard"), who tend to support more market-driven approaches. However, as this book argues, many YIMBYs are very supportive of public housing, tenant protections, and other government interventions in the housing market. Another term, "social housing," more common in Europe, has grown popular in the United States in recent years. This refers to a broad range of publicly built or subsidized housing types that may or may not be restricted to low-income households. Regardless of who calls the units home, high income or low, social housing residents typically pay a share of their income for rent, up to a maximum market-rate figure. In this way, public agencies are able to more flexibly support mixed-income buildings and communities. Public housing is arguably one branch under the umbrella term of "social housing."

This book does not include a detailed argument in favor of public or social housing, but only because the terms are so ill-defined—and also because I consider LIHTC and other publicly subsidized units to be a valuable form of social housing. I hope that the strong support expressed in this book for acquisition of existing housing, construction of low-income housing, and direct rental assistance conveys the message that we need housing at every income level and that poor and working-class households need the most support—even if I eschew some of the buzzwords surrounding the topic. Many of the policies in this book will lead to standardization of housing regulation, oversight, and enforcement, as well as greatly increased public and nonprofit ownership of housing. All of these efforts serve to make it easier, in the long run, to move a larger and larger share of homes off the private market, safe from the tumult of the economy and the whims of individual property owners. That is ultimately the goal of public housing, and these recommendations will help achieve it.

53 Increase Funding for Direct Rental Assistance

Rental assistance complements affordable housing construction by providing immediate, flexible relief to vulnerable households.

While a greater emphasis on affordable housing construction is needed, rental assistance such as Housing Choice Vouchers, which help very low income households pay their rent, are also essential. Vouchers administered by the US Department of Housing and Urban Development (HUD) help approximately 2.3 million low income households each year, with three-quarters targeted at extremely low income households.[41] Rental assistance programs have been identified as one of the most effective and efficient ways to serve vulnerable households and prevent homelessness. They serve those with some of the greatest needs, bridging the gap between immediate needs and long-term solutions such as low-income and supportive housing development, but only about one-quarter of those eligible for housing or rental assistance receive any. We should significantly increase funding for vouchers and make them available to all who need them. Rental assistance should be established as an entitlement similar to food stamps or Medicare: if you're eligible, you receive it—simple as that.

There are numerous rental assistance programs, but the largest by far is the Housing Choice Voucher Program (Section 8). This program provides supplementary rent payments to help low-income renters cover the gap between what they can afford (30 percent of their income) and what their landlords charge for rent. There is overwhelming evidence that rental assistance is a good investment, with positive impacts on overcrowding and food insecurity, homelessness, health, transportation, education, and more. Households that are severely cost-burdened (paying more than 50 percent of their income on rent) spend far less on average on these essential goods and services—less than one-third as much as non-cost-burdened households in some spending categories.[42]

Rental assistance is impressively effective at reducing homelessness. In a twelve-city study, families living in homeless shelters were offered several types of assistance, including housing vouchers. Only 22 percent of voucher recipients experienced another episode of homelessness or of living doubled up with others over the next eighteen months, compared with 50 percent of those who were offered only continued shelter (the control group), and 47 percent and 42 percent, respectively, of those who received rapid rehousing and transitional housing. Voucher recipients were also 55 percent less likely to report incidents of domestic violence and 42 percent less likely to have their children placed in foster care or housed with other family members, relative to the control group.[43]

Tenant-based housing vouchers, which renters can carry with them as they move within a city, receive approximately $20 billion in funding each year.[44] This is less than the amount spent on either the capital gains exclusion or the property tax deduction in 2015, and it is less than one-third of what is spent on the mortgage interest deduction. Along with increased funding for subsidized housing construction through programs such as LIHTC and project-based rental assistance, tenant-based housing voucher funding should also rise dramatically.

Phased implementation could start by offering housing vouchers as an entitlement only to extremely low income households, those earning 30 percent or less of the area median income, or AMI. This would be a sensible approach, especially because extremely low income (ELI) renters are most vulnerable to homelessness and other negative outcomes. Currently, households are eligible if they earn 50 percent of AMI or less (very low income, or VLI), and the Congressional Budget Office estimates that providing vouchers to all 8 million eligible households would cost $41 billion per year. This would be in addition to current spending, for a total cost of around $60 billion per year. Limiting the expansion of the program to only ELI households, at least initially, would help 4.5 million households and increase costs by $29 billion per year.[45]

As the supply of publicly subsidized affordable housing grows over time, from both new construction and acquisition, it could be possible to rein in tenant-based rental assistance. More homes would be "off-market" and offering more affordable rents. Conversely, ELI renters might be preferentially housed in newly built affordable housing, reducing the burden on the tenant-based voucher program and preserving funds to help VLI renter households. Households earning less than 30 percent of AMI require deeper subsidies than those earning 50 percent of AMI, so each ELI household moved out of the voucher program could potentially support the housing costs for two or more VLI households.

54 Fund Low- and Zero-Interest Loans for Housing Acquisition and Development

—

The cost of housing construction and acquisition could fall precipitously with access to low-interest loans.

As discussed in the introduction to this section, monthly payments on a zero-interest loan are roughly one-third less than on a 2 percent interest loan and one-half those on a 5 percent loan. The federal government could improve affordability by offering low- or zero-interest loans to developers in exchange for setting aside some of their units for low-income households.

Interest on construction loans, which provide the capital to pay contractors as a project is being built, is estimated to account for about 6 percent of the cost of new developments. Eliminating this cost by eliminating interest payments would have the effect of reducing rent by at least $100 per month in the typical market-rate apartment in many high-cost cities. Construction loans are short-lived, so they don't put a great strain on the government budget: they're drawn down as funds are needed, and they are usually paid back within just a few years. Interest rates are quite low, around 5.5 percent to 6 percent in 2019,[46] reflecting the relatively limited risk that lenders take when issuing construction loans. (Equity investors' money is usually the most at risk, and the vast majority of projects that begin are eventually completed.) Subsidized affordable housing developments, which charge far below market rates and always lease up immediately, would be prime targets for loan guarantees used to lower construction loan interest rates.

Government-backed construction loans would be a relatively low-cost, low-risk way to reduce the cost of development and provide more affordable homes, but it could also distort the market in potentially harmful ways. For example, if such loan guarantees were limited to "conforming" developments, it could serve to slow down innovative housing such as micro-units, co-living, parking-free apartments, and the like—this is already a problem in the private loan market, and governments should be wary of making it worse. It would be important to design a program such that it wouldn't ossify development practices in the face of changing demographics, tastes, and needs.

A less distortive and potentially more efficient low-interest loan program could focus on take-out loans: the long-term, mortgage-like loans that replace construction loans when a development is completed and leased up. These loans account for the bulk of a property owner's monthly costs, and offering them at reduced rates could cut their expenses by 20–30 percent or more. These savings could be contingent on setting aside a share of units for low- or moderate-income households, in addition to the requirements of local inclusionary zoning or density bonus laws.

Because take-out loans have long terms, often of fifteen years or more, this would be a role that only the federal government could realistically fill. A program of this nature would cost many billions of dollars in up-front capital. State and local governments lack the liquid capital and deficit-spending ability to make this work, but it's an ideal role for the federal government. The Treasury already offers bonds and low-interest loans in the context of banking and fiscal policy, so extending this to housing loans wouldn't be such a stretch. The up-front cost in absolute dollars would be high, but the long-term cost would be quite low and could secure a large number of affordable units at a very reasonable cost.

Another benefit to this approach is that it would bypass the expensive, complex, and time-consuming process required for financing 100 percent affordable projects, reducing cost and delay. It would also support more market-rate development by pulling high-cost units off the market and into the affordable housing stock: it would be a counterweight to oversaturation at the high end of the housing market, spurring private developers to build more housing and providing even more affordable housing in the process.

Part III

Bringing It All Together

Simultaneously enacting every recommendation in this book would be an impossible task for any local government, and it would also be undesirable in terms of the economic and social upheaval it would entail. Before proceeding, advocates, planning professionals, community stakeholders, and elected officials will need to set priorities for policy reform, based on impact as well as ease of adoption.

The following is a blueprint for prioritizing the housing policies discussed in part II, categorized by priority and with limited details included for each. This proposal is not intended to take the place of local decision-making processes, coalition building, or stakeholder input, but my hope is that this prioritization paired with concrete details will help you advance the conversation in your own community.

Immediate Priority

The following policies require limited funding or study. They should be adopted without delay.

Eliminate Density Limits in Most Places

Eliminate density limits within one-half mile of any transit stop (bus, rail, ferry, etc.). Maintain setbacks, floor area ratio, height restrictions, lot coverage, and other design constraints as desired. Consider a moderate floor area bonus for multifamily buildings—for example, a maximum of 2,000 square feet for single-family units, 2,500 square feet for duplexes, 3,000 square feet for triplexes.

Allow the development of accessory dwelling units (ADUs) and conversion of existing space (e.g., recreation rooms, garages) into ADUs on parcels that permit residential uses.

Eliminate Parking Requirements Everywhere

Eliminate parking requirements for all new development. Consider incentivizing the use of on-site parking spaces for car sharing and allowing for their use by the general public (not just residents of the new building). Also consider establishing paid parking districts in areas concerned with overuse of on-street parking, and allocate parking passes according to street frontage (i.e., a parcel with 100 feet of street frontage would be eligible for twice as many parking passes as one with 50 feet of street frontage).

Let Renters Decide What They Value

Allow micro-units—individual, fully separated housing units (including their own kitchen facilities and bathrooms) as small as 250 square feet—and co-living spaces (which include bathrooms, kitchens, and other shared spaces) as small as 150 square feet anywhere housing is permitted.

Place Moderate Restrictions on Rent Increases for Nearly All Housing

For any dwelling unit made available for occupancy five years ago or more (often determined by issuance of a certificate of occupancy), restrict the ability for tenants' rent to be increased by more than the consumer price index (CPI) plus 5 percent in any twelve-month period. This limitation applies even if the tenants' lease expires and they are renting month to month.

Place Stronger Restrictions on Rent Increases for Older Housing

For any dwelling unit made available for occupancy fifteen years ago or more, restrict the ability for tenants' rent to be increased by more than the CPI in any twelve-month period. This limitation would apply even if the tenants' lease expires and they are renting month to month. A standardized explanation of rent stabilization regulations should be included with all new leases of affected properties.

Make Affordability Requirements Permanent

When state or local funds are used (or public land is contributed) for the development of income-restricted affordable housing, or when affordable units are required of privately financed developments by density bonus or inclusionary zoning programs, require that affordability covenants be made permanent. Buildings that include covenanted affordable housing may still be redeveloped in the future but must include one-for-one replacement, at a minimum, or fees adequate to wholly subsidize the construction or acquisition of replacement units in the vicinity.

Use Just-Cause Protections to Discourage Evictions

Establish just-cause eviction protections, which limit the legal reasons for which tenants may be evicted from their rental home. Included in these protections should be a prohibition against evictions for the purpose of owner or family member move-ins except in narrowly prescribed circumstances.

Eliminate Discrimination against People with Housing Choice Vouchers

Establish rules prohibiting discrimination against users of Housing Choice (Section 8) Vouchers in rental housing, and adopt stiff penalties for landlords who violate them.

Don't Sell Public Land; Lease It

End the practice of selling off public land for a one-time payment, and transition to offering ground leases to private or nonprofit developers instead. Public land may, of course, still be used for other publicly beneficial uses such as parks or donated for the construction of 100 percent affordable or mixed-income housing upon the condition that income-restricted units be made permanently affordable.

Medium-Term Priority

These policies are still a high priority, but they may require additional time for planning or study before being adopted, or additional revenues may need to be identified to fund their activities.

Increased Zoning Capacity

Rezone to allow for a housing capacity at least double—ideally triple—that of the existing population and housing stock. This should take into account demolitions that may be necessary in the course of redevelopment. It must also ensure that rezoned areas are viable for development—for example, that they are not former industrial waste sites, physically infeasible sites such as hillsides, publicly owned parcels that government doesn't intend to redevelop, located where land assembly is essentially impossible, or already intensively used or developed.

Upzone Many Places at Once

Distribute increased development capacity broadly, to many different neighborhoods and across large parts of each neighborhood for which zoning is changed. This does not mean spreading rezoning evenly across the entire city; rather, it means avoiding concentrating most or all increased capacity in a small number of neighborhoods.

Focus Upzones in Accessible and High-Opportunity Areas

When distributing increased housing capacity across the city, allocate a disproportionate share to areas where residents have higher income or wealth, jobs are more concentrated, and transit or transportation options are most accessible. This does not mean that lower-income or less job-rich communities should be avoided entirely. Cities might consider developing a scoring matrix that weights neighborhood affluence, job concentration, and transit accessibility approximately equally, ranking neighborhoods on the basis of their scores, and then allocating increased housing capacity disproportionately to those neighborhoods that rank highest.

Find the Upzoning Sweet Spot: Not Too Big, Not Too Small

At the parcel level, increase development capacity to a level that is financially feasible for redevelopment on the basis of the land and development costs. Except in highly urbanized locations, a maximum floor area ratio (FAR) between 2.5 and 4.0 should be appropriate in most cases. Height restrictions, density limits, setbacks, and other regulations will generally be unnecessary.

Allow Housing in Commercial Zones

Allow residential uses in commercial zones, including 100 percent residential buildings along secondary commercial corridors, where there is a risk of oversupplying retail and office space.

Make It Expensive to Reduce the Supply of Homes

Prohibit services such as Airbnb and Vrbo from renting out entire units except in limited circumstances. Allow homes to be fully rented out for a maximum of one month per year, and allow partial unit (bedroom) rentals for no more than three months per year.

Make Development Approvals "By Right"

Streamline review processes and eliminate discretionary approvals to the greatest extent possible. This can be accomplished by incorporating resident and stakeholder feedback into clear and objective community planning documents rather than individual projects.

Speed Up the Entitlement Process

Set a goal of approving the vast majority of projects (and housing units) within three months of application submittal. Allow developers to pay for additional staff hours to process applications faster, including third-party consultants hired to fill gaps in staffing or surges in applications.

Explore Other Ways to Bring Down Development Costs

Establish a public agency division dedicated to researching and approving new construction methods and materials and assisting developers who wish to try innovative strategies. Work closely with private-sector partners to identify opportunities, and consider establishing a rigorous "unsolicited proposal" program to generate ideas for new approaches.

Be Careful with Vacancy Control

Consider enacting vacancy control on all homes subject to rent stabilization, but don't apply it to individual units until the next time the unit is vacant. As with rent stabilization, limit annual rent increases to the consumer price index (CPI). Allow for modest increases beyond the CPI for a preapproved list of upgrades and renovations made to units between tenancies. Given the untested nature of vacancy control, also consider applying it to only a small share of rental units in the first several years.

Implement Inclusionary Zoning and Density Bonuses

Enact a density bonus program that allows for increased density, floor area, lot coverage area, and height, as well as reduced parking, setbacks, fees, and open or common space, in exchange for on-site affordable units. Density and floor area bonuses of 50–80 percent and height bonuses of one to two stories may be secured in exchange for 10–15 percent of units affordable to low-, very low, or extremely low income households, or 20–30 percent of units for moderate-income households. Los Angeles's Transit Oriented Communities (TOC) program is an excellent model.

Enact a low inclusionary zoning requirement—around 5–10 percent of units reserved for low-income households—to prevent any non-mixed-income projects from slipping through the cracks. Ideally, all projects will take advantage of the density bonus program, providing more of both affordable and market-rate units.

Consider an in-lieu fee instead of on-site affordable units for both the density bonus and inclusionary zoning programs. Note: the in-lieu fee (per unit not provided on-site) should be high enough to cover most or all of the subsidy needed to develop an affordable unit, including the pro rata cost of land.

Discourage Redevelopment That Requires Renter Displacement

When tenants are evicted for the purpose of residential redevelopment, require that they be offered a right of return to a comparable unit in the new building at the same rent paid in their previous dwelling. Their rent in the new unit must be stabilized and cannot count toward the development's income-restricted affordable unit requirements. During construction, the developer must also pay the difference between the tenant's previous rent and the rent the tenant pays for temporary housing. The temporary unit must be of similar quality and located within a short distance of the original home unless the tenant prefers a home elsewhere.

Require Transparency from Voluntary Tenant Buyouts

In place of a right of return and temporary rental assistance during redevelopment, or at any other time, tenants may also be offered a voluntary lump-sum buyout. Developers or property owners must disclose to the city their intent to negotiate a buyout before beginning discussions with tenants, and all mutually agreed-upon buyouts must be reported in a public database. Tenants have complete freedom to refuse any voluntary buyout offer, but in cases of redevelopment they must accept either a buyout or right of return.

Prioritize Displaced Tenants for Affordable Housing Placement

Low-income tenants displaced by redevelopment prior to the adoption of rules such as right of return and temporary rental assistance should receive priority placement in new and existing affordable housing developments. To the extent this can be made mandatory for nonprofit-operated affordable housing, it should be. Where state or federal laws prohibit such preferential treatment, public officials should work with private multifamily owners with income-restricted units that have been produced without public subsidy (such as through density bonuses) to encourage preferential placement for displaced low-income households.

Limit the Ability of Landlords to "Go Out of Business"

Prohibit owners from "going out of the rental business" within the first five years after purchasing their property for any reason except redevelopment into higher-density housing.

Prohibit property owners from converting to nonresidential uses, condominiums, or tenancies in common (TICs) without the consent of all existing renter households. Acceptance of a voluntary buyout offer should qualify as consent.

Require Government Notification for All Eviction Notices and Rent Hikes

Create a state or local registry of rental units, and require that landlords submit notification of any rent hikes or eviction notices before serving them to tenants. Allow tenants to access the registry to confirm that such notices have been formally submitted. The actions submitted to the registry should not require government approval; they exist for the purpose of tracking and enforcement. Governments may also use the registry to track basic data, including lease rates for individual rentals.

Offer Free or Reduced-Cost Legal Counsel to Residents Facing Eviction

Establish a right to counsel (RTC) program for tenants facing eviction. If funding is limited, consider initially restricting the program to households earning 30 percent or 50 percent of area median income (AMI) or less. As a starting point, the program may also be piloted in communities with the highest rates of eviction or eviction filings; a benefit of this approach is that it creates a control group against which a city can measure the effectiveness of the program. Over time, grow the program to assist more households with free counsel for those earning 100 percent of AMI or less, with partial assistance up to 150 percent of AMI and no assistance beyond that.

Enforce Housing and Building Codes

Increase code enforcement staffing to a reasonably high ratio of staff to rental units.

Require residential property-owning limited liability companies (LLCs) to reveal the identities of their owners and agents.

Institute high fines for property owners who violate code enforcement standards, with escalating fines for repeat offenders.

Create a process for owners of unpermitted dwelling units (UDUs) to bring their units into the formal housing market. Consider income restrictions or price controls or both that are high enough to encourage enrollment in the UDU program but low enough to discourage future development of unpermitted units.

Institute a Progressive Tax on Home Sales

Adopt a 1.0 percent tax on the sale of homes valued at less than $500,000; 1.5 percent for the portion of value from $500,000 to $750,000; 2.0 percent for value from $750,000 to $1 million; 3.0 percent for value from $1 million to $2 million, and 5.0 percent for value above $2 million. These rates should be based on average cost per unit rather than total property value. Be sure to include an automatic inflation adjustment each year.

Note: cities and states with high property tax rates (especially progressive property tax rates) should minimize taxes on home sales. High property taxes achieve all of the same goals as a progressive tax on home sales without discouraging household mobility.

Tax "Flipped" Houses at Higher Rates

Institute a 50 percent tax on profits earned from the sale of a home bought and resold in three years or less. Properties located on parcels zoned for single-family homes that are also at least one-half mile from a transit stop may be exempted from the tax, if desired.

Tax Underutilized and Vacant Property

Assess a fee equal to 1 percent of property value on any home left unoccupied for at least six months in a given year.

Minimize Impact Fees and Charge Them Equitably

Convert all existing fees into per-square-foot fees rather than per dwelling unit or per bedroom. Consider reducing or eliminating fees for projects that agree to specified rent levels (not "affordable" rates but less than the prevailing market rate in a given location).

Assess impact fees at the issuance of a certificate of occupancy or, at worst, at issuance of a building permit, not at the time of application or any other preconstruction phase.

Don't Let Small Buildings off the Hook

In places with linkage fees or inclusionary zoning, or both, for larger multifamily buildings, also include a fee of equal or greater value on smaller multifamily and single-family construction. Cities may consider exempting small multifamily buildings in high-cost, high-opportunity neighborhoods to encourage more housing construction than in lower-cost, lower-opportunity locations. They may also consider limiting this exemption to only those properties that maximize a parcel's allowable density.

Reform and Increase Funding for Affordable Housing Construction

Increase combined funding for the Low-Income Housing Tax Credit (LIHTC) and Section 8 project-based vouchers to at least

$50 billion per year. Alternatively—in fact, preferably—maintain current LIHTC and project-based voucher funding and establish a direct grant program to supplement existing programs: at least $50 billion per year in total funding for all programs.

Increase Funding for Direct Rental Assistance

Establish the Housing Choice Voucher Program (Section 8) as an entitlement for all households earning 30 percent of the area median income (AMI) or less (extremely low income). Later, increase the eligibility threshold to 50 percent of the AMI (very low income, or VLI). As VLI households are phased into the entitlement program, ensure that existing voucher holders earning between 30 percent and 50 percent of the AMI are able to retain their vouchers.

Long-Term Priority

The following policies are technically complex, politically challenging, expensive, or all of these. They will likely require more time to plan, fund, and build support for passage.

Promote Counter-cyclical Home Building

Utilize federal funds to support home construction during recessions, borrowing against future revenues or simply printing currency to maintain production and keep construction workers employed. At a minimum, offer zero- or low-interest federal loans to private developers who build during recession and recovery periods.

Buy Naturally Occurring Affordable Housing with Public Funds

Utilize local, state, and federal funds for acquisition of existing low-cost housing. Individual properties may be operated with a mix of market-rate and below-market units with a target of zero operational surplus revenues (i.e., any surplus is spent on deeper and broader subsidies for below-market units). Alternatively, properties may be operated at a surplus that is used to repay up-front acquisition costs, *to* acquire additional properties, or both.

Prioritize Stability over Wealth Creation

Create or reform down payment assistance programs that share in appreciation on the basis of government's share of the down payment, not on their share of the original purchase price. That is, for a $450,000 home with a $10,000 down payment from the buyer and $90,000 in down payment assistance from the government, the government would collect 90 percent of appreciation rather than 20 percent.

Utilize Property Taxes

Increase property taxes in lieu of other taxes such as sales taxes, income taxes, and the like. If attempting revenue-neutral tax reforms, increase property taxes with offsetting decreases in sales taxes and income taxes on lower earnings (e.g., the first $50,000 of personal income). Consider delaying property tax increases on rental property for five years or until the property changes ownership, whichever comes first. Also establish an exemption program for low-income property owners, including those with fixed incomes such as Social Security. Consider delaying collection of increased property taxes for certain groups (seniors, low-income residents) until the sale or transfer of property.

Reform or Eliminate Most Homeowner Subsidies

Eliminate the mortgage interest deduction entirely. If this is viewed as too extreme, reduce the eligible mortgage value to $250,000 and make the deduction equal to a flat 25 percent of interest paid, regardless of the filer's income tax bracket. Also begin to phase out the deduction for individuals earning over $100,000 ($200,000 for joint filers) and phase it out entirely by $150,000 ($300,000 for joint filers).

Eliminate the property tax exclusion and the capital gains exclusion on home sales. If revenue-neutral reforms are a priority, consider redirecting the savings from these three programs toward expansion of fully refundable earned income tax credits (EITCs).[1]

Fund Low- and Zero-Interest Loans for Housing Acquisition
and Development

Explore the possibility of municipal, county, state, or federal programs to offer low- or zero-interest construction or take-out loans,
or both, in exchange for reductions in rent or the setting aside of additional units for low- or moderate-income households. Loan guarantees may also be considered.

Work with highly profitable corporations with large cash bal-
ances (Apple, Google, etc.) to deploy low- or zero-interest loans to
support affordable and mixed-income housing construction as well
as housing acquisition and stabilization.

Conclusion

—

Nearly all of these policies, big and small, can be designed to work together. And they must. Policy makers and advocates will be tempted to pick and choose from this list, supporting those that seem easiest or that best align with their political ideology and excluding those that seem difficult or misaligned with their politics. This is a recipe for failure—a conscious decision to promote scarcity over abundance or to sacrifice the well-being of some of our most vulnerable neighbors for the benefit of the many. Any approach that excludes Supply, Stability, or Subsidy will leave many people out in the cold, and this is neither acceptable nor necessary.

Housing policy is contentious, sometimes to the point of being vicious, because it is important. Having a safe, clean, accessible, and affordable place to call home is among our most essential needs. Anything that threatens to change people's relationship to their home, and their community—to say nothing of being displaced from it—will be the subject of intense and vital scrutiny. My hope is that this policy framework, the Three S's, can help readers appreciate the validity of their critics' viewpoints and recognize the shortcomings of their own. Housing policy is too important, and too complex, for anyone to have all the answers. That includes me, despite having seventy thousand words to say on the subject!

Some people will be focused on Supply policies, others on Stability or Subsidy. That's okay: people have different strengths, interests, backgrounds, and areas of expertise that can be applied to the problem of housing affordability. It's a big issue, and enacting the necessary solutions will require a big tent. Some of us are teachers; others are organizers. We may lead on one issue but follow on another. We don't need everyone to become a dedicated advocate in all three areas.

What we *do* need is to stop tearing people down for choosing a focus different from our own, or for emphasizing different priorities or speaking to different audiences. That starts with recognizing how our own personal focus, whether Supply, Stability, or Subsidy, intersects with those of others. From there, we can begin to build the constructive partnerships needed to make housing affordable and accessible to all.

Appendix

—

Development and Real Estate Economics 101

This isn't a book about development and real estate, but a basic understanding of some key concepts will help readers understand the motivation and nuance behind many of the policies. Here, I provide a simplified overview of some of the most important concepts.

Who Profits from Housing Development

Many people assume that most of the cost of new housing is somehow a consequence of developer greed. This would imply that developers are taking a huge cut of their tenants' rent checks, which isn't borne out by the evidence. An analysis by Michael Andersen for the Open:Housing journalism collaborative looked into how a $2,000 rent check was divvied up for a new apartment in Portland, Oregon.[1] What he found might surprise you.

First, "developers" received only about 10 percent of that $2,000. "Developers" is in quotation marks because this is not just one group. It includes the development companies that actually manage the project from land acquisition to lease-up; they take about 3 percent. The remaining 7 percent goes to early investors, the people (or pension funds, or insurance companies, or whoever) who invest in the project at its earliest stages—this funding is known as equity, in contrast to debt issued by lenders.

In Portland, property taxes account for 11 percent of the rent check—more than the developers—plus the city collects another 5 percent through fees for parks, roads, sewer lines, and other public assets. (Note that property taxes and fees vary considerably among states and cities, but this is a good ballpark estimate for most places.) Materials and construction labor are the biggest cost drivers by far, accounting for 43 percent of the development's expense. Property management, construction lending, architecture, brokerage, and marketing all combine for another 18 percent. The remaining 13 percent goes to purchasing the land from the previous property owner.

There's no mind-blowing takeaway here. The simple truth is that many factors contribute to the expense of new housing, and a meaningful reduction in cost must address them all. We accomplish very little by focusing on "developer greed" because developers account for just 10 percent of the cost, give or take. Developer greed also doesn't explain why new housing in Phoenix or Houston costs so much less than in New York or Seattle. Like anyone else, developers deserve to be paid for their work. And, as you'll see, developer profits play an important role in determining what kind of housing gets built.

Development Risk and Its Impact on Supply

Equity, discussed earlier, is the riskiest money in real estate. It goes into a project before any other money, before construction has even started, and there's always a chance the investment could be lost if the project doesn't work out. Because of that risk, equity investors demand high returns on their investment, often around 15 percent per year or more. With a lower return, they'd be better off putting their money into a safer investment vehicle.

Real estate development—especially privately funded development, which accounts for the vast majority of new housing construction—depends on equity. Investors will require different minimum returns depending on how risky they view a project to be. This is known as the risk premium. Building near the end of an economic cycle (when a recession may be approaching) can be riskier, as can building in an area with less demand (e.g., Chicago compared with New York). A common risk in high-cost cities is project delay, whether a result of NIMBY ("not in my backyard") opposition, lawsuits, or simple bureaucracy.

Regardless of the cause, a higher risk premium makes projects more expensive. Apartment owners can't arbitrarily set their rents at whatever price they'd like—that's decided by the market—so when projects get more expensive to build, developers must target tenants within a narrower (and higher) income band. The higher up the income ladder you go, the smaller the pool of potential tenants, so fewer homes get built. And when governments enact rules that make housing less profitable, investors may find other, safer places to put their money. This is why putting the squeeze on developers often just leads to less development overall, with a greater portion targeted at the most affluent residents.

The Impact of Upzoning

Sometimes when zoning changes are proposed, opponents will argue that upzoning actually *increases* the cost of land and therefore makes cities less affordable, not more. A study by Yonah Freemark on the impact of upzoning transit-adjacent land in Chicago found evidence that this is true: upzoning appeared to increase the value of the affected parcels, but it didn't result in additional housing production.[2] The study was seized upon by opponents of new housing, but Freemark himself has acknowledged the limitations of this research and advised against applying its lessons too broadly.[3] For one, demand for new housing in Chicago is quite low because its population has been stagnant for over three decades. The study also looked only at development activity for five years after the zoning changes, and projects can take many years to complete.

Upzoning opponents who point to increased land values are arguing in bad faith. They're correct that land values often go up when upzoning occurs, but they're deliberately looking at the wrong number. When zoning capacity increases, the relevant number isn't the total property value but the property value *divided by the development capacity*.

Take, for example, land that is zoned only for single-family housing and that already has a home built on it, valued at $700,000. Now upzone it to allow four homes, and the value increases to $800,000. Is it less affordable? It depends on what the buyers want to do with it.

If the new owners want to continue using it as a single unit, they're paying more for the same thing; we've reduced affordability. But if the new owners want to replace that home with a four-unit condo, they're now paying $200,000 per developable unit. If they can build those condos for $400,000 per unit or less, they've just replaced one $700,000 home with four $600,000 homes. If you look at your local real estate listing website, you'll find that single-family homes are almost always the most expensive homes in a given neighborhood. This is because they must absorb the entire cost of land into a single unit, whereas condos and apartments can share that cost among multiple households.

The affordability benefit increases as the development capacity grows. If that same $700,000 parcel is zoned for twenty units instead of four, the property value might increase to $1 million, or $50,000 per developable unit. At the same development cost of $400,000 per unit, we've now replaced a $700,000 home with twenty $450,000 homes. We might also be able to mandate that two or three of those homes be set aside for low-income households, further increasing economic diversity in the neighborhood.

What Gets Redeveloped

Critics also ask whether upzoning will actually lead to equitable development. Even if you upzone the whole city, won't communities of color bear the brunt while whiter, more affluent neighborhoods continue to exclude—as they always have? Won't developers just build in lower-income areas, where land is cheaper?

There's a lot more to this critique than meets the eye because it isn't only a question of economics. Economics aside, political power matters. Wealthier communities have more influence over decision makers and more resources enabling them to sue or appeal projects, and this risk makes development more expensive. Some of the recommendations in this book seek to address that imbalance of power, most especially the need to rely more heavily on by-right planning approvals. The earlier and more objective the planning process, the less influence wealthier neighbors will have over it. I won't pretend this means that lower-income communities and communities of color will have equal power to richer neighborhoods, but it's an important starting point.

Limiting ourselves to the question of financial feasibility, however, the answer is no: developers do not prefer to build in low-income communities. Given the choice between redeveloping a single-family unit into a fourplex in a high-income neighborhood and doing the same in a low-income neighborhood, it will almost always be more profitable to build in the high-income area.

Within a metropolitan area, the cost of construction is essentially the same whether it's in a working-class or higher-income neighborhood. Land costs more in high-income neighborhoods, but that's offset by higher rents and sale prices. Here's an example. Start with a $600,000 single-family home in a high-income neighborhood and a similar $300,000 home in a working-class neighborhood. Rezone both parcels for up to ten units. In this scenario, construction costs in the region are about $200,000 per unit, so it will cost $2 million to build in either neighborhood. Total development cost, including land, is $2.6 million in the high-income area and $2.3 million in the working-class community. That works out to $260,000 per unit versus $230,000.

The cost of development in the high-income neighborhood is only marginally higher than that in the working-class community; yet, as discussed earlier, homes sell for about twice as much. A condo in the affluent area would likely sell for at least $400,000 to $500,000, a profit of more than $100,000 per unit. Meanwhile, new condos in the working-class neighborhood (where single-family homes are worth $300,000) might sell for only $250,000—barely any profit at all. Building homes in the high-income neighborhood is the clear winner. It should also be noted that bigger upzones are more favorable to development in high-income neighborhoods; increasing density only slightly, say, from one unit to two units per parcel, may not be enough to encourage much redevelopment because land accounts for such a large share of development costs in more affluent communities.

Note that if the construction cost increases to $250,000 or $300,000 per unit, the developer literally cannot earn a profit on housing built in the working-class neighborhood. As a result, no (unsubsidized) housing will be developed there. This is often the case in lower-income neighborhoods in expensive cities, where construction labor, materials, entitlements, fees, and other development costs are very high.

Residual Land Value

The previous example isn't the whole story because it doesn't ac-count for residual land value. In practice, land values vary according to local economic conditions such that a development opportunity in one location usually won't be wildly more profitable than an oppor-tunity elsewhere.

Let's return to the example just given, where two sites—one in a high-income neighborhood and the other in a low-income neigh-borhood—are each zoned for a ten-unit housing development. We'll also increase the construction cost to $300,000 per unit. If condos sell for $500,000 in the wealthier neighborhood, the land will almost cer-tainly be valued above $600,000, or $60,000 per developable unit. The owners of the site, knowing what new condos are worth and what it costs to build in the region, will adjust their sale price accordingly. They might expect $1.5 million for their land, knowing that the de-veloper can afford to spend $3 million on construction, sell the ten condos for $5 million, and still earn a healthy profit. The developer knows this, too, and therefore might agree to the $1.5 million price.

This is the concept of residual land value in a nutshell. A de-veloper has an idea of what to build, how much it will cost to de-velop, how much it will sell or rent for, and how much profit will be needed to attract investors. After deducting the projected costs (and profit) from the development's expected sale price, we're left with how much the developer can afford to spend on land. It looks something like this:

$5,000,000	Sale price of condos
− $3,000,000	Construction
− $500,000	Developer fees and profit
$1,500,000	Residual land value

Value Capture

Residual land value plays an important role in value capture. If you have land zoned for detached single-family units and upzone it to allow ten homes instead, you've increased the value of that parcel significantly. Rather than allow the landowner to collect that additional value as a windfall profit, you might wish to "capture" it in the form of affordable housing or funding for other community benefits. The city created the additional value, after all, so why shouldn't the entire community benefit from it? Understanding residual land value will help you design a successful value capture program.

Imagine the single-family parcel's value grows from $600,000 to $1.5 million after being upzoned. Ideally, you could capture 100 percent of the additional value, $900,000. You might do this by requiring that three of ten units be subsidized for very low income households, or simply have the developer cut a $900,000 check to the city. In reality, value capture programs can't be so precise, and they shouldn't aspire to be. If you manage to design a value capture program that captures exactly 100 percent of the additional value, a developer will be willing to pay exactly the same as a buyer who wants keep the single-family home and live in it (or rent it out): $600,000. Development is a complex, risky, time-intensive process, so there's a good chance that the property will remain a single-family home despite the upzoning.

Also, accurately predicting the price impact of an upzoning is nearly impossible. If your goal is 100 percent value capture, you may very well overshoot your aim. In that case, it's virtually guaranteed that the existing use will remain and redevelopment will be stymied. Not only do you not get more homes, you also don't get the community benefits funded by value capture.

It's best to think of two separate values being assigned to every parcel of land: its development value and its existing use value. Development value (DV) is what the land is worth to someone who wants to build something new on the site. Existing use value (EUV) is what it's worth based on its existing use, whether that use is a single-family home, an apartment, an office building, or a strip mall. When DV is greater than EUV, redevelopment is likely. When EUV is greater, the site will likely continue in its current use.

Advocates and city leaders should always consider how value capture and other development requirements will affect DV in relation to EUV. Of course, there may be circumstances in which it's worthwhile to deliberately reduce DV—for example, by enacting displacement protections to prevent the demolition of affordable rental housing. In this case, the community benefit comes not from redevelopment but from the preservation itself.

A good target for value capture is probably in the range of 50 percent to 70 percent of added value. At this level, it's unlikely that the cost of a value capture program will exceed the value created by the zoning change, even if you miscalculate a bit. It also gives existing property owners an extra incentive to sell. This is perhaps most important in single-family neighborhoods: homeowners in these communities may not have a right to keep their entire neighborhood zoned as low density (given all the social and economic costs of banning multifamily housing), but they *did* buy into a single-family neighborhood and may deserve some compensation if that changes. Some residents will still be angry about the change, but with an extra bump in home value they'll be well compensated for the inconvenience. If they don't like the direction in which the neighborhood is headed, they can take their windfall and buy a single-family home in another, less job-rich or transit-accessible neighborhood where low densities are more appropriate.

Speculation and the Price of Multifamily Housing

In Dallas, Texas, the mortgage payment for a duplex (which includes principal, interest, property taxes, and homeowner's insurance) might be $3,000 per month, and you might expect to lease each unit for around $1,500. In Detroit, Michigan, a similar mortgage might cost just $700 per month, and each unit might rent for $800. In Los Angeles, the mortgage might run $4,000, with each tenant paying $1,600 per month. The Dallas property owner is essentially breaking even each month, the Detroit owner is earning a profit, and the Los Angeles landlord is taking a significant loss. Why the discrepancy?

Operating costs are a part of the answer, but the much more influential factor is speculation. Put simply, the buyer in Dallas has a greater expectation of property value appreciation than the Detroit buyer, and the buyer in Los Angeles has a higher expectation still. In housing-scarce markets where prices can be expected to climb year after year, investors are willing to take an early loss on monthly cash flow with the hope of a bigger payoff when they either resell the property or are able to raise rents in the years to come. Large-scale investors, such as Invitation Homes (owned by the Blackstone Group), explicitly identify low housing supply and strong job growth as key to their success in reports to investors and the Securities and Exchange Commission (SEC).[4]

This is one of the clearer examples of why housing supply is so fundamental to affordability, and it has very serious implications for who can buy homes, rental and otherwise. When expectations of home value appreciation are high, those expectations are at least partially capitalized into the purchase price, raising costs for buyers. This makes housing a good investment for those who can afford to buy in high-cost, low-supply markets, but it closes the door to potential buyers of lesser means. From 2000 to 2013, homes in the most expensive markets increased in value by approximately 80 percent, while those in the cheapest markets grew in value by just 20 percent. You did quite well if you could afford the average home price of $364,000 in the expensive markets in 2000. If you could afford only the average price in the less expensive markets, $172,000, your investment probably didn't pay off nearly as well. In this way, scarce housing (and expectations of continued scarcity) serve to widen the gap between rich and poor regions and between rich and poor people.[5]

Notes

—

Introduction

1. Salvo Paper, "Tenant Power from Below: The Los Angeles Tenants Union," reposted on It's Going Down, March 29, 2018, https://itsgoingdown.org/tenant-power-from-below-la-tenants-union/.
2. Emily Alpert Reyes, "L.A. Housing Measure Has An Unexpected Foe: Tenant Activists," *Los Angeles Times*, July 19, 2016, https://www.latimes.com/local/lanow/la-me-ln-ballot-measure-20160719-snap-story.html.
3. Los Angeles Housing and Community Investment Department, "Relocation Assistance," Rent Stabilization Bulletin, July 25, 2019, http://hcidla.lacity.org/system/files_force/documents/relocation_assistance_english.pdf?download=1.
4. Los Angeles Homeless Services Authority, "2013 Greater Los Angeles Homeless Count," updated August 20, 2013, https://documents.lahsa.org/planning/homelesscount/2013/HC13-Results-LACounty-COC.pdf; Los Angeles Homeless Services Authority, "2016 Homeless Count Results, Los Angeles County and LA Continuum of Care," updated May 10, 2016, https://documents.lahsa.org/Planning/homelesscount/2016/factsheet/2016-HC-Results.pdf.
5. Los Angeles Homeless Services Authority, "2017 Greater Los Angeles Homeless Count Results, Los Angeles County and Continuum of Care," updated August 14, 2018, https://www.lahsa.org/documents?id=1873-2017-greater-los-angeles-homeless-count-presentation-los-angeles-county-and-continuum-of-care.pdf.
6. Dennis Romero, "3 L.A. Rental Horror Stories," *LA Weekly*, March 29, 2016, https://www.laweekly.com/news/3-la-rental-horror-stories-6766402.

7. Because of California state law, rents in rent-stabilized units are allowed to reset to the neighborhood's prevailing rates the instant an existing household leaves. Covenanted affordable units, which the Champion project proposed to provide, are required to charge well below market rate for at least fifty-five years.

8. Mac Taylor, "California's High Housing Costs: Causes and Consequences," Legislative Analyst's Office report, March 17, 2015, https://lao.ca.gov/reports/2015/finance/housing -costs/housing-costs.pdf.

9. At least in theory. In practice, many households don't stick around for the years-long process of demolition and re-development.

10. Important note: NIMBYs themselves are on a separate axis from most pro-housing and tenants' rights advocates. Well-meaning people, concerned about the impacts of development or overregulation, may be convinced that more housing and tenant protections can go hand in hand. NIMBYs, however, dress their language up in the clothes of social justice or property rights, but they are motivated first and foremost by opposition to new homes and new people. This book is not targeted at NIMBYs because they're not motivated by a desire to increase affordability, protect vulnerable residents, or improve access to opportunity for those most in need of support. A political movement that successfully improves housing affordability must wield sufficient power to overcome the entrenched power of those who oppose positive change.

11. Pew Charitable Trusts, "American Families Face a Growing Rent Burden," April 2018, https://www.pewtrusts .org/-/media/assets/2018/04/rent-burden_report_v2.pdf.

12. Emily Badger, "Whites Have Huge Wealth Edge Over Blacks (but Don't Know It)," *New York Times*, September 18, 2017, https://www.nytimes.com/interactive/2017/09/18 /upshot/black-white-wealth-gap-perceptions.html.

13. Joint Center for Housing Studies of Harvard University, "America's Rental Housing 2017," https://www.jchs

.harvard.edu/sites/default/files/harvard_jchs_americas
_rental_housing_2017_0.pdf.

14. Erika C. Poethig, "One in Four: America's Housing
Assistance Lottery," *Urban Wire: The Blog of the Urban
Institute*, May 28, 2014, https://www.urban.org/urban-wire
/one-four-americas-housing-assistance-lottery.

15. "Terner Center Research Series: The Cost of Building
Housing," Terner Center for Housing Innovation at the
University of California, Berkeley, Construction Cost
Series, January 17, 2018, https://ternercenter.berkeley.edu
/construction-costs-series.

16. US Government Accountability Office, "Low-Income
Housing Tax Credit: Improved Data and Oversight
Would Strengthen Cost Assessment and Fraud Risk
Management," Report to the Chairman, Committee on the
Judiciary, US Senate, September 2018, https://www.gao
.gov/assets/700/694541.pdf.

17. Federal Reserve Bank of St. Louis, "Housing Starts: Total:
New Privately Owned Housing Units Started," updated
December 17, 2019, https://fred.stlouisfed.org/series/HOUST.

18. Joint Center for Housing Studies of Harvard University,
"The State of the Nation's Housing 2018," https://www
.jchs.harvard.edu/sites/default/files/Harvard_JCHS_State
_of_the_Nations_Housing_2018.pdf.

19. National Alliance to End Homelessness, "State of Homelessness," latest counts from January 2018, https://end
homelessness.org/homelessness-in-america/homeless
ness-statistics/state-of-homelessness-report/.

20. Los Angeles Homelessness Services Authority, "Greater
Los Angeles Homeless Count, 2019 Results," updated
August 5, 2019, https://www.lahsa.org/documents?id=
3437-2019-greater-los-angeles-homeless-count-presentation
.pdf.

21. Chris Salviati, "Housing Shortage: Where Is the Under-
supply of New Construction Worst?," Apartment List,
July 26, 2017, https://www.apartmentlist.com/rentonomics
/housing-shortage-undersupply-of-new-construction/.

22. American Community Survey (ACS) 2017, "1-Year San Francisco City Occupancy Characteristics," US Census Bureau, data.census.gov.

23. ACS 2017, "1-Year San Francisco City Housing Units."

24. Zillow, "San Francisco Home Prices and Values," data through December 31, 2019, https://www.zillow.com/san -francisco-ca/home-values/.

25. ACS 2017, "1-Year San Francisco City Income over Past 12 Months."

26. ACS 2017, "1-Year Austin Housing Units."

27. Chris Salviati, "Housing Shortage: Where Is the Under-supply of New Construction Worst?," Apartment List, July 26, 2017, https://www.apartmentlist.com/rentonomics /housing-shortage-undersupply-of-new-construction/.

28. Zillow, "Austin Home Prices and Values," data through December 31, 2019, https://www.zillow.com/austin-tx /home-values/.

29. ACS 2017, "1-Year Austin Income over Past 12 Months."

30. Zillow, "Austin Home Prices."

31. Zillow, "San Francisco Home Prices."

32. Michael Wilt, "The Basics of Inclusionary Zoning," Texas State Affordable Housing Corporation, November 13, 2015, https://www.tsahc.org/blog/post/the-basics-of-inclu sionary-zoning.

33. Texas Housers, "State Bans Another Local Affordable Housing Tool with Anti-linkage Fees Legislation," May 24, 2017, https://texashousers.net/2017/05/24/state-bans -another-local-affordable-housing-tool-with-anti-linkage -fees-legislation/.

34. Eviction Lab, Princeton University, 2016 eviction statistics for San Francisco County, California, and Austin, Texas, https://evictionlab.org/map/#/2016?geography=counties& bounds=-123.037,37.647,-122.334,37.912&type=er&location s=4805000,-97.791,30.48%2B06075,-122.686,37.78.

35. National Low Income Housing Coalition, "The Gap: A Shortage of Affordable Homes," March 2017, https://nlihc .org/sites/default/files/Gap-Report_2017.pdf.

36. American Community Survey (ACS) 2005–2017, "1-Year Austin City Physical Housing Characteristics," US Census Bureau, data.census.gov.

37. ACS 2005–2017, "1-Year Austin Metro Physical Housing Characteristics."

38. ACS 2005–2017, "1-Year Dallas Metro Physical Housing Characteristics."

39. ACS 2005–2017, "1-Year Seattle Housing Units and Physical Housing Characteristics."

40. Zillow, "Seattle Home Prices & Values," data through December 31, 2019, https://www.zillow.com/seattle-wa /home-values/.

41. ACS 2005–2017, "1-Year Denver Housing Units."

42. Nadia Balint, "Which States Have the Best and Worst Laws for Renters?," *RENTCafé* (blog), March 14, 2018, https://www.rentcafe.com/blog/renting/states-best-worst -laws-renters/.

43. Zillow, "Denver Home Prices and Values," data through December 31, 2019, https://www.zillow.com/denver-co /home-values/.

44. Henry Grabar, "Minneapolis Confronts Its History of Housing Segregation," Slate, December 7, 2018, https:// slate.com/business/2018/12/minneapolis-single-family -zoning-housing-racism.html.

45. Zillow, "Minneapolis Home Prices and Values," data through December 31, 2019, https://www.zillow.com /minneapolis-mn/home-values/.

46. Amy Plitt, "Major Rent Law Reform Strengthening Tenant Protections Moves Forward in Albany," Curbed New York, updated June 12, 2019, https://ny.curbed.com /2019/6/12/18661872nyc-rent-stabilization-reform-legisla tion-universal-rent-control.

47. New York City Rent Guidelines Board, "Changes to the Rent Stabilized Housing Stock in New York City in 2017," May 24, 2018, https://rentguidelinesboard.cityofnewyork .us/wp-content/uploads/2019/08/2018-Changes.pdf.

48. Emily Nonko, "New York Apartment Guide: Rent Control vs. Rent Stabilization," Curbed New York, updated January 3, 2020, https://ny.curbed.com/2017/8/28/16214506/nyc-apartments-housing-rent-control.

49. Timothy B. Lee, "Tokyo May Have Found the Solution to Soaring Housing Costs," Vox, August 8, 2016, https://www.vox.com/2016/8/8/12390048/san-francisco-housing-costs-tokyo.

50. Lee, "Tokyo."

51. Robin Harding, "Why Tokyo Is the Land of Rising Home Construction but Not Prices," *Financial Times*, August 3, 2016, https://www.ft.com/content/023562e2-54a6-11e6-befd-2fc0c26b3c60.

52. Robin Harding, "Is This the Solution to Japan's Glut of Empty Homes?," *Financial Times*, July 17, 2015, https://www.ft.com/content/79297b7e-24c6-11e5-bd83-71cb60e8f08c.

53. James Gleeson, "How Tokyo Built Its Way to Abundant Housing," blog post, February 19, 2018, https://jamesjgleeson.wordpress.com/2018/02/19/how-tokyo-built-its-way-to-abundant-housing/.

54. Demographia, "14th Annual Demographia International Housing Affordability Survey: 2018. Rating Middle-Income Housing Affordability," Performance Urban Planning, data for third quarter 2017, http://www.demographia.com/dhi2018.pdf.

55. Barbara Eldredge, "Why the Average Family in Tokyo Can Own a New House for $850/Month," Curbed, February 3, 2017, https://www.curbed.com/2017/2/3/14496248/tokyo-real-estate-affordable-homes.

56. Japan Property Central, "Tokyo Apartment Sale Prices Increase for 68th Month," posted June 12, 2018, http://japanpropertycentral.com/2018/06/tokyo-apartment-sale-prices-increase-for-68th-month/.

57. Adam Forrest, "Vienna's Affordable Housing Paradise," HuffPost, updated February 25, 2019, https://www.huffpost.com/entry/

vienna-affordable-housing-paradise_n_5b4e0b12e4b0b15a
ba88c7b0.

58. Mercer Global, "Vienna Tops Mercer's 21st Quality of
Living Ranking," March 13, 2019, https://www.mercer
.com/newsroom/2019-quality-of-living-survey.html.

59. Eve Blau, "Re-visiting Red Vienna as an Urban Project,"
Austrian Embassy, Washington, DC, https://www.austria
.org/revisiting-red-vienna, abridgment of an article
published in Anton Falkeis, ed., *Urban Change: Social
Design—Art as Urban Innovation* (Basel, Switzerland:
Birkhauser, 2017).

60. Veronika Duma and Hanna Lichtenberger, trans. Loren
Balhorn, "Remembering Red Vienna," *Jacobin*, February
10, 2017, https://jacobinmag.com/2017/02/red-vienna
-austria-housing-urban-planning.

61. US Department of Housing and Urban Development,
Office of Policy Development and Research, "Vienna's
Unique Social Housing Program," PD&R Edge, https://
www.huduser.gov/portal/pdredge/pdr_edge_featd_arti
cle_011314.html.

62. City of Vienna, Austria, "Growth of the City—History of
Vienna," accessed April 9, 2020, https://www.wien.gv.at
/english/history/overview/growth.html.

63. Elliott Njus, "Oregon Legislature Passes Nation's First
Statewide Rent Control Policy, Eviction Protections,"
Oregon Live, updated February 26, 2019, https://www
.oregonlive.com/politics/2019/02/oregon-legislature-pass
es-nations-first-statewide-rent-control-policy-evictions
-protections.html.

64. Laurel Wamsley, "Oregon Legislature Votes to Essentially
Ban Single-Family Zoning," National Public Radio, July 1,
2019, https://www.npr.org/2019/07/01/737798440/oregon
-legislature-votes-to-essentially-ban-single-family-zoning.

65. Henry Kraemer, "Oregon and the Progressive Kitchen Sink
Approach to Housing," Data for Progress, July 12, 2019,
https://www.dataforprogress.org/blog/2019/7/11/oregon
-amp-the-progressive-kitchen-sink-approach-to-housing.

66. Gale Holland and Doug Smith, "L.A. Votes to Spend $1.2 Billion to House the Homeless. Now Comes the Hard Part," *Los Angeles Times*, November 9, 2016, https://www .latimes.com/local/lanow/la-me-ln-homeless-20161108 -story.html; Sarah Krueger, "Durham Affordable Housing Bonds Pass; Mayor Re-elected," WRAL, November 5, 2019, https://www.wral.com/durham-affordable-housing -bonds-pass-mayor-re-elected/18746416/.

67. Patrick Condon, "Rep. Ilhan Omar Proposes $1 Trillion for Affordable Housing," *Minneapolis Star Tribune*, November 21, 2019, http://www.startribune.com/rep-ilhan -omar-proposes-massive-affordable-housing-program /565274002/.

68. "Housing Finance at a Glance," July 2016, Urban Institute, Housing Finance Policy Center, https://www.urban.org /sites/default/files/publication/83016/2000879-Housing -Finance-at-a-Glance-A-Monthly-Chartbook-July-2016. pdf; "Housing Finance at a Glance," July 2019, Urban Institute, Housing Finance Policy Center, https://www .urban.org/sites/default/files/publication/100723/july_ chartbook_2019_1.pdf.

69. Approximately 1.2 million new homes were built each year during this period. Assuming an average value of $300,000, these new homes account for approximately $360 billion, or 28 percent of the increase in residential real estate value. Using Black Knight's repeat-sales year-over-year home appreciation estimate of 3.48 percent for May 2019, home appreciation accounted for approximately $920 billion of the rise in residential real estate values.

70. Phillip Reese, "California Homeownership Rate Jumps after Years of Decline," *Sacramento Bee*, October 16, 2018, https://www.sacbee.com/news/business/real-estate-news /article220008080.html.

71. This assumes that $500 per month is spent paying down a thirty-year loan and $500 is needed to cover operational expenses and long-term capital set-asides.

72. Joint Center for Housing Studies of Harvard University, "The State of the Nation's Housing 2019," https://www.jchs.harvard.edu/sites/default/files/Harvard_JCHS_State_of_the_Nations_Housing_2019.pdf.

Part I: Principles and General Recommendations

1. City of Seattle, Housing Affordability and Livability, "What Is HALA?," https://www.seattle.gov/hala/about.
2. Randy Shaw, "Can Building Housing Lower Rents? Seattle and Denver Say Yes," chap. 4 in *Generation Priced Out: Who Gets to Live in the New Urban America* (Berkeley: University of California Press, 2018).
3. *Abundant Housing Los Angeles* (blog), "Don't Call It a Boom: Despite Uptick, LA Still Adding New Housing at a Snail's Pace," January 3, 2017, https://abundanthousingla.org/dont-call-it-a-boom-despite-uptick-la-still-adding-new-housing-at-a-snails-pace/.
4. Zillow home values.
5. Liyi Liu, Douglas A. McManus, and Elias Yannopoulos, "Geographic and Temporal Variation in Housing Filtering Rates" (January 27, 2020), available at SSRN: https://papers.ssrn.com/sol3/papers.cfm?abstract_id=3527800 or https://dx.doi.org/10.2139/ssrn.3527800.
6. Lawrence Lessig, *America, Compromised* (Chicago: University of Chicago Press, 2018), xi.
7. Richard Rothstein, *The Color of Law: A Forgotten History of How Our Government Segregated America* (New York: Liveright, 2017), 222.
8. Erica C. Barnett, "How Seattle Is Dismantling a NIMBY Power Structure," Next City, April 3, 2017, https://nextcity.org/features/view/seattle-nimbys-neighborhood-planning-decisions.
9. Jon Goetz and Tom Sakai, "Guide to the California Density Bonus Law," Meyers Nave, revised January 2017, https://www.meyersnave.com/wp-content/uploads/California-Density-Bonus-Law.pdf.

10. City of Seattle, "Multifamily Tax Exemption," https://www.seattle.gov/housing/housing-developers/multi family-tax-exemption.

11. City of Chicago, "Affordable Requirements Ordinance: Proposed Enhancements," December 2014, https://www.chicago.gov/content/dam/city/depts/dcd/general/housing/ARO_Proposed_Enhancements_Dec_2014_Web_Final.pdf.

12. NYC Planning Inclusionary Housing Program, https://www1.nyc.gov/site/planning/zoning/districts-tools/inclu sionary-housing.page.

13. Michael Maddux, "Apr 5 #25%," *#Hashtag* (blog), accessed November 18, 2019, http://hashtaghashtag.org/blog-1 /2017/4/5/25.

14. Los Angeles Department of City Planning, "Housing Progress Report: Quarterly Report; October–December 2018," https://planning.lacity.org/odocument/42cb2634 -2885-4c33-9ff4-31c8f33c34d1.

15. City of Seattle, "How MHA Works," updated March, 2019, https://www.seattle.gov/Documents/Departments /HALA/Policy/How_MHA_Works.pdf.

16. Andrew G. Biggs, "No, Half of Older Americans Aren't without Retirement Savings," *Forbes*, March 28, 2019, https://www.aei.org/articles/no-half-of-older-americans -arent-without-retirement-savings/.

17. Laurie Goodman, "Setting the Stage on Housing and Retirement," presentation at 2018 Housing Wealth in Retirement Symposium, Washington, DC, March 23, 2018, http://retirement.theamericancollege.edu/sites/retirement /files/Housing_Symposium.pdf, 21.

18. Daniel Hertz, "Housing Can't Both Be a Good Investment and Be Affordable," City Observatory, October 30, 2018, http://cityobservatory.org/housing-cant-be-affordable _and_be-a-good-investment/.

19. Francisco Gonzalez, quoted in Shaw, *Generation Priced Out*, chap. 2, "A Hollywood Ending for Los Angeles Housing Woes?"

20. Zoltan L. Hajnal, "Why Does No One Vote in Local Elections?," *New York Times*, October 22, 2018, https://www.nytimes.com/2018/10/22/opinion/why-does-no-one-vote-in-local-elections.html.

21. Portland State University, "Who Votes for Mayor?," http://www.whovotesformayor.org/.

22. FairVote, "Voter Turnout," accessed November 29, 2019, https://www.fairvote.org/voter_turnout#voter_turnout_101.

23. Hajnal, "Why Does No One Vote?"

24. Tara Golshan, "Young People, Women, Voters in Cities: How Democrats Won in 2018, by the Numbers," Vox, April 26, 2019, https://www.vox.com/2019/4/26/18516645/2018-midterms-voter-turnout-census.

25. Mike Maciag, "Millennials Let Their Grandparents Decide Local Elections," Governing, January 2017, https://www.governing.com/topics/elections/gov-voter-turnout-generations-millennials.html.

26. Portland State University, "Who Votes for Mayor?"

Part II: Policies
Supply: Why Housing Matters

1. Jed Kolko, "5 Truths of Tech-Hub Housing Costs," Trulia, February 6, 2014, https://www.trulia.com/research/price-and-rent-monitors-jan-2014/.

2. Jeff Tucker, "Home Values Grew Most in Markets with Strictest Land Use Regulations," Zillow, August 1, 2018, https://www.zillow.com/research/home-values-land-use-regs-20860/.

3. Shane Phillips, "Increased Apartment Housing in Seattle Likely to Stabilize Rent Prices," *Better Institutions* (blog), September 27, 2012, http://www.betterinstitutions.com/blog/2012/09/increased-apartment-housing-in-seattle; Shane Phillips, "It's the Vacancy Rate, Stupid: Why New Development Has Little to Do with Rising Rents," *Better Institutions* (blog), April 25, 2016, http://www.betterinstitutions.com/blog/2016/4/24/its-the-vacancy-rate-stupid-los-angeles.

4. "Toyota Models," Kelley Blue Book, https://www.kbb
   .com/toyota/?vehicleclass=newcar&intent=buy-new.

5. Timothy Cain, "Toyota Camry Sales Figures," Good Car
   Bad Car, http://www.goodcarbadcar.net/2011/01/toyota
   -camry-sales-figures/.

6. Timothy Cain, "Toyota Sales Figures—US Market," Good
   Car Bad Car, http://www.goodcarbadcar.net/2012/10
   /toyota-brand-sales-figures-usa-canada/.

7. Mac Taylor, "Perspectives on Helping Low-Income
   Californians Afford Housing," Legislative Analyst's
   Office, LAO Brief, February 9, 2016, https://lao.ca.gov
   /Reports/2016/3345/Low-Income-Housing-020816.pdf, 8.

8. Dan Bertolet, "Video: Cruel Musical Chairs (or Why Is
   Rent So High?)," Sightline Institute, October 31, 2017,
   https://www.sightline.org/2017/10/31/video-cruel-musical
   -chairs-why-is-rent-so-high/.

9. Evan Mast, "The Effect of New Market-Rate Housing
   Construction on the Low-Income Housing Market,"
   Upjohn Institute Working Paper 19-307, July 2019, https://
   www.dropbox.com/s/zuzxvupdbqcvhql/Mast%20Luxury
   %20Housing.pdf?d1=0.

10. Brian James Asquith, Evan Mast, and Davin Reed, "Panel
    Paper: Does Luxury Housing Construction Increase
    Nearby Rents?," Association for Public Policy Analysis
    and Management, November 10, 2018, https://appam
    .confex.com/appam/2018/webprogram/Paper25811.html.

11. Gregory D. Morrow, "The Homeowner Revolution:
    Democracy, Land Use, and the Los Angeles Slow-Growth
    Movement, 1965–1992" (PhD diss., University of Califor-
    nia, Los Angeles, 2013), https://escholarship.org/uc/item
    /6k64g20f.

12. Shane Phillips, "Single-Family Homes Are Luxury
    Housing," *Better Institutions* (blog), July 10, 2019, http://
    www.betterinstitutions.com/blog/2019/7/10/single-family
    -homes-are-luxury-housing.

13. Health Effects Institute, "Traffic-Related Air Pollution: A
    Critical Review of the Literature on Emissions, Exposure,

and Health Effects," Special Report 17, January 2010, https://www.healtheffects.org/publication/traffic-related-air-pollution-critical-review-literature-emissions-exposure-and-health.

14. This is a vast oversimplification of the Strong Towns way of thinking, and anything lost in translation is the fault of this author. Strong Towns is a wonderful organization that has led to a more rigorous, thoughtful approach to city planning across the country, especially in smaller cities that are often overlooked in the national discourse on urban issues. I recommend reading more at https://www.strong towns.org if you're not familiar with Charles Marohn and his organization.

15. Shane Phillips, "Keep Los Angeles Affordable by Repealing Proposition U," *Better Institutions* (blog), May 16, 2016, http://www.betterinstitutions.com/blog/2016/5/16/keep-los-angeles-affordable-repeal-proposition-u.

16. Jeremy Rosenberg, "How Downtown L.A. Became a Place to Live (without Parking)," KCET, April 2, 2012, https://www.kcet.org/history-society/how-downtown-la-became-a-place-to-live-without-parking.

17. Sarah Holder, "The Airbnb Effect: It's Not Just Rising Home Prices," CityLab, February 1, 2019, https://www.citylab.com/equity/2019/02/study-airbnb-cities-rising-home-prices-tax/581590/.

18. Emily Badger and Quoctrung Bui, "Cities Start to Question an American Ideal: A House with a Yard on Every Lot," *New York Times*, June 18, 2019, https://www.nytimes.com/interactive/2019/06/18/upshot/cities-across-america-question-single-family-zoning.html.

19. Mikaela Sharp and John Burns, "Home Sharing: 44 Million Empty Bedrooms Await," John Burns Real Estate Consulting, February 13, 2018, https://www.realestateconsulting.com/home-sharing-44-million-empty-bedrooms-await/.

20. Daniel Parolek's new book, *Missing Middle Housing: Thinking Big and Building Small to Respond to Today's*

Housing Crisis (Washington, DC: Island Press, 2020), provides a compelling and much more thorough overview of this approach.

21. Henry Grabar, "Minneapolis Confronts Its History of Housing Segregation," Slate, December 7, 2018, https://slate.com/business/2018/12/minneapolis-single-family-zoning-housing-racism.html.

22. Rachel Monahan, "Oregon House Passes Bill to End the Exclusive Use of Single-Family Zoning in Cities," *Willamette Week*, updated June 20, 2019, https://www.wweek.com/news/state/2019/06/20/oregon-house-passes-bill-to-end-the-exclusive-use-of-single-family-zoning-in-cities/.

23. Kenneth Chan, "Laneway Homes Can Now Be More Easily Built in Vancouver," Daily Hive, July 24, 2018, https://dailyhive.com/vancouver/vancouver-laneway-house-program-change-july-2018.

24. Los Angeles Department of City Planning, "Accessory Dwelling Units: Housing Progress Report, January 2015–September 2018," https://planning.lacity.org/odocument/7b7f2d26-d4a2-428b-8c19-0e846fd443a4.

25. Los Angeles Department of City Planning, "The Big Picture: Housing Progress Report, January–March 2019," https://planning.lacity.org/odocument/c82e412b-9d5a-4306-8e19-48bd17ebd752.

26. Alan Durning, "Wide Open Spaces: Thousands of Parking Slots; Vacant, Unwanted, Mandatory," Sightline Institute, July 25, 2013, https://www.sightline.org/2013/07/25/wide-open-spaces/.

27. Saumya Jain, "ITE Takes On Parking Minimums and Manuals," State Smart Transportation Initiative, February 26, 2019, https://www.ssti.us/2019/02/ite-takes-on-parking-minimums-and-manuals/.

28. Nick Magrino, "What Happens When You Ease Parking Requirements for New Housing," January 30, 2018, https://www.nickmagrino.com/blog/2018/1/30/when-you-dont-have-to-build-so-much-parking; Rob Manning, "No Room for Parking at Many New Apartment Complexes,"

OPB, August 15, 2012, https://www.opb.org/news/article
/no-room-parking-many-new-apartment-projects/?
utm_source=August+20%2C+2012&utm_campaign=Tracks
-Aug-15&utm_medium=email?utm_source=August+20%2C+
2012&utm_campaign=Tracks-Aug-15&utm_medium=
email.

29. I wrote about micro-units in greater detail, including their
specific benefits for urban centers and downtowns, in a white
paper for the Central City Association of Los Angeles. See
Jessica Lall et al., "Micro-Units in DTLA: New Housing
Choices for LA's Fastest Growing Neighborhood," March
2018, http://ccala.org/microunitwhitepaper.

30. Moira O'Neill, Giulia Gualco-Nelson, and Eric Biber,
"Examining the Local Land Use Entitlement Process in
California to Inform Policy and Process," Working Paper
2, February 2018, Berkeley Law and IURD, University of
California, Berkeley, and GSAAP, Columbia University,
https://iurd.berkeley.edu/uploads/WorkingPaper_2_Final
_web.pdf.

31. Steven Sharp, "Caruso Agrees to Downsize Beverly Grove
Development," Urbanize Los Angeles, January 18, 2017,
https://urbanize.la/post/caruso-agrees-downsize-bever
ly-grove-development; Elijah Chiland, "Downsized Mixed
Use Complex Would Bring 242 Units of Housing to
Granada Hills," Curbed Los Angeles, October 9, 2017,
https://la.curbed.com/2017/10/9/16451538/granada-hills
-development-housing-retail; Steven Sharp, "L.A. City
Council Approves Western/Franklin Development," Urbanize Los Angeles, April 24, 2018, https://urbanize.la/post
/la-city-council-approves-westernfranklin-development.

32. Sarah Mawhorter and Carolina Reid, "Local Housing
Policies across California: Presenting the Results of a New
Statewide Survey," Terner Center for Housing Innovation,
University of California, Berkeley, December 2018, http://
californialanduse.org/download/Terner_California_Resi
dential_Land_Use_Survey_Report.pdf.

33. Scott Wiener and Daniel Kammen, "Why Housing Policy Is Climate Policy," *New York Times*, March 25, 2019, https://www.nytimes.com/2019/03/25/opinion/california-home-prices-climate.html.

34. O'Neill, Gualco-Nelson, and Biber, "Land Use Entitlement Process."

35. Kimberly Burnett and Tyler Morrill, "Development Process Efficiency: Cutting through the Red Tape," report prepared by Abt Associates for the National Association of Home Builders, November 30, 2015, https://www.nahb.org/~/media/NAHB/advocacy/docs/top-priorities/housing-affordability/development-process-efficiency.

36. The White House, "Housing Development Toolkit," September 2016, https://www.whitehouse.gov/sites/whitehouse.gov/files/images/Housing_Development_Toolkit%20f.2.pdf.

37. Alan Greenblatt, "Why Rents Are Actually Lowering in Some Big Cities," Governing, March 2018, https://www.governing.com/topics/urban/gov-rents-coming-down.html; Mike Rosenberg, "Apartment Rents Dropping in Seattle, Landlords Compete for Tenants as Market Cools," *Seattle Times* via Associated Press, updated January 6, 2019, https://www.oregonlive.com/business/2019/01/apartment-rents-dropping-in-seattle-landlords-compete-for-tenants-as-market-cools.html; Lance Hernandez, "Metro Denver Rents Decline as More Apartments Come Online," Denver Channel 7 website, updated January 23, 2019, https://www.thedenverchannel.com/news/our-colorado/metro-denver-rents-decline-as-more-apartments-come-online.

38. Steven Sharp, "Modular Apartment Building Takes Shape in Leimert Park," Urbanize Los Angeles, June 12, 2019, https://urbanize.la/post/modular-apartment-building-takes-shape-leimert-park.

39. 4252 Crenshaw Apartment Homes, "Floor Plans," accessed April 9, 2020, https://www.4252crenshaw.com/floor-plans.

40. I wrote extensively about mass timber in a white paper for a former employer, the Central City Association of Los

Angeles. See Jessica Lall et al., "Mass Timber: A Faster, More Affordable, and More Sustainable Way to Build Housing," 2019, https://www.ccala.org/masstimberwhite paper.

41. Federal Reserve Bank of St. Louis, "All Employees, Construction," updated January 10, 2020, https://fred.stlouisfed.org /series/USCONS.

42. Brittany De Lea, "Construction Worker Shortage Tops Sector Concerns in 2019," FoxBusiness, January 2, 2019, https://www.foxbusiness.com/economy/construction -worker-shortage-tops-sector-concerns-in-2019.

43. US Census Bureau, "Construction Price Indexes," accessed December 14, 2019, https://www.census.gov/construction /cpi/.

44. Federal Reserve Bank of St. Louis, "Average Hourly Earnings of All Employees: Construction," updated January 10, 2020, https://fred.stlouisfed.org/series/CES200 0000003.

Stability: Why Tenant Protections and Rental Housing Preservation Matter

1. See the US Supreme Court case that gave birth to modern zoning, *Village of Euclid, Ohio v. Ambler Realty Co.*, 272 US 365 (1926), in which Justice George Sutherland, speaking for the majority, had this to say about apartment housing (emphasis mine): "With particular reference to apartment houses, it is pointed out that the development of detached house sections is greatly retarded by the coming of apartment houses, which has sometimes resulted in destroying the entire section for private house purposes; that, in such sections, *very often the apartment house is a mere parasite*, constructed in order to take advantage of the open spaces and attractive surroundings created by the residential character of the district."

2. Rebecca Diamond, Timothy McQuade, and Franklin Qian, "The Effects of Rent Control Expansion on Tenants,

Landlords, and Inequality: Evidence from San Francisco," *American Economic Review* 109, no. 9 (2019): 3365–3394, https://doi.org/10.1257/aer.20181289.

3. Rebecca Diamond, Tim McQuade, and Franklin Qian, "Who Benefits from Rent Control? The Equilibrium Consequences of San Francisco's Rent Control Expansion," unpublished paper, 2018.

4. Diamond, McQuade, and Qian, "Effects of Rent Control Expansion," 3392.

5. Stout Risius Ross, "Economic Return on Investment of Providing Counsel in Philadelphia Eviction Cases for Low-Income Tenants," prepared for the Philadelphia Bar Association's Civil Gideon and Access to Justice Task Force, November 13, 2018, https://www.philadelphiabar .org/WebObjects/PBA.woa/Contents/WebServerResources /CMSResources/PhiladelphiaEvictionsReport.pdf.

6. Elliot Njus, "How Does Oregon's First-in-the-Nation Rent Control Law Work? A Quick Guide," *Oregonian*, posted March 6, 2019, https://www.oregonlive.com/busi ness/2019/03/how-does-oregons-first-in-the-nation-rent -control-law-work-a-quick-guide.html.

7. Liam Dillon, "California Tenants Will See Cap on Rent Increases Under Bill Sent to Newsom," *Los Angeles Times*, September 11, 2019, https://www.latimes.com/california /story/2019-09-11/california-renters-relief-legislation -gavin-newsom-rent-cap.

8. I wrote about rolling rent control at greater length on my blog, *Better Institutions*: "Rent Stability, Part 2: How 'Rolling' Rent Stabilization Might Preserve Affordability in LA," September 11, 2016, http://www.betterinstitutions .com/blog/2016/9/11/rent-stability-part-2-rolling-rent -control.

9. Dan Bertolet, "Modifications to Washington's Condo Law Could Give Production a Shot in the Arm," Sightline Institute, January 9, 2019, https://www.sightline.org/2019 /01/09/modifications-to-washingtons-condo-law-could -give-production-a-shot-in-the-arm/.

10. The Local, Sweden, "Almost 580,000 Now Waiting for Apartments in Stockholm," August 16, 2017, https://www.thelocal.se/20170816/almost-580000-now-waiting-for-apartments-in-stockholm.

11. Kevin Schofield, "Understanding Rent Control," Seattle City Council Insight, April 25, 2019, https://sccinsight.com/2019/04/25/understanding-rent-control/.

12. The Local, Germany, "Germany's Controversial Rent Control Law Works After All (At Least in Central Berlin)," February 14, 2018, https://www.thelocal.de/20180214/controversial-rent-control-law-does-work-after-all.

13. Feargus O'Sullivan, "Berlin's Massive Housing Push Sparks a Debate about the City's Future," CityLab, November 27, 2018, https://www.citylab.com/equity/2018/11/berlin-germany-affordable-housing-construction-rents/576469/.

14. Los Angeles Housing and Community Investment Department, "Relocation Assistance," Rent Stabilization Bulletin, July 24, 2019, http://hcidla.lacity.org/system/files_force/documents/relocation_assistance_english.pdf?download=1.

15. Wikipedia, "99-Year Lease," accessed December 3, 2019, https://en.wikipedia.org/wiki/99-year_lease.

16. The equation for calculating the present value of future revenues is Present Value = Future Value * (1 − Discount Rate) ^ Years.

17. Robert Hickey, Lisa Sturtevant, and Emily Thaden, "Achieving Lasting Affordability through Inclusionary Housing," Lincoln Institute of Land Policy, https://www.law.du.edu/documents/rmlui/conference/handouts/2015/ElliottDRisingInterestInclusionaryHousingOrdinances.pdf.

18. Shane Phillips, "Increasing the Duration of Affordability Requirements for New Affordable Housing," Policy Brief, UCLA Lewis Center for Regional Policy Studies, 2020, https://escholarship.org/uc/item/9fs1m0tt.

19. Rosalind Greenstein and Yesim Sungu-Eryilmaz, "Community Land Trusts," Lincoln Institute of Land Policy, *Land Lines*, April 2005, https://www.lincolninst.edu/pub lications/articles/community-land-trusts.

20. Shane Phillips, "Private Development, Public/Non-Profit Ownership: Recipe for Long-Term Housing Affordability," *Better Institutions* (blog), June 19, 2016, http://www .betterinstitutions.com/blog/2016/6/19/private-develop ment -public-ownership-housing-affordability.

21. *The Pruitt-Igoe Myth*, 2011 film directed by Chad Freidrichs, http://www.pruitt-igoe.com/about.html.

22. City and County of San Francisco Rent Board, "Topic No. 263: Buyout Agreements," February 2019, https://sfrb.org /topic-no-263-buyout-agreements.

23. DataSF, "Map of Buyout Agreements," accessed December 20, 2019, https://data.sfgov.org/Housing-and-Buildings /Map-of-Buyout-Agreements/aa2m-ehxd.

24. City of Fremont, "Rent Control and Just-Cause Eviction: Review of Programs," Management Partners, June 2017, https://www.fremont.gov/DocumentCenter/View/35249 /Fremont—-Rent-Control-Just-Cause-Eviction-Report —-final?bidId=.

25. Eviction Lab, Princeton University, "National Estimates: Eviction in America," May 11, 2018, https://evictionlab .org/national-estimates/.

26. Andrew Flowers, "How We Undercounted Evictions by Asking the Wrong Questions," FiveThirtyEight, September 15, 2016, https://fivethirtyeight.com/features/how-we -undercounted-evictions-by-asking-the-wrong-questions/.

27. If it turned out that the eviction or rent increase complied with law and the only infraction was failure to submit the notification to the database, the landlord could be offered a one-time exemption from the fine.

28. Los Angeles Housing and Community Investment Department, "Rent Registry," accessed December 6, 2019, https://hcidla.lacity.org/rentregistry.

29. Kriston Capps, "New York City Guarantees a Lawyer to Every Resident Facing Eviction," CityLab, August 14, 2017, https://www.citylab.com/equity/2017/08/nyc-ensures -eviction-lawyer-for-every-tenant/536508/.

30. The *Times* Editorial Board, "L.A. Renters Deserve a 'Right to Counsel' for Evictions," *Los Angeles Times*, April 23, 2019, https://www.latimes.com/opinion/editorials/la-ed -right-to-counsel-eviction-lawyers-20190423-story.html.

31. Stout Risius Ross, "Economic Return on Investment."

32. Jake Blumgart, "Philly Renters Guaranteed Lawyers in Eviction Court under New City Council Bill," WHYY, May 9, 2019, http://planphilly.com/articles/2019/05/09 /philly-renters-guaranteed-lawyers-in-eviction-court -under-new-city-council-bill.

33. Nadra Nittle, "Free Legal Help for Tenants Who Get Eviction Notices? LA Poised to Budget $3M for It," Curbed Los Angeles, May 16, 2019, https://la.curbed.com /2019/5/16/18623160/right-to-counsel-los-angeles-evictions -free-attorney.

34. Oksana Mironova, "NYC Right to Counsel: First Year Results and Potential for Expansion," Community Service Society, March 25, 2019, https://www.cssny.org/news/entry /nyc-right-to-counsel.

35. Gale Holland, "L.A. Spent $619 Million on Homelessness Last Year. Has It Made a Difference?" *Los Angeles Times*, May 11, 2019, https://www.latimes.com/local/california /la-me-ln-homeless-housing-count-20190511-story.html.

36. Los Angeles Homeless Services Authority, "Greater Los Angeles Homeless Count: 2019 Results," updated August 5, 2019, https://www.lahsa.org/documents?id=3437-2019 -greater-los-angeles-homeless-count-presentation.pdf.

37. Stout Risius Ross, "The Financial Cost and Benefits of Establishing a Right to Counsel in Eviction Proceedings under Intro 214-A," presentation to the Pro Bono and Legal Services Committee of the New York City Bar Association, March 16, 2016, https://www2.nycbar.org/pdf /report/uploads/SRR_Report_Financial_Cost_and_Bene

fits_of_Establishing_a_Right_to_Counsel_in_Eviction
_Proceedings.pdf.

38. Stout Risius Ross, "Economic Return on Investment."

39. Report from the New York State Senate Committee on Investigations and Government Operations, "Final Investigative
Report: Code Enforcement in New York State," August 5,
2019, https://www.nysenate.gov/sites/default/files/article
/attachment/final_investigative_report_code_enforcement_
senator_skoufis_igo_committee.pdf, I. Executive Summary.

40. Aaron Mendelson, "Deceit, Disrepair, and Death Inside a
Southern California Rental Empire," LAist, February 12,
2020, https://laist.com/projects/2020/pama/.

41. Alex Johnson, Andrew Blankstein, and Stephanie Gosk,
"Oakland Warehouse Fire: 'Ghost Ship' Sailed through
Regulators' Fingers for Years," NBC News, updated
December 5, 2016, https://www.nbcnews.com/news/us
-news/oakland-warehouse-fire-ghost-ship-sailed-through
-regulators-fingers-years-n692306.

42. Peter Fimrite, Hamed Aleaziz, and Rachel Swan, "Oakland Official: Ghost Ship Building Not Inspected in 3
Decades," SFGate, December 8, 2016, https://www.sfgate
.com/bayarea/article/Search-of-Oakland-warehouse-fin
shed-as-fire-death-10780261.php.

43. Chava Gourarie, "Buyers of All-Cash LLC Purchases
above $300K in NYC Must Be Disclosed, under Updated
Rule," 6sqft, November 19, 2018, https://www.6sqft.com
/buyers-of-all-cash-llc-purchases-above-300k-in-nyc
-must-be-disclosed-under-updated-rule/.

44. Los Angeles Department of City Planning, "Unapproved
Dwelling Unit Ordinance: Background and Frequently
Asked Questions," updated July 2018, accessed April 5,
2020, https://planning.lacity.org/ordinances/docs/unap
proveddwellingunit/UDUQuickGuide.pdf.

45. Alicia Mazzara and Brian Knudsen, "Where Families
with Children Use Housing Vouchers: A Comparative
Look at the 50 Largest Metropolitan Areas," January 3,
2019, Poverty and Race Research Action Council, Center

on Budget and Policy Priorities, https://www.cbpp.org /research/housing/where-families-with-children-use -housing-vouchers.

46. Edgar Walters and Neena Satija, "Section 8 Vouchers Are Supposed to Help the Poor Reach Better Neighborhoods. Texas Law Gets in the Way," *Texas Tribune*, November 19, 2018, https://www.texastribune.org/2018/11/19/texas -affordable-housing-vouchers-assistance-blocked/.

47. Andrew Khouri, "Housing Vouchers Can Save People from Homelessness. But Landlords May Not Accept Them," *Los Angeles Times*, March 29, 2019, https://www.latimes.com /business/la-fi-section-8-landlords-20190329-story.html.

48. Alison Bell, Barbara Sard, and Becky Koepnick, "Prohibit- ing Discrimination against Renters Using Housing Vouchers Improves Results," Center on Budget and Policy Priorities, updated December 20, 2018, https://www.cbpp .org/research/housing/prohibiting-discrimination-against -renters-using-housing-vouchers-improves-results.

49. Bell, Sard, and Koepnick, "Prohibiting Discrimination."

50. Bell, Sard, and Koepnick, "Prohibiting Discrimination."

51. Mazzara and Knudsen, "Where Families with Children Use Housing Vouchers."

52. FY2019 Fair Market Rents Documentation System, HUD User, https://www.huduser.gov/portal/datasets/fmr/fmrs /FY2019_code/select_Geography.odn.

53. "Study Supports Use of Small Area Fair Market Rents," National Low Income Housing Coalition, June 11, 2018, https://nlihc.org/resource/study-supports-use-small-area -fair-market-rents.

54. City and County of San Francisco, Mayor's Office of Housing and Community Development, "Downpayment Assistance Loan Program," accessed December 4, 2019, https://sfmohcd.org/dalp-details.

55. Los Angeles Housing and Community Investment Department, "Helping Low-Income, First-Time Home- buyers," accessed December 4, 2019, https://hcidla.lacity .org/help-low-income-first-home-buyers.

56. Down payments can be particularly difficult to cobble together in high-cost, housing-scarce cities. A household might manage to sock away $10,000 in a year only to see home prices rise by more than $50,000, putting them further behind than when they started if their goal is a 20 percent down payment.

Subsidy: Why Government Spending and Public Programs Matter

1. Will Fischer and Barbara Sard, "Chart Book: Federal Housing Spending Is Poorly Matched to Need; Tilt toward Well-Off Homeowners Leaves Struggling Low-Income Renters without Help," Center on Budget and Policy Priorities, March 8, 2017, https://www.cbpp.org/research/housing/chart-book-federal-housing-spending-is-poorly-matched-to-need.
2. Marisol Cuellar Mejia and Vicki Hsieh, "A Snapshot of Homelessness in California," Public Policy Institute of California, February 19, 2019, https://www.ppic.org/blog/a-snapshot-of-homelessness-in-california/.
3. Matt Levin, "To Create Affordable Housing, Lawmakers Eye Ending Tax Breaks for Vacation Homes," Cal Matters, March 15, 2017, https://calmatters.org/articles/to-create-affordable-housing-lawmakers-eye-ending-tax-breaks-for-vacation-homes/.
4. Congressional Research Service, "An Introduction to the Low-Income Housing Tax Credit," updated February 27, 2019, https://fas.org/sgp/crs/misc/RS22389.pdf.
5. Novogradac, Affordable Housing Resource Center, "State LIHTC Program Descriptions," https://www.novoco.com/resource-centers/affordable-housing-tax-credits/application-allocation/state-lihtc-program-descriptions.
6. Fischer and Sard, "Federal Housing Spending."
7. Western Regional Advocacy Project, "History of Slashing HUD Budget," n.d., http://weap.org/uploads/fact%20sheets/WRAP-HistoryofSlashingHUDBudgetFactSheet-Final.pdf.

8. Alison Bell and Douglas Rice, "Congress Prioritizes Housing Programs in 2018 Funding Bill, Rejects Trump Administration Proposals," Center on Budget and Policy Priorities, July 19, 2018, https://www.cbpp.org/research /housing/congress-prioritizes-housing-programs-in-2018 -funding-bill-rejects-trump.

9. Joint Center for Housing Studies of Harvard University, "America's Rental Housing: Meeting Challenges, Building on Opportunities," 2011, https://www.jchs.harvard.edu /sites/default/files/americasrentalhousing-2011.pdf.

10. Shane Phillips, "Reviewing LA's Homelessness Report, Pt. 2: Efficacy and Cost of Housing Strategies," *Better Institutions* (blog), January 12, 2016, http://www.better institutions.com/blog/2016/1/12/los-angeles-comprehensive -homeless-strategy-housing-part-2.

11. Dennis R. Capozza, Richard K. Green, and Patric H. Hendershott, "Taxes, Mortgage Borrowing, and Residential Land Prices," chap. 5 in *Economic Effects of Fundamental Tax Reform*, ed. Henry J. Aaron and William G. Gale (Washington, DC: Brookings Institution Press, 1996), 186, https://books.google.com/books?hl=en&lr=&id=7bxfBHc grtEC&oi=fnd&pg=PA171&dq=info:j91xBvJQse4J:scholar .google.com&ots=1H66PVOTiw&sig=R_gx4ZVIfMHT sjwrrSpY4_N4zgE#v=onepage&q&f=false.

12. James M. Poterba, "Tax Reform and the Housing Market in the Late 1980s: Who Knew What, and When Did They Know It?," in *Proceedings, Federal Reserve Bank of Boston Conference Series*, 1992, vol. 36, 230–261, https://pdfs .semanticscholar.org/0129/484dabe3fc471098d6966421b33 2185d612c.pdf.

13. Jeffrey Prang, "2018 Annual Report," Los Angeles County Office of the Assessor, https://assessor.lacounty.gov/wp -content/flipbook/annual_report_2018/?page=1.

14. Note that the market value increased by more than $93 billion, but California state law (via Proposition 13) restricts taxable value increases to 2 percent each year except when a property is sold to a new owner, at which

time it is reassessed at market value. It's difficult to know exactly how much the market value of homes in Los Angeles County increased from 2017 to 2018, but it was significantly more than $100 billion.

15. Los Angeles County Registrar-Recorder/County Clerk, "General Information: Additional Tax Rates for Specific Cities," accessed November 30, 2019, https://www.lavote .net/home/records/property-document-recording/docu mentary-transfer-taxes/general-info.

16. City and County of San Francisco, Office of the Assessor-Recorder, "Transfer Tax," accessed November 30, 2019, https://www.sfassessor.org/recorder-information /recording-document/transfer-tax.

17. City and County of San Francisco, California, Office of the Controller, "Comprehensive Annual Financial Report: Year Ended June 30, 2018," https://sfcontroller.org/sites /default/files/Documents/AOSD/CCSF%20CAFR%20 FY2018%20v6%20%28FinalV4%29.pdf.

18. City of Los Angeles, Office of the Controller, "Comprehensive Annual Financial Report, Fiscal Year 2018," https:// lacontroller.org/wp-content/uploads/2019/02/FY18_CAFR _Final_1.31.19_v3.pdf.

19. Note: The $1.51 trillion property valuation is for Los Angeles County, whereas the $209 million in real estate transfer tax revenues is for the City of Los Angeles, which represents about 40 percent of the county's population.

20. State of Washington, "Engrossed Substitute Senate Bill 5998," 66th Legislature, 2019 Regular Session, May 21, 2019, http://lawfilesext.leg.wa.gov/biennium/2019-20/Htm /Bills/Session%20Laws/Senate/5998-S.SL.htm.

21. Mark Huffman, "Sales of 'Flipped' Homes Declined in the First Quarter," Consumer Affairs, June 10, 2019, https:// www.consumeraffairs.com/news/sales-of-flipped-homes -declined-in-the-first-quarter-061019.html.

22. Chicago Metropolitan Agency for Planning (CMAP), "Stability of Major Tax Revenue Sources," January 18, 2012, https://www.cmap.illinois.gov/updates/all/-/asset

_publisher/UIMfSLnFfMB6/content/stability-of-major-tax
-revenue-sources.

23. Henry Aaron and William G. Gale, eds., *Economic Effects
    of Fundamental Tax Reform* (Washington, DC: Brookings
    Institution Press, 1996), https://books.google.com/books
    ?hl=en&lr=&id=7bxfBHcgrtEC&oi=fnd&pg=PA171&d
    q=info:j91xBvJQse4J:scholar.google.com&ots=1H66PV
    OTiw&sig=R_gx4ZVIfMHTsjwrrSpY4_N4zgE#v=on
    epage&q=municipal&f=false.

24. Gillian B. White, "Millennials Who Are Thriving Finan-
    cially Have One Thing in Common . . . Rich Parents,"
    Atlantic, July 15, 2015, https://www.theatlantic.com/busi
    ness/archive/2015/07/millennials-with-rich-parents
    /398501/.

25. Steven Sharp, "Op-Ed: Downtown Has a High Apartment
    Vacancy Rate? The Rest of L.A. Should Be So Lucky," *Los
    Angeles Times*, February 13, 2018, https://www.latimes.com
    /opinion/livable-city/la-oe-sharp-vacancy-dtla-luxury
    -development-20180213-story.html.

26. Shane Phillips, "Does the Los Angles Region Have Too
    Many Vacant Homes?," UCLA Lewis Center for Regional
    Policy Studies, February 2010, https://escholarship.org/uc
    /item/87r4543q.

27. Canadian Press, "City of Vancouver Says 2018 Empty
    Homes Tax Eased Tight Rental Market," updated Febru-
    ary 6, 2019, https://www.cbc.ca/news/canada/british
    -columbia/city-of-vancouver-says-2018-empty-home-tax
    -cut-number-of-homes-sitting-vacant-1.5008365.

28. Discount rates are used by investors to measure the value
    of future earnings relative to present-day earnings. For
    example, a 10 percent discount rate would mean that a
    dollar of income one year in the future would be valued
    the same as 90 cents of income today (a 10 percent "dis-
    count" on the present-day value). It's a crucial number for
    determining whether to proceed with an investment, and
    higher-risk investments will typically be accompanied by
    higher discount rates. Governments are necessarily more

conservative in their investments and thus have lower discount rates (even if they rarely, if ever, use such terms), so future revenue is of greater value to them than to most other entities.

29. American Community Survey, "ACS Demographic and Housing Estimates," 2017, ACS 5-Year Estimates Data Profiles, Marina del Rey CDP; County of Los Angeles, "Annual Report, 2015–16," https://www.lacounty.gov /wp-content/uploads/Complete_Annual_Report.pdf.

30. Rosalind Greenstein and Yesim Sungu-Eryilmaz, "Community Land Trusts," Lincoln Institute of Land Policy, *Land Lines*, April 2005, https://www.lincolninst.edu/publi cations/articles/community-land-trusts.

31. Chris Lentino, "Chicago to Pay $20 Million to Parking Meter Company in 2018," Illinois Policy, November 2, 2017, https://www.illinoispolicy.org/chicago-to-pay-20 -million-to-parking-meter-company-in-2018/.

32. Better Government Association, "Chicago's Parking Meter Deal a Lesson in 'Worst Practices,'" March 15, 2009, https://www.bettergov.org/news/chicagos-parking-meter -deal-a-lesson-in-worst-practices/.

33. Sarah Mawhorter, David Garcia, and Hayley Raetz, "It All Adds Up: The Cost of Housing Development Fees in Seven California Cities," Terner Center for Housing Innovation, University of California, Berkeley, March 2018, http://ternercenter.berkeley.edu/uploads/Development _Fees_Report_Final_2.pdf.

34. Joint Center for Housing Studies of Harvard University, "America's Rental Housing 2017: Renter Households," https://www.jchs.harvard.edu/sites/default/files/02_har vard_jchs_americas_rental_housing_2017.pdf.

35. Amelia Josephson, "Changes to State and Local Tax Deduction—Explained," SmartAsset, February 11, 2020, https://smartasset.com/taxes/trumps-plan-to-eliminate-the -state-and-local-tax-deduction-explained.

36. Joint Center for Housing Studies of Harvard University, "America's Rental Housing: Meeting Challenges, Building

on Opportunities," 2011, https://www.jchs.harvard.edu
/sites/default/files/americasrentalhousing-2011.pdf.

37. Bree J. Lang, "Cost Inefficiency in the Low-Income
Housing Tax Credit: Evidence from Building Size," https://
www.novoco.com/sites/default/files/atoms/files/lihtc_cost
_inefficiency_032615.pdf.

38. Jeff Stein, "In Expensive Cities, Rents Fall for the Rich—
but Rise for the Poor," *Washington Post*, August 6, 2018,
https://beta.washingtonpost.com/business/economy/in
-expensive-cities-rents-fall-for-the-rich--but-rise-for-the
-poor/2018/08/05/a16e5962-96a4-11e8-80e1-00e80e1fdf43
_story.html.

39. Simón Rios, "Affordable Housing Credit Remains, but
Could Be Less Effective," WBUR, December 21, 2017,
https://www.wbur.org/bostonomix/2017/12/21/affordable
-housing-gop-tax-plan.

40. Laura Sullivan and Meg Anderson, "Affordable Housing
Program Costs More, Shelters Fewer," National Public
Radio, May 9, 2017, https://www.npr.org/2017/05/09
/527046451/affordable-housing-program-costs-more
-shelters-less.

41. Corianne Payton Scally et al., "The Case for More, Not
Less: Shortfalls in Federal Housing Assistance and Gaps in
Evidence for Proposed Policy Changes," Urban Institute,
January 2018, https://www.urban.org/sites/default/files
/publication/95616/case_for_more_not_less.pdf.

42. Scally et al., "More, Not Less."

43. Douglas Rice, "Major Study: Housing Vouchers Most
Effective Tool to End Family Homelessness," Center on
Budget and Policy Priorities, July 14, 2015, https://www
.cbpp.org/blog/major-study-housing-vouchers-most
-effective-tool-to-end-family-homelessness.

44. Department of Housing and Urban Development, "Congressional Justifications," 2019, 4-1, https://www.hud.gov
/sites/dfiles/CFO/documents/FY%202019%20Congression
al%20Justifications%20-%20Combined%20PDF%20-%20
Updated.pdf.

45. Congressional Budget Office, "Federal Housing Assistance for Low-Income Households," September 2015, http://www.cbo.gov/sites/default/files/114th-congress-2015-2016/reports/50782-lowincomehousing-onecolumn.pdf.

46. Paul Emrath, "Interest Rates on Construction Loans Showed Rising Trend in 2018," National Association of Home Builders, February 18, 2019, http://eyeonhousing.org/2019/02/interest-rates-on-construction-loans-showed-rising-trend-in-2018/.

Part III: Bringing It All Together

1. Dylan Matthews, "Democrats Have United around a Plan to Dramatically Cut Child Poverty," Vox, updated May 2, 2019, https://www.vox.com/future-perfect/2019/3/6/18249290/child-poverty-american-family-act-sherrod-brown-michael-bennet.

Appendix: Development and Real Estate Economics 101

1. Michael Andersen, "Why Are New Apartments So Expensive?," Medium, April 5, 2018, first published March 27, 2018, by the *Portland Tribune* and KGW as part of the Open:Housing journalism collaborative, https://openhousing.net/why-are-new-apartments-so-expensive-c84904003966.

2. Yonah Freemark, "Upzoning Chicago: Impacts of a Zoning Reform on Property Values and Housing Construction," *Urban Affairs Review*, January 29, 2019, https://journals.sagepub.com/doi/abs/10.1177/1078087418824672?journalCode=uarb&.

3. Matt Levin, "Does 'Upzoning'—Allowing Taller, Denser Housing to Be Built—Actually Work?," CalMatters, February 22, 2019, https://calmatters.org/articles/upzoning-housing-study-pitfalls-california/.

4. Invitation Homes Inc., Form S-11 for Registration under the Securities Act of 1933 of Securities of Certain Real

Estate Companies, United States Securities and Exchange Commission, Washington, DC, https://www.sec.gov /Archives/edgar/data/1687229/000119312517004519/d26012 5ds11.htm.

5. Shane Phillips, "Home Values in the New Millennium: The Rich Get Richer," *Better Institutions* (blog), August 22, 2013, http://www.betterinstitutions.com/blog/2013/08 /home-values-in-new-millenium-rich-get.

Island Press | Board of Directors